George Jackson

The diaries and letters of Sir George Jackson from the Peace of Amiens to the Battle of Talavera

Edited by Lady Jackson. Vol. 1

George Jackson

The diaries and letters of Sir George Jackson from the Peace of Amiens to the Battle of Talavera
Edited by Lady Jackson. Vol. 1

ISBN/EAN: 9783337107871

Printed in Europe, USA, Canada, Australia, Japan

Cover: Foto ©ninafisch / pixelio.de

More available books at **www.hansebooks.com**

THE

DIARIES AND LETTERS

OF

SIR GEORGE JACKSON, K.C.H.,

FROM THE PEACE OF AMIENS TO THE BATTLE

OF TALAVERA.

EDITED BY LADY JACKSON.

IN TWO VOLUMES.

VOLUME I.

LONDON:
RICHARD BENTLEY AND SON,
Publishers in Ordinary to Her Majesty.
1872.

LONDON :

PRINTED BY WILLIAM CLOWES AND SONS,

STAMFORD STREET AND CHARING CROSS.

CONTENTS.—VOL. I.

CONTENTS.

xii   CONTENTS.

APPENDIX.

INTRODUCTORY CHAPTER.

SIR GEORGE JACKSON was the youngest son of Dr. Thomas Jackson—one of the canons of the Abbey of Westminster, rector of Yarlington, chaplain to Francis, fifth Duke of Leeds, and subsequently canon residentiary of St. Paul's. He was born in October, 1785, and was destined for the church; but the death of his father, at a comparatively early age, caused a change in the family arrangements. At the close of 1801, he left Westminster to join the special mission to Paris, as unpaid attaché; Mr. Francis Jackson, his brother, and senior by many years, being the minister appointed to reside in that capital during the negotiation of the Treaty of peace at Amiens.

In the same capacity, he accompanied Mr. Francis Jackson's mission to Berlin, in October, 1802—pursuing there his general studies under professors while gaining experience in the line of life he had entered upon.

VOL. I.   *   B

In 1805, he was presented at the Prussian court as Chargé d'Affaires, during his brother's temporary absence; and was afterwards sent on special service to the electoral court of Hesse Cassel.

Early in May, 1806, Mr. Francis Jackson was ordered to quit Berlin without taking leave; the definitive occupation of Hanover by Prussia having just taken place, and war, in consequence, being determined upon on the part of Great Britain.

Later in the year, overtures were made to the British Cabinet for a renewal of friendly relations between the two powers, and at about the same time that Lord Morpeth was appointed to negotiate with Prussia, Mr. George Jackson received orders from Mr. Fox to leave England for the north of Germany.

He returned, in February, 1807, with the Treaty with Prussia, signed by Lord Hutchinson, at Memel; and in the following April he was sent back by Mr. Canning, with the ratification of the Treaty, and instructions to Lord Hutchinson to appoint him Chargé d'Affaires on his lordship's return to England.

In July, he was gazetted secretary of Legation to Mr. Frere's mission to the Court of Prussia. This mission however was put an end to by the Treaty of Tilsit.

Recalled to England, he took Copenhagen on his way; witnessed the bombardment of that city, and brought home the account of the capitulation, and the surrender of the Danish fleet to the British forces.

In 1808-9, he was one of the secretaries of Legation to the mission to the Spanish Junta. He was afterwards appointed to Washington—Mr. Francis Jackson being minister—but a suspension of diplomatic relations ensued between Great Britain and the United States before he could join that mission.

In 1813, he accompanied Sir Charles Stewart— Lord Londonderry — to Germany, as secretary of Legation, and remained at the head-quarters of the allied armies throughout the campaigns of 1813-14; finally entering Paris with the allies.

On the return of the King of Prussia to Berlin, Mr. George Jackson was accredited Chargé d'Affaires to that Court, with the appointments of minister, and resided there until 1816, when he was gazetted Secretary of Embassy at St. Petersburg.

Subsequently he was sent by Mr. Canning on special and confidential service to Madrid.

From 1823 to 1827 he resided at Washington, as commissioner, under the first article of the Treaty of Ghent, for the settlement of the American claims.

In 1828, he was named Commissary Judge to the several mixed commissions established at Sierra Leone.

In 1832, the cross of civil commander of the Guelphic order, with the further honour of knighthood, was conferred on him by His Majesty William the Fourth.

From 1832 to 1859, he was Chief Commissioner— under the Convention for the abolition of the African slave trade—first, at Rio Janeiro, until 1841, whence he was transferred to Surinam, and afterwards, from 1845, at St. Paul de Loanda.

Sir George Jackson retired on a pension in 1859, having been fifty-seven years in the diplomatic and foreign service of the crown. He died at Boulogne-sur-Mer, May 2nd, 1861.

The following extracts from his diaries and family letters date from the close of 1801, when he made at Paris the first step in diplomacy, and extend over the period of his residence at Berlin—and other parts of Germany, to which the Prussian Court was subsequently driven by the events of the war—to his return from Spain, at the end of 1809, to join his brother at Washington.

Those eight years were eventful ones in the history of Europe; to no nation more deplorably eventful than to Prussia—the aggressive policy of Napoleon, and the submissive one of Frederick William the Third, having well nigh brought about the total overthrow of the Prussian monarchy.

The great interest taken by Mr. G. Jackson in public affairs, from the very outset of his career, and the especial advantage he possessed of a thorough diplomatic training, under his brother—a man of considerable talent, and distinction in his profession—give to the observations and opinions contained in the diaries and letters of this young attaché, a certain value, as outlines of the events of the above-named period, which are traced, it is thought, with sufficient firmness to convey a fairly correct notion of the scenes depicted and the characters portrayed.

The appointment of the elder Mr. Jackson as
minister to the French Republic was made known by
him to his mother in the following letter.

York Hotel, Albemarle Street,
23rd October, 1801.

MY DEAR M.,

The die is at length cast, and as favourably as
I could possibly have expected or wished, by which
you will understand that I do not go to America.
That post is said to be now offered to Mr. Wickham,
but it has been proposed to me, in the most gratifying
terms, to reside at Paris as plenipotentiary whilst
Lord Cornwallis is at Amiens, where the definitive
Treaty will be negotiated, and until Lord Whitworth,
who is to have the embassy, arrives.

I owe this entirely to Mr. Addington's determined
preference of me; not that Lord Hawkesbury was
opposed to it, but he would not, probably, of himself
have thought of giving me the appointment. "It
is but a temporary mission," Mr. A. said, "and, in
point of diplomatic rank, not so much as your just
claims entitle you to, yet in offering it to you at this
critical moment I consider that we give you a very
strong proof of our confidence in you."

Lord Cornwallis takes with him, Lord Bruce,
Colonel Littlehales, and F. Moore. Mr. Merry will
be secretary to the embassy. Probably Mr. Hill,
Webb, and another friend, as well as George, will go
with me; but all this is not yet decided, and indeed
the whole business is at present a secret, so pray do
not talk about it.

Now, as to time, I am to follow Lord C., so as to be in Paris a few days before he leaves it, as he goes there first, on a particular invitation from Bonaparte, and then returns to Amiens. He will set off, I should say, about the 1st of November, and I leave in time to reach Paris for the fête of the 9th, about which I confess to feeling no sort of curiosity, as I think it looks a little like showing us off.

As to the *details* of this business, such as allowances, &c., &c., I feel pretty confident, from what is now passing, that everything will be very pleasantly and easily settled.

You need have no anxiety about George, he is not going to Paris on a mere party of pleasure. I intend that he shall fag, and lose none, if I can help it, of the advantages which I trust this appointment will produce.

Adieu, my dear M.,

Your affectionate and dutiful son,

F. J. J.

DIARIES AND LETTERS

OF

SIR GEORGE JACKSON.

1801.

Letters— Oct. 31*st*.—Three hours ago, my dear
mother, my brother received orders to hold himself
in readiness to leave England by the middle of next
week. He desires me to tell you so; also that he
is, and will be, so fully employed, that, with the
exception of what he calls "a gleaner," which he
intends to write you before he starts, you must
henceforth—meaning not only here but also in Paris
—look chiefly to me for the history of our doings.

You may now take your revenge, he says, for
having so long been tongue-tied, and may talk of
our mission at all your Bath tea-tables to your
heart's content; the reason no longer existing for
the great secrecy that was for a time necessary.

You will be glad to know that the Office has
behaved very liberally and handsomely to him, and
that he has heard there is a prospect of Parliament

providing, ere long, for the payment of the arrears
of salaries and pensions; so that he hopes, on his
return, to touch the full amount of the seven quarters
now due to him.

Since the news got abroad that a special mission
is about to be sent to Paris, my brother has been
beset by all sorts of people—for the most part utter
strangers—urging him to take charge of letters and
parcels, enough to freight a ship. A great many
emigrants think it a good opportunity for sending
safely to friends. There are boxes and packages
without end at the Foreign Office, addressed to his
care; but strict orders have been given that no
more are to be received, and, of course, we are not
going to carry over those already deposited there.
He has also commissions innumerable, from the ladies
of his acquaintance, for the purchase of French silk,
laces, and cambric; in short, he says, were he to
comply with all these modest requests he must
appoint a deputy to perform the duties of his office.
Nevertheless, he will bear *your* wants in mind, and
assures you that you may rely on receiving a lace
cloak that shall be envied by all the ladies of Bath.

· My brother has twice been with Lord Cornwallis,
and likes him very much. I believe Major Dalton
will go with our party.

Nov. 6th.—I think it will please you, dearest M.,
to hear that I have eaten what I call my first diplomatic dinner. I need hardly explain that it was neither
at Mr. Addington's nor at Lord Hawkesbury's. It was
at M. Otto's, the French Chargé d'Affaires. My brother

and Mr. W. only were invited; but when M. Otto, who called to speak with Francis on business, heard that I too was going to Paris, he begged that my brother would allow me also to dine with them. He and his wife, an American lady, are both very pleasant people, perhaps what you would call of the old school, for they are excessively polite, and unlike in manners what I should have expected to find citizens of either of the modern republics. We had, however, in a very lively lady just arrived from Paris, a specimen of the new French school, both in dress and deportment. Perhaps she would have shocked you a little, but she amused us a good deal.

There was also of the party a great *célébrité*, Mademoiselle d'Eon, the famous chevalier, who served as a man, for nearly forty years, in the French service. My brother told me he remembered paying at Bath, in 1795, a half-crown to see her take part in a public exhibition of fencing.

Our dinner was a very handsome one; and of course in the French style—everything *très recherché*. The French and English flags floated together over the centre *plateau*, and we drank prosperity and stability to their union in foaming bumpers of champagne.

8th.—My brother's arrangements are nearly complete, and the greater part of his packages sent off. He took leave of Mr. Addington on the 5th, and again saw Lord Cornwallis, before he set out for Paris last Monday. We follow on the 11th, and I cannot tell you, my dear M., how much I regret not being able to run down to Bath, as you wish, to bid

you and my sisters good-bye. But remember, your
absentees will return with the swallows, and that
there is but the narrow Channel between us, instead
of the wide Atlantic you lately dreaded to hear
would divide us. Twice a week, there is a post to
and from Paris, besides messengers from the Office.
I intend, however, to follow my brother's suggestion
of keeping a diary, both for your benefit and my own.
                        Adieu, my dearest mother,
                                    G. J.

Diaries—Dover, Nov. 12*th.*—We left London for
Dover yesterday at 8 A.M. At Dartford, we were
overtaken by a messenger sent in pursuit of us by
Madame Otto, from whom he brought a note, and
a small box that had been taken to our hotel almost
immediately after we had left it. The box was
recommended to my brother's especial care, its important contents being a cap for Madame Bonaparte.
After promising that the millinery should be well
looked after, we posted on with all speed and arrived
here to dinner at half-past five.

We sail to-day at noon; the wind is fair, and we
hope to reach Calais before dark.

Calais, 13*th.*—Our passage was a tedious one,
for there was so little wind that we did not get in
until 1 A.M. Notwithstanding the lateness of the
hour, several official people were waiting to receive
my brother on his debarkation. Carriages were in
attendance, and he was conducted to Dessein's, where
a handsome saloon and suite of rooms had been

prepared for him and his party. A supper was also
ready to be served up—an attention fully appreciated
by all of us—and when the mutual complimentary
and congratulatory speeches were ended, the weary
voyagers were left to themselves, to enjoy the good
cheer, or to seek repose if they preferred it.

This morning is a busy one for my brother. He has
to receive many visitors, and to address a deputation
of the principal persons of the town, who are to wait
upon him presently, to compliment him on his
arrival, and to express their satisfaction at the
happy prospect they have before them of a lasting
peace.

A guard of infantry is stationed in the courtyard
of the hotel ; carriages and relays of horses are provided, and we leave at twelve o'clock for Boulogne.

Boulogne, 14*th*.—When about to leave Calais, my
brother became aware that an escort of cavalry,
commanded by an officer, was to accompany him,
and that the same mark of respect was to be paid
to him until he reached Paris. This surprised him,
the more so, as Lord Cornwallis had so recently preceded him. He was anxious to dispense with, without
seeming to reject, the intended honour ; he therefore
sent to the military commandant, and thanking him
for his great courtesy, begged leave to decline the
attendance of the escort. The commandant replied
that he acted on special orders from the French
Government, which he dared not depart from, to
show this and every other possible mark of respect
and attention to His Majesty's Envoy. This settled

the question; the escort galloped up, and off we clattered at a dashing pace. But it did not last long, for the roads soon became rough, and towards the last stage were steep and heavy, so that Boulogne was not reached until the evening.

An enthusiastic greeting awaited the British Minister, and there was a general and brilliant illumination of the upper and lower towns.

The avenue of the house at which he alighted was lined on either side by the National Guard. And this reception was not merely an official one; a large concourse of people of all classes had assembled to welcome him, and did so, apparently, from a real feeling of gladness.

This morning there are again many visits to receive before we continue our journey. The most interesting one has already taken place. *Monsieur le Ministre* was presented with a bouquet of choice flowers by *Mesdames les Matelotes*. Twelve of them formed a sort of deputation; two elderly fish-wives and ten young ones; the latter very pretty specimens of their class. All were dressed in a quaint and most picturesque costume; beautiful white lace caps with broad frills, red, or red and white striped petticoats, worked muslin aprons and neckerchiefs, violet coloured stockings, and charmingly natty *sabots*, lined with white wool and ornamented, in some instances, with carvings on the front. Besides this, large oval-hooped gold earrings, crosses, and chains. There was a numerous attendance of men and women who were not in grand gala; the former wore the ordinary dress of the day, with no indications of their calling but their bronzed faces and hands; the latter had the wide frilled caps, and large black cloaks with enormous silver clasps. Their procession was a very pretty sight, and the compliment they paid my brother pleased him more than any other of the civilities he has received.

One of the elder women spoke a short address, and her daughter—*sa fille unique,* as she called the very pretty girl who walked by her side and bore the *bouquet*—presented the floral offering. No doubt the reply was most appropriate; but I did not hear it, for my attention was quite taken up by the lively bright-eyed young *matelotes.* They seemed to be well satisfied with the proceedings, which concluded with the hearty blessing of the ancient dames, and reiterated wishes for a *bon voyage* and a speedy peace.

Paris, 17*th.*—My brother being anxious to hasten on to his destination, as well as to escape from the honours so liberally heaped upon him, arranged to sleep but two nights, instead of three—as at first proposed—between Boulogne and Paris. Yet, as far as time allowed, the same attentions were paid him throughout the journey as at Calais and Boulogne.

We arrived very late on the 14th at Abbeville, and were off early the following morning, to the great disappointment of the people; stopped two hours at Amiens for refreshment, congratulations, visits, and speeches, and slept at a very pretty château at Wavigny, where we were received with much cordiality, and were very hospitably enter-

tained by a private family, who had offered their
house for the occasion—the inn not affording the
requisite accommodation.

Yesterday evening, between five and six, we
arrived in Paris, having travelled the last two posts
over a remarkably fine road, and through a magnificent avenue of lofty elms, extending from the
cathedral town of St. Denis to the gates of the city.
Rooms had been secured at the Hotel Pajol, where
Lord Cornwallis and suite have also taken up their
quarters.

21*st.*—We remain at Pajol's, the hotel most in
vogue here, until the departure of Lord Cornwallis
and the rest of the plenipotentiaries for Amiens,
which will be in the course of next week, when we
remove to a fine apartment in the Hotel Caraman,
Rue St. Dominique, Faubourg St. Germain.

My brother, for the present, purposely keeps in
the background, for Lord C. is a little sore at his
arrival in Paris—being an independent envoy—
before he and his party have left it.

He does not wish to ruffle the good old gentleman's feelings, nor will he allow him to know, lest it
should further annoy him, that M. Talleyrand has
taken advantage of his exceedingly small acquaintance
with the French, language to declare himself to have
been at a loss to understand the distinct nature of
my brother's functions, as attempted to be explained
to him by his lordship.

This, however, he says, is not important for the
moment, as he cannot have his audience of the First

Consul until he receives his letters of credence, which
have been delayed on account of some hesitation
here—on the part of M. Talleyrand it is supposed—
in forwarding similar credentials to M. Otto.

Meanwhile, the French Government are endeavouring to get the seat of congress changed from Amiens
to Paris—though it is not likely their wishes will
be consented to—and my brother, while holding
aloof from politics and diplomacy, is fully occupied
in paying first visits and assisting at great dinners.
He finds Paris greatly changed since he was here with
Major Mitchell on his way to the Hague in 1787.
Everything, he says, appears new to him, and the
few objects he does recollect are so much altered as
scarcely to be recognized.

Not even the squares and streets, still less the public
and private buildings, bear a resemblance to those
of former times, and only a few melancholy remnants
remain of what *was*, what *is* by no means making
up for the loss. But as I see Paris for the first time,
it seems to me a very fine city, however much it may
be shorn of its former splendour.

The public buildings are certainly far handsomer
than those of London; the houses much higher, and
the white stone they are built of looks lighter and
more cheerful than bricks. There are good streets
and magnificent houses, or hotels as they are called,
in the quarter we are to live in. Yet the widest
streets can hardly be called very wide, and none are
very pleasant for walking, owing to the rough mode
of paving them. They have a gutter in the centre,

no footways, and are mostly covered with a thick mud of inky blackness, through which you have to pick your way with some difficulty, and even danger to life and limb; for the *fiacres* and other vehicles are driven in the most careless and reckless way; they come suddenly floundering out of the gutters and sloughs close up to the houses, so that if you are not nimble, or cannot make good your retreat to some courtyard or open doorway, it will be a lucky chance if you escape getting crushed, and are only half smothered with mud.

Before we left England my brother said to me, " For walking take only the thickest boots; Paris mud and dirt, I remember, was heavy and penetrating; and but one pair of leathers, for there was little or no riding." I can answer for these hints to travellers, founded on his recollections of 1787, answering equally well for 1801.

We—that is, Mr. Hill, my brother's secretary, and myself—are going to explore Paris with Mr. Dorant as cicerone. He is the proprietor of the York Hotel in Albemarle Street, and of another hotel in Jermyn Street. Being more than half a Frenchman, the manners and language of this country are very familiar to him. He says he came to claim a sum of 2000*l.*, which, being in *assignats*, proves to be worth about twelve francs, but, if I may venture to guess, some secret political object was the reason of his coming over with us.

22nd.—My brother dined yesterday at M. Talleyrand's. All the ministers of the country were there, as well as Generals Moreau, Berthier, Massena, and some others. He was placed at dinner next to the First Consul's brother, Joseph Bonaparte, who is to be plenipotentiary at the congress, and who showed him much civility and attention, and conversed a good deal with him. Francis thought him a pleasant gentlemanlike man.

I went with some of our party to the opera. A good many English were there; those whom we knew, and who joined us, pronounced the singing execrable, and the house inferior to ours. But I thought the decorations and dresses very beautiful; the women very pretty, and the dancing the most graceful I have seen. The celebrated Vestris was the principal dancer; he is said to be getting too old for his work, and to feel fatigued very soon. There was, however, no appearance of age; he bounded over the stage with the most perfect ease and grace, but I remarked that he danced but little. The corps de ballet was really excellent and effective. The house was lighted by two circular rows of lamps suspended from the centre of the ceiling. The company in the boxes was more like what you would expect to see in a two shilling gallery, especially the male part of it. Madame Bonaparte and her daughter, Mademoiselle Beauharnois, were there in a sort of state box. The First Consul was also present for a short time, but in a *loge grillée,* so that he could not be seen by the audience.

23rd.—Yesterday I saw the First Consul at a parade in the courtyard of the Tuileries. It is his custom to hold one every tenth day, or revolutionary week, and yesterday being Primodi, or number one of the first decade of the third month, Frimaire, Mr. Hill and I, for whom one of the ministers had sent tickets— without which no one, on these occasions, is admitted either to the palace or court—took the opportunity of seeing this military spectacle. And a very grand affair it was. The space, was, perhaps, rather small for the number of troops present; cavalry, infantry, and artillery, besides numerous field officers, generals, and commanders of different grades. Their uniforms were splendid; for the most part ornamented with elaborate embroideries in gold and silver. Even the upper part of the boots of some of the officers had tracings or inlayings of gold, others had gold spurs most beautifully wrought.

The proceedings commenced by the French colours being carried by the Consular Guard, to the audience-chamber, where the First Consul was waiting their arrival. As they were borne through the ante-room, the guard on duty saluted them, the bands in the courtyard at the same time playing the war-inspiring Marseillaise hymn. Soon after, with a grand *fracas*, the wide doors of the audience-chamber were thrown open, and the standards were carried back with the same ceremonies, but, now, preceding the *grand guerrier* in person. He descended to the court, where a white charger, with very rich trappings, was held in readiness for him. As soon as he had mounted, and his brilliant staff of generals had surrounded and saluted him, the inspection commenced.

I have heard some English officers say, that these
parades are not nearly so well conducted as some far
less pretentious ones in England.   Of that, I know
nothing; but I do know, that the parade of this
Republican General was a right royal one, and, on a
small scale, an unrivalled display of the " pomp and
circumstance of war."

I was much struck by the personal appearance of
Bonaparte; for the caricatures, and the descriptions
which the English newspapers delight to give of him,
prepare one to see a miserable pigmy; hollow-eyed,
yellow-skinned, lantern-jawed, with a quantity of
lank hair, and a nose of enormous proportions.
But, though of low stature—perhaps five feet five
or six—his figure is well-proportioned, his features
are handsome, complexion rather sallow, hair
very dark, cut short, and without powder.   He
has fine eyes, full of spirit and intelligence, a firm,
severe mouth, indicating a stern and inflexible
will—in a word, you see in his countenance, the
master-mind; in his bearing, the man born to
rule.   After the parade, we passed through the
palace of the Tuileries into the gardens.   At
present the three Consuls reside in the palace, but
on dit, that Bonaparte finds this arrangement *très
gênant*; that he wants a house to himself, and that
numbers two and three will most likely soon be
ousted, to accommodate him.   Then—but this is only
whispered—that large flaunting inscription on the
centre pavilion of the palace, " *République Française*,"
may vanish, as well as the republican clock that

c 2

stands above it, with the hour divided into ten, instead of twelve parts.

The garden is one of the few places in Paris where a little cleanly walking can be had. It is pleasant, but formal, with long straight walks, and clipped trees. In summer, it is said to be thronged by all classes of people ; and even now there is no lack of lively groups and gay promenaders, when the weather is bright.

It is very bright now, without the slightest fog or haziness in the atmosphere. This, however, as I have lately discovered, is not considered an advantage by everybody. For, a few days ago, a rather eccentric old fellow we had here, an Englishman, called to see my brother, and met with an acquaintance, who, in the course of conversation, asked him how he liked Paris. "To tell you a good deal in a few words," he answered, "I don't like the climate."

"No !" said his friend ; "why, we are in the midst of November, and have clear bright sunshine, while I hear from home that London is wrapped in its usual gloom and fog."

"I am not one of those who find fault with that," answered the old gentleman. "It's the right thing at this time of the year ; and if they had a little more of it in this country, it would be a good thing for them. You may depend upon it, that a reasonable degree of weight in the atmosphere steadies the brain, and that we Englishmen owe much of our solid good sense, our respect for God and His Majesty, and the laws of the land, to the—the—I'll call it the sedateness of our climate.

" Now, I've been ten days in this country, and I should be sorry to stay in it ten more. For I notice that the kind of thin, light, and, I'll even say, flippant sort of air you get here, makes a man light-headed. It's like taking too much of their champagne wine —flimsy stuff, without body, that excites to folly, and makes you feel ready for any sort of mad spree."

" Why, H.!" said his friend, laughing, " is that the effect of Paris air on your constitution?"

" Not quite come to that yet," he said, " but I can't say what might happen soon. I speak of the effect it has on the native constitution. It brings on in time a sort of moral *delirium tremens*—they get savage—knock down their kings and nobles—smash their palaces—tear down their churches—anything that comes in their way, till the fit wears itself out. Then any man, that has been able to keep his head clear and steady, may put his heel on them. He, I've an idea, who now has them well under his heel, will keep them there for some time to come. But there'll be another tussle by-and-by—it's in the air, I tell you, they can't help it, and in time the fit will be on again, and the present man be kicked over for another.

" I'm off to-morrow. There's no place can compare with old England. A snug fireside, a fine sirloin, and a bottle of old mellow port, I look on, as pleasant things, as peculiarly her own, as the fogs that are a necessary ingredient of her winter. I find none of them here, and am too old, and too much of an Englishman to put up with a flickering bit of wood, froth, and stewed frogs as substitutes.   Good-bye, my friend.   I hope soon to shake hands with you again in Bond Street."

"Good-bye, H.," said his friend, "I agree with you entirely, barring the fogs.   I take one thing with another," he answered, "and I find they make up a very good whole."

There are many English in Paris as much out of their element as this blunt old John Bull, and who wish themselves at home again as heartily as he did.

As regards the French ladies, my brother thinks, that, even in what is called the very best Parisian society, our countrywomen find in their own sex much that offends English notions of propriety and good taste.   While the case is even worse with the men, for there are some, who fill very high offices, whose manners are not only repulsive to women, but who are so excessively vulgar and ill-bred that no gentleman would voluntarily associate with them.

The very few English ladies we have here seem half frightened at the free and lively manners of the French women; and as they are rarely strong enough in the language to appreciate the piquancy and playful wit of the Parisiennes in conversation, they are too apt to set down to boldness and effrontery what is merely the effect of great natural vivacity.   The dresses now in vogue are of the scantiest pattern, and, it must be confessed, scarcely consistent with modesty of demeanour; yet what there is of them is worn with so much grace and elegance that one really soon learns to think them becoming. The men, on the other hand, repel by their utter disregard of the ordinary decencies of the toilet. I saw the other evening, at a reception at Madame Fouché's, more than one pair of spattered boots, and a good deal of linen far from clean, the wearers being not the least important personages present. The roughnesses of the revolution are not yet polished off.

But the First Consul begins, they say, to set his face against this lingering taste for republican manners, and those about him follow the example he sets them; so that, by degrees, should peace continue, republican contempt for decency and good-breeding may give place to an excess of ceremony and formality. Cambacérès, the Second Consul, was at the Théâtre Français last evening with a very considerable retinue, in fact, quite in state.

About the same time, several regiments of infantry were marching into Paris to intimidate the populace, who have been riotous, and threaten further disturbances, in consequence of the high price of bread. In ordinary times, it appears, and after a fair harvest, the usual price is about a penny per pound. Lately it has been three halfpence, and a further rise to twopence halfpenny is expected. This causes much misery, and the police have been unable to prevent the discontent of the people from showing itself in acts of violence. By way of throwing them a crumb of comfort, the price of the English quartern loaf has been quoted in the " Moniteur."

Dec. 5th.—The plenipotentiaries are all off to
Amiens, and to-day we have got into our new
abode. It belongs to M. Caraman—Marquis, before
the revolution—and is a very fine mansion, with a
very good garden.

6th.—My brother's letters of credence arrived
yesterday, one day too late, unfortunately, for the
First Consul receives only on the 15th of the republican month.

We went, therefore, to Sèvres, to the china manufactory, where we saw some beautiful specimens, but
fewer than we had expected. This establishment,
like most others, for want of skilled workmen, is not
in the flourishing state it was some years back.
About fifty workmen are now employed, formerly
there were nearly three hundred. Most of their
choicest productions are sent to Paris. We called at
the *depôt* on our return, and my brother bought a
centre *plateau* of biscuit-ware—very handsome—also a
dinner-service of Angoulême china, the whole cost
being little more than a hundred pounds.

. *10th.*—As dinners are to be the extent of his
civilities to the many English now here—a rather un-
interesting set at present, but who must nevertheless be
fed—he has arranged to give, every week, two dinners
of fourteen covers, and one of twelve. The first has
passed off *à merveille*. Most of the guests seemed to
have left their native isle for the first time, and
nearly all expressed themselves disappointed, and
anxious to be at home again.

The chief drawback to enjoyment is, as was ac-

knowledged, that the greater part of the English
visitors are constrained to be dumb, and might almost
as well be deaf. French must be, they say, henceforth more generally studied, and the French people
seem to expect it, for though *they* rarely speak any
language but their own, I have heard the remark,
" Ces Anglais sont excessivement bêtes; ils no
savent pas un mot de Français !"

After dinner we went to the opera. Madame
Bonaparte was there, and was grossly insulted on
leaving. Very obscene language was addressed to
her, and, strange to say, the police took no notice
of the offenders. Dorant—who by some means con-
trives to know everything—says the insult was a
mere stratagem of the police, to induce the belief that
the commotion among the poorer class, on the increasing price of bread, is of a more serious nature than it
really is; it being an object with Fouché just now to
keep the First Consul in Paris, in order to prevent
Talleyrand—between whom and Fouché a continuous
struggle goes on for priority in Bonaparte's good
graces — from accompanying him on his projected
journey to Lyons to meet the cis-Alpine deputies.

12*th.*—Rumours are afloat of a conspiracy being
on foot to overthrow the existing government. In-
flammatory handbills have been extensively distributed, and great freedom of language is openly
used in speaking of the present state of affairs.

13*th.*—To enable the First Consul to watch these
proceedings, the journey to Lyons has been postponed,
which is a source of great mortification to Talleyrand,

while all the vigilance of Fouché is said to be employed to detect the supposed conspirators, and to
overthrow their plans. But it is believed that he
endeavours to magnify the real danger that may
exist, and to create the appearance of a good deal
that does not, that a higher degree of merit may be
claimed by him for suppressing it. It is however very
certain that society, generally, is rife with intrigue,
plots, and counterplots.

18th.—Since it has become generally known that
the minister is my brother, some attempts have been
made to convey information to him through me, on
subjects of public interest, which he might be
supposed not unwilling to lend an ear to, or to let
him know by mysterious hints that there are sources
whence valuable intelligence may be drawn, if a
suitable price were paid for it.

But from the first, my brother has warned me
against being drawn on to speak of any public affairs
that might either have been mentioned in my presence, or of which I had, otherwise, any sort of
knowledge.

To hear, see, and say nothing, he says, is my *rôle*
—not quite so easy an one, as it seems to be, when
exposed to the *rusé* attacks of one of the many
fascinating political *intrigantes* to be met with in
Parisian society.

Several very perplexing communications have
recently been made to me by a lady, whose notice
ought to be flattering—she being a great *belle*, and
in high favour in influential quarters. She always

begins her *tirades* with some compliment. The last was, " Il est rare, je sais bien, qu'un jeune homme de votre age possède si remarquablement les qualités de discrétion, et de réticence, dont par caractère vous êtes doué ; ainsi, je vais vous confier, sans crainte, un secret qu'il sera peut-être utile qu 'un de nos connoissances, soit informé." Then followed a pretended revelation, with the question, " *Croyez vous que cette nouvelle importante lui est déjà parvenu ?*"

My brother laughs heartily at some of these secrets, and says I must try to turn to good account the lessons of this lady-diplomatist, and justify her high opinion of my discretion and reticence.

23rd.—I am, at least, in a good school for acquiring them. Not a day passes but I am reminded of the necessity for caution and circumspection in every act and word ; for Fouché has established a system of espionage equalling that, my brother says, of Le Noir. There is not a family in Paris, considered worthy of his notice, that has not one or more servants in his pay. It is almost impossible for any foreigner, and quite so for a foreign minister, to procure a servant who is not a spy upon him. This part of his plan is carried on with so little concealment as to seem likely to defeat its own object by putting persons so much upon their guard. It is, however, certain that Fouché is made acquainted with the most private transactions of every individual, not excepting even the First Consul, who has had the mortification to find himself on more than one occasion the object of his minister's vigilance, and has thought it advisable to smother his resentment under a feigned approbation of his zeal for the public service.

I confess that I find it an uncomfortable thing, that deprives one of a good deal of pleasure, to sus-pect everybody of being a spy. It is constantly drilled into me that I must beware of the professor—a pleasant man, full of information—with whom I read and study French for two hours daily; also of the fencing-master—a jovial fellow, with a gay sort of swagger—such persons being frequently secret agents of police. I am told to bear in mind that there exists in some quarters a desire to know in what light the events that are passing here are represented to the English Government, as well as to find out my brother's private sources of infor-mation; and although it could hardly be expected that this knowledge is possessed by me, or, if so, would be imparted; yet, so subtle are the French, that one might, unawares, be drawn into a conversa-tion that would afford a hint of which advantage would be taken.

It is, however, rather amusing to know that while M. Fouché is employing every possible means to find out what others are doing and saying, and, perhaps, even thinking, an unsuspected person, of a kindred genius, has discovered that he is concerting with an officer of high standing—though of a character so opposite, that it makes the affair seem almost doubtful—the best means for giving France another form of government and a new ruler. But as the aims of the General in question are as honourable and unselfish as those of the minister of police are the reverse, they are at present, it appears, divided as to the measures to be employed for bringing about their object.

24th.—Mr. Dorant, who returned to England some days ago, and took with him my brother's despatches, has written from Dover to say that the violence of the late storm was so great, that the chaise in which he travelled was overturned by the wind near Boulogne. He had hoped to find a vessel to cross in from that port, none being able to leave Calais. Failing in that, he engaged an open boat which had landed him safely at Dover, after a passage of fourteen hours and a half. Bruised and battered by land, somewhat kicked about and weather beaten at sea, he was yet setting out for London as soon as the horses could be harnessed ; resolved to do his courier's work after a fashion that should put to shame the official messengers, who were dawdling at Calais for a fair wind and a smooth sea.

M. Talleyrand set out yesterday morning for Lyons. The First Consul was to follow on the 29th, but as he wished to arrive on the last day of the year—when all the members of the Consulta are to assemble—it left but forty-eight hours for the journey, and it being impossible to accomplish it in that time, his departure is now fixed for the 28th. Many persons doubt that it will take place then. My brother will have his audience on the 5th of January —the 15th of the month *Nivose.* Several presentations are appointed for that day, and it is supposed

that that circumstance will favour another postponement of the journey; for Bonaparte is unwilling to
leave Paris at this moment, on account of the numerous
embarrassments which the intrigues of discontented
Generals and Jacobin plotters occasion him, and
which frustrate, for the present, his original object in
going to Lyons.   This was to obtain from the
deputies the sovereignty of the cis-Alpine republic,
with the title of Imperator, to be followed up on his
return by a similar act in France; by which the
Second and Third Consuls should be set aside, but provided for, by being appointed ministers of justice and
finance.

27th.—We had an English party on Christmas day,
consisting, besides ourselves, of Sir Elisha and Lady
Impey, with their son and daughter, and a Miss Foster.
Sir E. is come to Paris to try to recover some
property in the French funds, in which he is
not very likely to succeed.   Besides, her ladyship
is quite out of sorts, dissatisfied with everything,
and anxious for nothing but to be at home again.
She admires neither Madame Bonaparte nor her
daughter, and thinks the First Consul supercilious
and conceited.   She pronounces the men, generally,
ill-mannered bears; the women, disgustingly forward.   The Apollo, the Diana, and all the art
treasures which, as saith the catalogue, " Un héros
guidé par la victoire fit conduire et fixer à jamais
sur les rives de la Seine," she refuses to admire, and
sighs for her English home and its comforts.   Yet
we made an arrangement to go to Versailles yester-

day, and as the day was very fine, and not too cold,
we set off at nine, in two carriages ; changed horses
at Sèvres, and enjoyed the drive much, the country
looking pretty, notwithstanding the leaflessness of
the season.

The wide road by which we approached Versailles,
was dreary and desolate in the extreme.   Traces
of former grandeur remain, yet the town is gloomy
and poverty-stricken.   The palace itself is a stately
edifice, but bearing too evidently those marks of
destruction that ruthless revolutionary hands have
left on most things that were grand and beautiful.
The exterior of the building is much defaced.   All
ornamental work, especially where a crown, a cipher,
or other royal emblem appeared, has been utterly
destroyed.

In the interior, the smashing, tearing down, and
demolishing has been carried on to a greater extent
still ; most likely it was easier work.   The splendidly
painted ceilings of the large saloons, with their
elaborate and gilded cornices, have been fearfully
damaged, and in some parts are mouldy and rotting
with damp, the rain having made its way through
apertures in the roof ; while there is scarcely a window
with a whole pane in it, or a shutter or a door left
standing.

Many magnificently carved frames remain on the
walls, without either mirrors or pictures.   All of the
latter that were most valuable have been taken away,
the inferior ones left.   We saw very little of the
once splendid furniture, and that little wofully

damaged.   Most of the apartments were empty; and
should the palace continue in its present neglected
state, its ruin must soon be complete.

With the exception of a few soldiers, a sergeant's
guard, who lounge about the entrance, it is inhabited
only by some half-dozen dirty fellows who call themselves guides and attendants.

The gardens are indescribably desolate and dirty,
and, from the formality of their style, look the more
forlorn in their humiliation, like a stately personage
in rags.   The fountains are choked with mud, and
the bronze gods and goddesses seem to be looking on
the changed scene around them in comical helpless-
ness and despair.

The figure of the great and magnificent Louis himself, as Apollo, issuing from a cave with a suite of
belles dames, representing the Muses, I believe, has
been treated by the filthy *canaille* with the most dis-
gusting indignity.   One of the tattered and torn
ciceroni, who had persisted in quartering himself
upon us, took much pains to explain to Sir Elisha
that this was done to show the Grand Monarque—
should he ever take a fancy to revisit this scene of
his former courtly revels—the contempt in which the
citizens of republican France held his extravagant
follies.   He evidently thought this a dreadfully
severe cut at poor Louis Quatorze.   Sir E. answered,
that the shade of the monarch might feel somewhat
consoled when he saw how far beneath contempt the
virtuous citizens placed themselves by their manner
of expressing contempt.   " Vous êtes monarchiste !

royaliste !" said the man. " Moi, je suis citoyen et bon républicain; payez moi ma journée et je me retirerai." He had engaged himself, and had followed us about for the last half hour; but a *franc* was tossed to him, which he condescended to pick up, and walked off with an air of offended dignity.

We went on to the *Grand Trianon;* it was like the rest of the show, in a miserable condition. The *Petit Trianon* is fitted up as a *restaurateur! Fêtes* and balls take place there in the summer.

30th.—Talking with my brother about the ruinous state of the palace of Versailles, he told me he had heard it was the First Consul's intention that the reparation of Versailles and other buildings should be shortly commenced, as also some projected improvements in Paris, but that he imagined he was at this moment intent only on securing the establishment of his authority, on which everything else depended. That in effecting this he had the opposing interests of various factions to contend with, which was the cause of the uncertainty and apparent inconsistency in the acts of the government. The First Consul, he said, had made the replacing of the country in a state of peace, after a successful war, an object of the first importance to him. He believed he would persevere in it. Still, allowing him all possible credit for sincerity, his views, he considers, are subject to contingencies, which do not depend altogether either upon him or the powers with whom he is treating. His Generals are dissatisfied with what is going on at Amiens, and desire war that they may enrich themselves by plunder. General Massena has openly boasted of the ease with which he could have effected the invasion of England, and considers his career of victory and glory cut short by the negotiations for peace. If Bonaparte does not find himself strong enough to overcome these plotters and intriguers, it is my brother's opinion that he will, to preserve his own position, gratify his Generals and once more plunge the country in war. But, he says, such is the restless nature of Frenchmen, especially since they have become legislators, that under whatever form of government they may live there will always be a strong party amongst them who will oppose everything, merely for the sake of opposing.

31*st*.—The journey to Lyons was again put off; the 6th or 7th of January is now named for the First Consul's departure. It is thought that he would be glad to give it up altogether, and send the Second Consul, Cambacérès, to Lyons in his stead ; but having once decided on a thing, and made his decision publicly known, it is in his character to persist in it, even if no other reason for doing so existed.

A circumstance connected with these postponements has afforded some amusement both to his friends and his enemies. The expenses of the journey were calculated at four millions of livres, and that sum was applied for : Barbé Marbois, the minister of public treasure, refused the advance ; " No law existed," he said, " authorizing him to make it." As the First Consul can brook no opposition to his will, the refusal of his minister to comply with it brought down on him a hurricane of invective and personal reproach, but, notwithstanding, he has remained firm, it is said, up to this time. Citoyen Barbé Marbois is reputed to be of inflexible integrity, and, on principle, an ardent republican. He devotes himself entirely to the business of his department, and it is considered that Bonaparte gave him the appointment in order to insure a faithful application of the public money to such services as he should direct. That he, who looks for so much subserviency to his views, should receive such a proof of his minister's independence of character, and fidelity in his office, causes much malicious mirth in society.

1802.

Jan. 2nd.—We had yesterday a dinner of different nations to celebrate the new year. Though it is not the republican *jour de l'an*, yet many of the French are fond of recurring to the pleasant memories connected with it, and do not heartily accept the 23rd of September as its substitute. Amongst other notabilities we had General Moreau, for whom my brother has a particular esteem. He resides at a short distance from Paris, at his country house, to which he retired at the end of the Continental War, and whence he makes only occasional visits to the capital. Between him and the First Consul a coolness has subsisted ever since the battle of Hohenlinden. The latter is supposed to be actuated by professional jealousy, and by an apprehension of the popularity which that event, as well as his acknowledged military capacity and

D 2

general high character, ensured to Moreau. On his return to Paris, after the battle, Bonaparte received him in the most frigid manner, and not only expressed no satisfaction on the occasion, but observed towards him, as he had towards the General's immediate connections and friends, a studied silence on the subject. As Moreau had never been very intimate with Bonaparte, he had not to suffer the loss of his friendship and favour; and the opinion generally entertained of him here has placed him as high in the public estimation as even a much more ambitious man could wish to stand.

A circumstance which occurred about a fortnight ago shows, I think, the general turn of his mind and character.

M. d'Orsay who, before the revolution, was a nobleman of high rank and considerable fortune, lost by it most of his landed property, which was sold, as belonging to the nation. One of his estates, adjoining that of Moreau was sold to the General, as has been usual in such cases, at a price infinitely below its real value. Moreau went to M. d'Orsay to inform him of it, and to request him to join in the conveyance, as well as to accept the amount of the difference between the purchase money agreed for with the government, and the known value of the estate.

These, and other transactions that have come to my brother's knowledge, give him a very high opinion of General Moreau's honour and principle in the affairs of private life.

Letters—Jan. 3rd.—The arrival yesterday of your

letter of the 27th ult., my dear M., brought me to a sudden halt in the account I was attempting to give you of two or three of the most distinguished guests at my brother's last dinner.

I cannot tell you how deeply it grieves me that you have thought it needful to alloy your congratulations and good wishes at this season with so many painful reproaches, and I doubt whether I shall have courage again to take up my pen in your service, as it appears I have caused you more displeasure than amusement.

You say, you perceive with regret, that the *conceit* which I, like so many other youths, acquired at Westminster, is rather growing greater than less, and that you have no doubt the imposing " Westminster strut " still does duty for the manly air we boys thought to take for ourselves, before the years of manhood conferred it.

You bid me, dear mother, bear in mind that I am *not yet a man;* that it requires the training of experience to form a correct judgment of public characters and political acts, and that it is presumption in a mere youth to pronounce an opinion on either one or the other, in the confident tone I have assumed.

You are sure, you say, that a sharp rap on the knuckles would await me were I attached to any other mission than my brother's ; and that even he would not let me off very easily, were you to give him a hint of the freedom of my observations on both men and women, and of my absurd admiration of the tyrannical disposition of Bonaparte, described by me as that of "a master mind, and of a man born to rule."

I have done, as I shall ever do, dearest mother, and as you have desired me, I have laid the advice you give me, for my guidance, to heart; but do not think me undutiful if I say that you have borne a little hard upon me. I did my best to supply what my brother has not time for; and he allowed me to do so, knowing the interest you take in all public matters, especially those in which he is in any way concerned. Now, like you, he thought the new year a proper season for warning and advice, and we had a long talk together on that day; in the course of which, it may surprise you to learn, he told me I must remember that I was *no longer a boy*, and reminded me that he had commenced life also in his seventeenth year, when he went to the Hague as Lord Malmesbury's secretary, and not long afterwards was left there as Chargé d'Affaires until appointed secretary of legation at Berlin. Why then does it seem so strange to you, my dear mother, that another son of the same age should take, at least, an equal interest in the affairs of the world.

It is my brother's wish that I *should* observe, even more than I do, what is passing on this great scene of political and military intrigue, gaiety, and ·dissipation. He allows that I possess, in some degree, energy of mind, which of itself is not enough, he says, to go creditably through the world with. Habits of *profitable* observation, of thought, and application, must be added; and to become really habits of the mind, must be cultivated, and cultivated early. He considers this a good school for acquiring some knowledge of mankind—I won't shock you by saying of womankind also—though " the ladies "— observe, these are your eldest son's words—" do play most adroitly a very great part in this interesting French drama."

The comments I venture to make on the actors are generally submitted to him, often he approves of them; when he does not he explains matters more fully to me, or mentions circumstances I of course could not be aware of, but which I fancy you give me the credit, or perhaps discredit, of fishing out for myself.

From time to time I have sent some pages of my journal, instead of letters. Because, although my *professional quill work* has hitherto amounted almost to nothing at all, yet my time is fully occupied, and will be until Mr. Hill—who, I am sorry to say, leaves my brother, but for a regular appointment— is gone; first by morning study, afterwards with fencing, riding, dancing, perhaps flirting, or rather being flirted with, so that I cannot always accomplish a formal letter. And, besides, we are so surrounded by spies, in servants, and others whom one scarcely likes to suspect, that when a messenger has been on the point of being despatched, my brother has said, " Send off those papers of yours, they will be safer in the family archives at Bath than in your room."

You are now convinced, I hope, my dearest

mother, that my political news is more worthy of your attention than you were willing to believe, though it may not be confirmed by that which is current in Bath circles. If I pluck up courage enough to send you another batch of it you must not be offended at my presumption.

My sister tells me, Bath never was so thin. I sympathize with her, knowing how voluminous her correspondence is, and that the thinness of Bath means "a dearth of *frank* men," there being, she says, only Lords Rosselyn and Harcourt to fly to. However, there can be no dearth of scandal for your tea-tables, as we know you have had an heiress entrapped into marriage by the emigrant, Count Lorge, and that her mother is actually dead from the intensity of her grief. Mrs. Fitz, too amongst you, flown to Bath after a quarrel with her prince; while that "pride of the nation," *en attendant* the clearing of the atmosphere in that quarter, is basking in the sunshine of Mrs. Billington's smiles.

I am afraid to undertake to supply my sister with the information she asks for respecting French fashions. "What materials are most in vogue?" she inquires: I really don't know. Mr. Dorant, when he makes his trips to London is always charged with many commissions for dresses, &c., from Mesdames Bonaparte, Luxembourg, Fouché, and other ladies, so that I should suppose English materials to be in vogue. But whatever they may be, a very small quantity can be required; for the dresses are so short, and so scanty, they are nothing to speak of; as a covering they cover very little, and conceal almost nothing.

As you ask for domestic news, you may perhaps care to hear that my brother, having made up his accounts to the end of the year, finds that, limiting himself to the very moderate style of living he has adopted here, 4000*l.* would barely bring him round the year. He has but one carriage and one pair of horses, no extra groom, and no saddle-horses, but those that are hired. This calculation proves, that the expense of living in Paris is increased by at least one-third since the revolution.

Diaries—Jan. 6th.—At last my brother has had his audience. Yesterday, being the fifteenth of the month, an intimation from the Bureau des Affaires Etrangères, that it was the day for presentations, was expected; but at 11 o'clock none having arrived, my brother wrote to the *préfet du palais*, who is here the master of the ceremonies, and received a verbal answer that if he were at the palace by two o'clock he would be introduced to the First Consul.

At the appointed hour he went to the Tuileries, and waited for some time with others in the room set apart for the reception of the *corps diplomatique* called La Salle des Ambassadeurs. At length the *préfet* and another officer of the household arrived, and, preceded by four messengers of state, conducted the ministers who were then assembled up the grand staircase, and through a suite of apartments to the saloon or audience-chamber, in which Bonaparte received them. He was standing between the Second and Third Consuls, surrounded by the ministers and officers of state, the officers who were members of the senate, and the principal officers of his household.

Grenadiers of the Consular Guard were stationed at short intervals on the staircase and in the suite of saloons leading to the audience chamber, and an officer's guard saluted the members of the *corps diplomatique* with military honours.

My brother, as directed by the *préfet*, advanced, on entering the room, a little before the other ministers, to present His Majesty's letter, which Bonaparte came forward a few steps to receive, and handed to the minister of finance, who officiated on the occasion for M. Talleyrand. He then said, "I am very glad to see here an English minister; it is most essential for the peace and prosperity of Europe, that there should be one." My brother bowed, and said he had been charged, on delivering his credential letter, to assure the First Consul of His Majesty's sincere desire to see the great work of peace, which had been so happily commenced, brought to a speedy conclusion. The First Consul made no reply, but conversed for some time with my brother on in-different subjects. He seemed to wish to make a difference between his reception of the English and the Etrurian minister, who was next presented to him, and to whom he spoke but a few words.

An invitation to dine with the First Consul that evening followed the presentation; and my brother was informed that, before the dinner hour, etiquette required that he should leave his card with the

Second and Third Consuls, the secretary of state, and the ministers of the country. It was therefore a busy day for him; as much as he could do, in fact, to get through the necessary visits and dress in time for the dinner, which was at six; the French, generally, having given up the custom of dining earlier.

In the great gallery of the Tuileries a table was prepared for two hundred and forty-eight persons. Bonaparte seated himself at the centre, Le Brun, the Third Consul, took the opposite seat, Cambacérès the upper end. My brother was requested to place himself next to the minister of marine, who was on the Third Consul's right hand; but he observed that with the exception of the president of the senate, who was on Bonaparte's right, and the president of the *corps législatif,* who was on his left, the company seated themselves promiscuously along the table.

The dinner was a very short one, compared with the time those repasts usually occupy in England, but it was most *recherché,* the wines of the finest description, and the decorations of the table of regal richness and elegance.

When it was ended, the First Consul took an opportunity of speaking to all the foreign ministers, but conversed with the English minister for a considerable time. He spoke of the negotiation at Amiens, which he said seemed to be in a satisfactory state of forwardness. Upon which my brother repeated the allusion he had made in the morning to His Majesty's desire for the speedy conclusion of peace. Bonaparte reflected for a moment, then answered quickly, " Eh, bien ! si vous faites la paix aussi bien que vous avez fait la guerre, elle sera bien faite." Presently he added, " A good understanding between France and England is necessary to ensure peace, prosperity, and progress in civilization to the rest of the world."

He mentioned the king, only to say, that " he was happy to find Mr. Addington enjoyed so much the esteem and confidence of His Majesty and the nation. " It was a good omen," he said, " of future prosperity to both nations."

He spoke several times, and in very high terms, of the Prince of Wales ; from which my brother is inclined to think that M. Otto has sent here a full account of his reception by the prince, which is said to have been particularly gracious, and that he has repeated something that passed between them with reference to the First Consul ; for, in speaking, of the prince, he seemed as if flattered by some compliment that had been paid to him by his royal highness.

He afterwards mentioned " Monsieur " Windham— who is indeed a mark shot at by every body here —asked many questions about him ; and said, " Why, if he was so fond of war, did not he take the field himself ?"

My brother answered that " there were enthusiasts in all countries ; that Mr. Windham was considered a person of that description ; but he believed that there was no man more ready to support the doctrines he professed, and no one who spoke, in this instance, from more respectable motives."

The First Consul probably mentioned Mr. Windham, because it is known to the police—through an
agent employed by Fouché, named Duthal, who
gains access by some means to our public offices—
that he has lately transmitted money to royalists; as
much as 2000*l.* has been sent over to one family, a
father and three sons.   It is thought too large a sum
for an act of private charity.   Mr. Dorant, through
whom the knowledge of this comes to my brother,
suggested that Mr. Windham might have *lent* his
name, or that it had been made use of unknown to
him.

On returning home, my brother dictated to me the
above particulars of his audience and subsequent
conversation with the First Consul, both of which he
considers, in appearance at least, satisfactory.

I am to add to the account of it I propose to send
my mother, that he was not presented to Madame
Bonaparte; she being at present somewhat indisposed, as well as much occupied with the preparations for the marriage of Mademoiselle Beauharnois
with the First Consul's brother, Louis Bonaparte.
The First Consul's manner was more like Lord
Malmesbury's, my brother says, than that of any
person he knows, consequently not the less acceptable to him.

I have made diligent search for prints, in order
to gratify the curiosity of friends at home; but,
as yet, I have met with none that give a tolerably
correct notion of the appearance of either *Monsieur*
or *Madame.*   Generally, they are less good of him

than of her. I fancy—though I must not tell it in Bath—that there is something in the countenance of Bonaparte that must be very difficult to transfer to either canvas or paper. You see, at the first glance, that he is a man of iron will, of dauntless force of character, and you seem to understand why his secret and inveterate foes, of which Parisian society seems to be wholly composed, *talk* only of " the removal of the tyrant," of his being " struck down," &c., and you understand—at least I do— that they might stab him in the back, but would never venture to confront him face to face.

9th.—The inflexible Barbé Marbois has probably been brought to see the advisableness of supplying the funds for the Lyons expedition ; for this morning the First Consul, accompanied by Madame Bonaparte, General Duroc, and a private secretary, set out on his long-projected journey. *On dit*, or rather as a frequent visitor here, who has remarkably sharp ears, always commences his stories, *on chuchote*, that Bonaparte and M. Talleyrand being now out of the way, General Moreau and M. Fouché, who are allies in a scheme to overthrow Bonaparte and give France a new form of government, will turn their absence to account, by endeavouring to come to a definite understanding on that subject.

There is a powerful party, it appears, who are convinced that the General is the only man to whom the nation can safely look for a moderate government, and who is capable of succeeding Bonaparte in the administration of affairs.

But my brother is of opinion that nothing will result from the coalition of two persons so opposite in character, views, and aims; and he is at a loss to understand how it has happened that an intimacy of that kind should have sprung up between them.

That Bonaparte shall be removed from his present position seems to be the only point on which they are fully agreed. The General is a royalist; but he will have no share in effecting the removal of Bonaparte unless monarchy be re-established in the person of Louis XVIII.; for he considers there is a prospect of peace and prosperity for France only in limited monarchy, and the restoration of the rightful dynasty.

He declares that he wishes for himself no exclusive power, no ostentatious position that might excite envy and enmity in his fellow-citizens. His sole object would be to protect the monarchy on its restoration; and, for that purpose, he would wish to have revived for him the office of High Constable of France.

By a short, though perhaps violent effort, he believes that success might be attained in this enterprise. Only a million and a half of livres, which he can command, would be required for it; but he strenuously maintains that on the above-named terms only will he have any personal share in the overthrow of the present government.

Fouché, coarse-minded, vulgar, and brutal, has not been able to bring himself to consent to this plan. It contrasts too glaringly with his known principles; it clashes with his personal interests; and it is indeed evident that, under such a change, he could only be indebted to his coadjutor, or to the force of circumstances, for a continuance in .any office of trust or honour.

11th.—Yet there are supposed to be strong reasons why Fouché should yield his own views and judgment to those of the General. He holds his present position entirely at Bonaparte's will; he could be removed from every source of power and influence by a stroke of the First Consul's pen, and, by a decree of banishment, not without precedent, be settled for life at Cayenne.

Fouché has acted as the friend and faithful supporter of Bonaparte as long as he could hope that he had the preference over his rival Talleyrand; but this motive of action may have been reversed, and, having failed in preventing the First Consul in following Talleyrand to Lyons, he may consider the die as cast. But on the other hand, the General's project being so little in harmony with his own views, he may choose to withdraw altogether from it.

It is known that Fouché induced Madame Bonaparte, who is under some obligations to him, to accompany her husband to Lyons, in order that her presence might, in some measure, counteract the influence of Talleyrand; and it is thought that Fouché, to attain his own objects, may even have given the First Consul some hint of General Moreau's proposed plan. For a short time ago the First Consul sent for the General, and asked him if there was anything he could do or could offer

that would be acceptable to him.   He answered, that
at present he was well satisfied ; he wished for
nothing more than he already had.   Bonaparte
replied, " I think you are mistaken, Moreau ; and I
can, at all events, do as much for you as Fouché."
Thus, almost every day, the *pros* and *cons* of new
plots are discussed.   *En attendant* the result of the
last one, we shall have some good skating, for the
weather has become excessively cold.   Our hearths
are piled up, log upon log, much crackle and flame,
but no heat; we shiver, and think enviously of the
coal fires now blazing away in old England.

14*th.*—We just learn that the First Consul arrived
at Lyons on the evening of the 11th, his journey
having occupied from fifty five to fifty six hours.

15*th.*—Mr. Hill and I, accompanied by Mr. Dorant,
went last evening for a stroll in the Palais Royal.
I had not before seen it in the evening lighted up.
It was a very gay scene ; noisy and lively ; the
arcades were thronged, and I noticed there several
of our countrymen.   To most of the English and
other foreigners, the Palais Royal is a spot of
peculiar attraction.   The Parisians look on it as a
sort of earthly paradise, though it has the reputation
of being also the "emporium of profligacy," which
gives, perhaps, a more correct idea of the kind of
pleasures to be found there.   The shops in the arcades that surround the gardens, vie with each other
in their brilliant lighting up.   The fine *cafés*, the
restaurateurs—the most famous in Paris—and the
gambling saloons, in the rooms above, form by their

united display of light, a general and brilliant illumination. The throng of loungers was immense, for no part of Paris is so much resorted to for amusement, promenading, dining, and supping.

There are subterraneous apartments, where unlicensed gambling goes on, and fearful scenes of dissipation take place.

The centre garden has well gravelled walks, and is nicely arranged; in the summer, a quantity of orange trees are placed in it. A very good view of the whole of the building may be had from the garden.

But, both gardens and arcades are infested by a crowd of profligate women, who, in Paris, are allowed only in the Palais Royal to display their profligacy openly; and so disreputable does the company appear to be, generally, that no ladies could possibly walk there in the evening. One tour of the arcades and the gardens satisfied us. Summer weather, and ices, would of course much add to their attractions.

This morning we looked in at the panorama of the city of Paris, and another of the town and port of Toulon, now being exhibited in the Jardin des Capucines. They are very effectively painted. We were, however, on our way to a far more interesting exhibition—the famous collection of pictures and monumental sculpture, saved from destruction when the wild rage of the revolution was at its height. When churches were profaned and pillaged, and all works of art that bore any reference to the memory of those who at any time had filled positions of honour, power, or influence, were madly torn down, mutilated, or demolished.

The collection is extensive ; and is chronologically arranged, in the Maison des Petits Augustins, in separate apartments lighted by windows of stained glass, in the style of each period. Some of the monuments date from the thirteenth century. Those that are perfect, or of which the injuries can be repaired, will be replaced in the cathedrals and other buildings whence they were taken, if peace should allow of the many works that are projected being carried out.

The only monument I have a distinct recollection of, is that of Diane de Poitiers. I thought it very beautiful—a kneeling figure, with a dog by her side. It was brought from the castle of Anet—but, on the whole, I looked on these remnants from the tombs with less interest than I had expected. Lord Aberdeen, who was with us, said, he seemed to regret more what had been destroyed by sacrilegious fury, than to admire what had been rescued; for he thought that those monuments, in their places, were contemplated with a feeling of veneration, that invested them with a sort of ideal beauty, which was lost to them when removed.

20th.—Now that " Der Fürst "—as the secretary of a German legation ventures, in private, to name the great man—is away, and those who will bow the knee to him, on his return, are plotting and laying their heads together to upset him in his absence, we, with some of our English visitors, are doing a little sight-seeing.

E 2

As everybody is talking of the wonderful skill of a Scotchman, with the Irish name of O'Reilly, as an engraver on glass, we went to see some fine specimens of his art, at the Manufacture des Cristaux. His work is said to be of the highest degree of perfection. It is, no doubt, very fine, and it fetches a very high price. My brother bought, for eighteen louis d'or, two small vases, with figures representing the seasons, beautifully executed. Other persons of our party also made purchases of these exquisite works.

21*st*.—This morning I was despatched on a shopping expedition, with her ladyship of Impey, who had been good enough to take pity on our ignorance, and to offer us the aid of her judgment, in the purchase of lace, as well as to explain for my brother a defect in the Duchess of York's satin shoes, which H. R. H. had commissioned him to get made for her in Paris. This accomplished, we proceeded to the celebrated manufactory of Gobelins tapestry, established in Paris, by two brothers, named Gobelins, of Rheims, so long ago as the reign of Francis I. Up to the time of the revolution it was exclusively a royal manufactory, and flourished accordingly. Now, it is very far from flourishing, and the beautiful hangings and rich carpets, with designs copied with marvellous fidelity from the works of French and foreign artists, find rarely a purchaser. Indeed, few persons can afford the great outlay; for the time, skill, and labour required for their production necessarily make their cost enormous. Besides, I am

told, they are no longer much sought after. But
there seems to be a good stock on hand, and many
beautiful works were unrolled for inspection. A few
looms were at work, but here, as elsewhere, the want
of skilled workmen was complained of. That want
alone has brought many manufactures almost to a
stand-still, and when strangers visit the factories, the
languishing state in which most of them are found,
is generally apologized for, as it were, by the
information that the wars have carried off all their
best hands, but that, on the re-establishment of peace,
they look for a more settled and prosperous state of
things.

The Gobelins workmen, notwithstanding the
artistic nature of their employment, are paid at
the rate of only four to four and a half livres per
day. But, if manufactures have suffered, art has
been a gainer. The collections of art treasures, now
brought together in Paris, are said to be unequalled
in the world. The shopkeepers will profit by them,
at all events; for, although the number of foreigners
they have already attracted is great, a far
greater number await the signing of the Treaty, to
gratify their desire of seeing them. I saw, yesterday,
the Pope's fine collection of medals, which has been
added to the Cabinet de Medailles; also the Roman
coins found near Amiens.

25th.—We were at a *re-union, chez* Madame
Joubert, yesterday evening. She is a very charming
woman, spoken of by every one as *une femme
infiniment aimable,* and it is scarcely an exaggera-

tion. She looks on me, I believe, as an especial *protégé*; having brought her from London some private letters, confided to me by her friend, Madame Otto, to deliver to her personally. Fouché was there for a short time, looking rather surly, and more repulsive than usual. He and the General have been unable, as yet, to combine their plans, and, as the First Consul is expected back shortly, they will most likely be quietly dropped, or for the present laid aside. As far as poor Louis XVIII. is concerned, it is doubtful whether even the royalists who remain here care much about him. "Were he to be now forced on the nation, it would cause"—this was said by Fouché himself—" a revolution more bloody than any that has taken place. The great difficulty which the present government has to contend with," he remarked, " is its newness ; it is yet in its infancy, it is the creation of the present age, and every man is convinced that he has a right to destroy what was, in a manner, his own work. But we will have no more revolutions," he exclaimed, " therefore we must strenuously oppose the return of Louis XVIII.; who could not remain three months in power, for the country is no longer the same, and would not tolerate the old principles of government by which he and his advisers would wish to govern."

The person with whom Fouché, of his own accord, had entered into conversation on this topic, answered that " were such an unexpected event to happen as that he had alluded to, the persons named would probably profit by past experience and regulate their measures according to the altered dispositions of the country."

Fouché rejoined quickly, " the event is impossible ! The country is determined to preserve its tranquillity;" adding, with some excitement, " Si Bonaparte, même, avec toute sa gloire, voulait se faire couronner, ou faire couronner un autre, il serait poignardé dans la journée."

It has transpired that Fouché has recently spoken in this sense to several foreign ministers ; and no one is better able than he to speak to this point, as he has now under his direction, in Paris, forty organized Jacobin clubs, by whose means he could put in motion an armed mob of eight thousand men.

Fouché's late dissatisfaction with the First Consul, was caused by a reproof he received from him, arising out of an appeal to the Tribunate made by a merchant of Brussels, who was a short time since arrested by the police of that town, with some circumstances of violence and injustice, on the alleged, but erroneous, charge of exporting corn.   The Tribunate, however, sanctioned the proceedings of the police ; but Bonaparte in his desire to throw public odium on the Tribunate, in revenge for its late opposition to his *projet* for a *code civile*, and to obtain, as his enemies said, popularity for himself, was obliged to make a partial sacrifice of his minister.   He declared his conduct in this case to be unconstitutional and not to be justified—insisting that " he will not suffer the police, in the execution of their duties, to trample upon individual liberty."

Fouché was stung to the quick by this high-handed act of the First Consul, and might have been willing to aid in any practicable scheme for his overthrow. But there can be but two changes—monarchy, or a Jacobin reign. Fouché would be at the head of the latter, yet only in the last extremity would he bring forward his party, for he knows them too well not to be aware that he himself might in the end be their victim.

But the city of Paris and the army would act, as I am told they have ever acted, a distinct part from the rest of the nation. That, as regards the first, so long as Bonaparte can rely on the attachment of his Guards, they will, under his direction, triumph over every exertion of open force that can be employed against him, while the Jacobins, though formidable by their numbers and organization, yet know well the difficulty of contending with regular troops, composed, as Bonaparte's guard is, of soldiers of the most approved bravery, and attached to him also by many ties.

The Generals who have become dissatisfied with Bonaparte on account of the " premature peace," have sought to alienate the affections of his Guards; and many well informed persons think the army is not to be relied upon. That a few colonels may bring over their regiments to act as they please, and thus decide the action of the whole army, which would abandon him, as it did Lafayette and Demourier, if hostile Generals should make it appear that he is acting contrary to the will of the nation.

It is however pretty sure that Bonaparte is, at

least, as popular with the army as any of the Generals who have taken an active part against him. He has besides superior abilities to improve his cause, and the only man who could vie with him in this respect, and who would be supported by that part of the army that has been under his command, has declared his determination to act only on a plan which meets with no other than his own individual support.

February 1st.—The First Consul returned from Lyons on Monday. He entered Paris under a salute of ninety guns, and attended by a brilliant retinue and military escort. The populace assembled in great numbers and welcomed him with loud acclamations. It is rumoured that M. Talleyrand has not been negligent during his absence of the means of strengthening his influence at the Tuileries, and that a marriage between Mademoiselle Archambeau, a niece of M. Talleyrand, and Eugène Beauharnois, Madame B's son, is in contemplation. The consent of the First Consul has not yet been given, and if Fouché resumes his influence probably it will be altogether withheld.

The Italian Republic is the name given to the new country. From the official narrative of the proceedings at Lyons, it would seem that they were conducted with much unanimity, but private letters say they were not; and the first impression made by the late transactions of the government on those who desire the tranquillity of France and Europe, is that of apprehension. For it is considered that other

powers cannot behold with indifference so considerable an extension of the French empire, or regard it
as a favourable specimen of the First Consul's pacific
disposition. "The government of France alone was
fully sufficient," they say, "to occupy his time and
attention." On the other hand, joy and exultation
prevail amongst those men who look only to the
gratification of personal ambition and the supremacy
of the French nation ; and who think them not too
dearly purchased at the expense of private suffering
and public calamity.

The "Moniteur" of to-day has a statement, the
object of which is to prove that the acquisition of the
territory now forming the Italian Republic was in-
dispensably necessary, in order to preserve to France
the same proportion of power and influence that she
formerly possessed.

4th.—The accounts from Lyons state that the
General Assembly made many objections to the constitution imposed on them, and many pertinent
remarks on the impropriety of choosing a stranger as
the head of it. This produced a considerable disturbance amongst the members, when some officers of the
regiments in garrison at Lyons appeared in the hall,
and enforced silence on all parties. Bonaparte has
sent one of his aides-de-camp—a son of the Third
Consul, Le Brun—to Naples with a letter to the king,
to thank him for the assistance afforded to some
French troops who were forced by stress of weather
to seek refuge in one of the ports of Sicily.

The real aim of this mission, as well as that of

General Duroc, who took a letter to the Emperor of Russia, is supposed to be to bring the First Consul into personal correspondence with the sovereigns of Europe by a sort of semi-official means.

Letters —Feb. 6th.— My brother, yesterday, presented several of our countrymen to the First Consul, amongst others Lord Aberdeen, a very agreeable young man, and a great, though a young, friend of Mr. Pitt, who wrote to my brother strongly recommending him, and begging he would show his lordship every attention in his power during his stay in Paris; consequently, we have seen a good deal of him. Also Mr. Caulfield, a young Irishman just come of age and into a fortune of 30,000*l.* a year, with 100,000*l.* besides, in his pocket to get rid of as fast as he can. As soon as he arrived, he engaged an apartment at an hotel, at ninety louis a month, hired sixteen servants, and has given dinners of thirty covers three times a week, of two louis per head, with innumerable etceteras. Almost any Englishman, Irishman, or Scotchman may drop in if he likes, and be welcome. In the midst of the jovial bachelor's life he is leading, he has received a letter from Lady Crofton—to one of whose daughters he is engaged— that informs him she will be in Paris in a few days with the bride elect and her sisters. The moment, it is thought, is rather ill-chosen ; however, the marriage is to take place in Paris they say.

Lady Crofton's letter was forwarded from London by Mr. Dorant, who was supposed to be at Amiens. But he has thought it advisable, he says, to cross the

Channel, and will return in the course of ten days, without his wife even knowing the why and wherefore of his journeys. In the execution of his amateur business as a secret agent he will be obliged, he says, to keep such extraordinary company when he arrives, and to do such mysterious things, that he foresees he shall barely escape a lodging in *Le Temple* as the result of his zeal for the interests of England.

Mr. Hill left us on the 2nd, and I have begun, as far as I am able, to supply his place in the confidential department. For, as the business at Amiens is expected to be completed very shortly, no one will be sent out to replace Mr. Hill. This throws, for the time, a good deal of drudgery on my brother—the state of things here obliging him to vie with M. Talleyrand in precaution.

We have had one " Milor " here, who kept a strict incog.—fortunately so, they say—Lord Camelford, who, not being able to obtain a passport, came to Boulogne as an American, and thence in the capacity of a gentleman's servant. He stayed here some time, but fearing that the police might get hold of him he went off to Vienna. It is feared he should attempt some personal mischief.

9th.—The stories of mysterious disappearances, masked midnight visitors, extensive robberies, and other similar events reported in some of the English papers, and which have caused my dear mother so much alarm, are mere inventions. We thought you would have known how little credit such reports are entitled to, and that you hear of us, and from us, often enough to be assured that we are not threatened with any such dangers as you have imagined. It is true that a number of persons have lately been arrested on the plea of a conspiracy against the life of the First Consul, and that Madame Champtenitz, whose husband was governor of the palace on the 10th of August, 1792, was yesterday sent for by the police and given into the charge of an officer who had orders not to leave her until she had passed the frontiers of Holland. With this exception, the arrests have been confined to some obscure individuals whose names are said to have been found amongst the papers of the emigrants seized at Bareuth some time since. But these measures are supposed to be taken with the view of intimidating the royalists, who have lately been very indiscreet in their conduct.

Last week, some of them were so inconsiderate as to vehemently applaud a play that contained many allusions to the revolution unfavourable to the present order of things. The government instantly ordered the withdrawal of the play.

12th.—We see that the English have also got a story of the written bulletins, and of Bonaparte having reprehended M. de Markoff. The fact is, he treated him as he a short time back treated M. de Lucchesini, and, as those opposed to him say, he is inclined to treat everybody who does not profess a wonderful admiration of all he does, and an implicit faith in all he says. As regards the bulletins, it appears there have always been written ones in circulation, professing to give more accurate information on public affairs than can be found in the newspapers.

It might be supposed that the total subjection of the French press would furnish a good chance of success to such an undertaking; but we are told that these bulletins differ from those of former times only in their conformity to the change of habits, manners, and language; and that they are still coarse in expression, but less good in intelligence.

However, the author of the present bulletins has been seized, and also his papers. On the list of his subscribers the name of M. de Markoff appeared, and at the last levée Bonaparte asked him whether the information he supplied to his government was derived from the written bulletins.

Everything that is said out of France unfavourable to the wishes or views of this government is always attributed to one or other of the foreign ministers, and I dare say they believe that the observations the English papers indulge in originate with my brother.

14*th*.—When Fouché dined here a few days ago, a reference was made to those reports which have been current of assassinations, &c., with the remark that "with a police so well organized, such a series of depredations as was said to have taken place would be almost impossible." I suppose Fouché considered this was said by way of paying him a compliment, for he answered with that brutal sort of indifference which characterizes him, " Oui, oui, cela va fort bien à présent; mais pour en venir là il m'a fallu abâttre au moins deux cents têtes !" One can readily believe, after this confession, all the horrors attributed to him at the most furious period of the revolution. I know that it caused a shock to the feelings of more than one person then present.

Diaries —Feb. 17*th.*— The hereditary Prince of Orange dined here last evening—afterwards we went to the Théâtre Français. The prince came about a week ago, for the purpose of ascertaining whether the interests of his family are likely to be benefited, or otherwise, by the peace.

General Duroc, governor of the Tuileries, waited upon him immediately, in the name of the First Consul. The prince has been promised a private audience from day to day, but from day to day M. Talleyrand has made some excuse for deferring it. Meanwhile, the prince is amusing himself with very little dignity, having consented to be introduced by M. de Lucchesini, the Prussian minister, to a lady of no very high repute, though very high in the favour of M. Talleyrand. M. de L. being aware that the prince was commissioned by the king of Prussia to ask Bonaparte whether he wishes him to be recalled or not—as his wish in either case would be complied with—in order to induce Talleyrand to advise a favourable answer, commenced paying the most servile court to the above-named lady, to whom he promised to introduce the prince. The princess, his mother, is most anxious about him, and has

written to my brother, who was known to her at the
Hague and at Berlin, expressing her fears for her
son *sur un pavé si glissant,* and apparently wishing
him to see that the prince does not make *un faux pas.*
A connection of his family, whom he would scarcely
like to meet—the pretended Prince of Nassau—
being one of *les intimes* of the lady in question, he
has been informed of the circumstance, and for the
rest, my brother says, the prince must look to his
steps himself.

The marriage that was, said to be, on the *tapis* is
no longer spoken of as at all likely to take place.
Bonaparte's success at Lyons has suggested, it is
supposed, other and more ambitious schemes, which
will be fatal to M. Talleyrand's hopes of strengthening his influence by uniting his niece to the First
Consul's stepson.

Madame Bonaparte, a few evenings since, introduced my brother to her daughter, now become her
sister-in-law, and has been most amazingly civil to
him since he was presented to her. She seems to be
so thoroughly good-natured that she might readily
be credited with a wish to show attentions, independent of the promptings of her lord and master.
But here, nothing is said or done, and least of all in
those high quarters, to which some hidden motive is
not assigned, and Madame Bonaparte's smiles and
words, as they are more or less sunny and gracious,
serve, some persons, as an index of the degree of
favour or disfavour, in which they and others are
held by the great man himself.

Those of her acquaintance, however, who know her most intimately, assert that her nature is too genial to be regulated after such a fashion—proud as she is of her hero—and that, in fact, Bonaparte does not impose such restraints upon her. Many people think her handsome. According to my own private opinion, she is not; but she is elegant, beautifully dressed, and captivates by her pleasant, good-humoured manner. A Frenchman, who knew her before her second marriage, spoke of her to some Englishmen, who were much pleased with her reception of them, as "une excellente femme, qui a plus de cœur que d'esprit; d'une tournure agréable, si vous voulez, mais dont la charme infinie de sa grace d'autrefois est effacé par l'air de dignité qu'elle affecte aujourd'hui."

Madame Louis has something of her mother's manner; my brother says she has less *bonhomie* in her disposition; but it may be that youth and better education restrain the free expression of it. It is generally thought that very little, if any, affection exists between her and her husband.

18*th*.—M. Talleyrand is now occupied with his own marriage, which awaits the arrival of the Pope's dispensation. Meanwhile, he is amassing wealth by making the Department of the Emigrants, which is under his control, as foreign minister, a source of considerable private emolument. He grants, very liberally, permissions to return to France, to those emigrants who can find means to pay him liberally ; whilst Fouché and his police are active in searching

out reasons for arresting a great number of these
unfortunate persons when they arrive.

The enmity that exists between these two ministers
is occasioned no less by the opposition of their
personal characters than by the difference in their
public views.

Talleyrand is considered the head of the aristo-
cratic party, Fouché that of the Jacobinical. Talleyrand has something of severity in his manners, and
from former habits is disposed to whatever partakes
of refinement, even in his vices. Fouché, on the
contrary, is as vulgar in deportment, as coarse-
minded, and ferocious in disposition. He is, more
or less, connected with every species of malefactor,
and gratifies his thirst of power and riches by the
favouring of one party to the prejudice of another.

20*th.*—How long, some people ask, can a government, circumstanced as this is, be expected to
last? Others answer, that the great energy and
activity of Bonaparte's mind form an almost in-
vincible barrier to the attacks of those who would
overthrow him. He secludes himself, now, almost
entirely from the public, lives in the Tuileries as
in a fortified castle — every possible avenue to it
being doubly guarded—and in the midst of a chosen
body of veteran troops, already much attached to
him, and with whom he employs every means to
ingratiate himself still further.

From the frequent change in the commanders of the
Consular Guard, it would seem to be Bonaparte's
policy not to leave the same officers amongst them

long enough to have the opportunity of gaining much influence with the men; whilst the officers he does appoint are, of course, those he considers most firmly attached to his interests.

General Lannes, who commanded the Consular Guard, and, like Massena, was much dissatisfied at the prospect of a peace, was suspected of tampering with the men for the purpose of ascertaining how far they would offer opposition in any attempt at revolt. He was dismissed from his command, put under arrest, and afterwards ordered to reside in the country at a fixed distance from Paris. But he has since given up the names of his friends, made known the circumstances of their plot, and accepted the embassy to Portugal, which he at first rejected.

The Abbé Sièyes was also at the head of a set that had combined to oppose Bonaparte's government. He was offered a national domain of considerable value, which he accepted, and received also the appointment of member of the Sénat Conservatem, thus, crushing himself; for as soon as it was said that his object was pecuniary recompence he fell into contempt, even amongst his warmest adherents, and has been deprived of the power of employing with effect that genius for intrigue for which he is so eminent. Nevertheless, his house is still the resort of all who are disaffected towards the government; he is easy of access, and gives liberal encouragement to all who think themselves entitled to complain.

But, notwithstanding all the means that are employed to annihilate Bonaparte and his government,

those most competent to give an opinion affirm that
he can only be overpowed by a much larger, and far
more united, force than is, at present, likely to be
brought against him; or by a far more general
change of sentiment throughout the country than has
hitherto taken place.

Letters—Feb. 25th.—My brother had a very kind
hint the other day from Mr. Abbot, as soon as he
knew of his intended election and Mr. Wickham's
appointment to Ireland, by which the Berlin mission
becomes vacant. Although he has a powerful com-
petitor in Mr. Frere, there is a very good chance
of my brother gaining the day, as he has learned
from trustworthy authority. At all events, he-
thinks you may rely on his not crossing the Atlantic,
for should Mr. F. get Berlin, he will then most
probably return to Madrid, for which post Mr. Frere
was destined. He would prefer that, he says, to
America, though with only the rank of envoy, as it
must be put, at least, on an equal footing in point of
emolument, and, besides, would not be so much out
of the way. He expects to hear soon from Mr.
Addington that it is settled provisionally. Vienna
will shortly be vacant; Mr. Paget who has been there
but six months, being, we hear, quite tired of his
residence in that capital.

There has been so much writing, that without
further assistance it could not be got through;
Mr. Wild, a nephew of Sir Isaac Heard, has therefore joined my brother, and will remain until the end.
People are beginning to think that the end has been

waited for long enough, and it is said that the delay
is on the English side. But it has been announced
that Lord Whitworth is ready to set out, and awaits
only the signing of the Treaty.

Mr. Dorant has got himself into a scrape. He
writes that he had embarked in the Dover packet on
his return to Paris, having in his possession five
hundred and sixty-nine guineas, but no order for
their exportation. By some means it became known
at the inn he had slept at, and information of the
circumstance was given by the landlord to the
Custom-House officer. When Dorant went on board
he was seized and searched ; the money was taken
from him, and he was compelled to return on shore.
He had a passport from M. Otto, who had given
into his charge a parcel, which Dorant describes, in
his odd way, as " about three feet long and as thick
as a man's thigh, and containing several pieces of
flannel for M. Talleyrand." Also he had a lace dress
for Madame Bonaparte, for which he had paid sixty
guineas ; two others for Mesdames Fouché and
Luxembourg, as well as green tea and cotton
stockings for the latter lady, with two or three
patent lace cloaks, and other articles for less distinguished personages. These he was compelled to
leave on board, but they were all addressed to the
English minister, and were to be passed through the
Customs as his. He had the folly to declare that the
guineas, as well as the packages, were for the use of
the British minister. However, his story was not
credited. He excused himself to my brother by

saying that it was really a fact, as they enabled him
to take a journey in his service, and to be useful to
him.

On returning to London he applied to the Foreign
Office for the restoration of his money.   But Mr.
Stone, the Dover agent, had already reported the
matter, with, as Dorant says, " the most unfounded
and exaggerated insinuations that ever entered into
the mind of man to make, and that brought on him,
from my Lord Hawkesbury, through Mr. Hammond,
reproaches that were most painful to bear.   He asked
for his money, not that he valued it more than if it
had been a bottle of wine, for he was not fond of
money, and had already more than he should live to
spend ; but it was the way of losing it that hurt him
so deeply.   My lord could not understand why he
should go to France in such a manner, nor what
secret there was between him and His Majesty's
minister, when he gave them information which,
they said, changed completely the face of the thing,
and Mr. H., who had declared that he had never
known an instance of money once seized being
restored, then promised him some compensation.
This he declined ; he would have the whole or none."
He is likely it appears to get none, for he has heard
nothing more on the subject, and has not made any
further application ; being well satisfied, he says, if
they will leave him alone.   He declares that he had
information that would have enabled Lord Cornwallis
to have the Treaty signed on his own terms within
forty-eight hours.

For the present, I suppose, he has given up his
self-imposed duty of collecting secret intelligence,
for he knows not, he says, when he may be able to
revisit Paris. This is a disappointment and loss to
others, no less than to himself; he has such a talent
for worming out secrets, and does it so thoroughly
con amore. I believe he has found it also not an
unprofitable pastime, even should he eventually not
recover in some form the value of the guineas seized
at Dover.

March 2nd.—What a dismal set of table-talkers
you have at Bath, my dear mother, with their stories
of the king's want of strength, and Mr. Addington's
want of strength ; themselves, I think, deficient in
that sort of strength they think the king wanting
in ; for my brother had yesterday a letter from
Mr. Harcourt, dated Windsor Lodge, in which he
says all the family is quite well. You have levées
and drawing-rooms as usual ; and as Mrs. Lawrell,
we hear, adds so much to the warmth of the latter,
their Majesties must be in good health to support the
fatigue of them.

It is not in the papers, but that is not very con-
clusive, that the Duke of York has recently lost
200,000*l.*, and is selling his town house and horses.
At all events you have the Duchess amongst you,
though, as you suggest, only to be out of the way,
he having brought her down and returned to town
the next day. We have a Bath letter of later date
than yours, which says that the Duchess has been
bitten in the hand by one of her dogs ; that the

wound will not heal, and that her physician has
recommended her to try the Bath waters.— Oh,
wonder-working waters!—Her royal highness, we
are told, " has her hand pumped upon, and then takes
one glass of water, after everybody has left the little
pump-room, as she would avoid as much as possible
being seen." I hope you will not fail to inform us
of the happy result, and my brother says you are
to lay him at her royal highness's *feet*, and inquire if
she wants any more shoes before he leaves Paris.

Diaries—March 4th.--Bonaparte is furious at what
is said of him in our papers. Pelletier's journal has
been complained of. M. Talleyrand has mentioned
with much dissatisfaction the hostile feeling which, as
he asserts, the English ministerial newspapers display
towards France. " Ce n'est pas là la manière d'agir,"
he said, " mais, malgré tout cela, nous ferons la paix."
He added, however, a sort of threat, if those un-
scrupulous attacks were not discontinued, to " lâcher "
his papers against us, which would produce, he said,
a by no means pleasant sort of warfare.

Both the " Times " and the " Morning Chronicle "
have copied articles respecting my brother, from
Montlivier's " Journal de Londres," a paper in the pay
of this government. All its articles on the public
and private affairs of France are supplied from the
Tuileries, and Fouché's office, and there is a person
here, connected with the " Morning Chronicle," whose
business is to explain what his colleague dares not
bring forward in his semi-official shape. Hence the
indecent paragraphs in the " Chronicle " respecting

persons high and low in this country. The story
of the king's intention to abdicate, has produced a
most unpleasant effect on the Continent, where there
are no means of knowing the falsehood of such like
reports.

10*th.*—We are to have Mrs. Damer and her friend,
Miss Berry, here in a few days. Two such connoisseurs in every way, would not, of course, lose the
first opportunity of visiting Paris to see the Apollo
Belvidere and other fine sights. Lord Pelham would
not give them a passport till now, and he does not
say what made him change his determination. They
will see pictures and statues enough here to satisfy
them, I hope.

M. David, the painter of the fine picture of the
passage of Mont St. Bernard, has completed one of
the Roman and Sabine warriors; the Sabine women
interposing to prevent the fight. The artist has
published an apology for the nakedness of these bold
warriors. Mont St. Bernard, with Bonaparte and his
heroes, pleases me better than this scuffle of naked
savages and wild women—so much for my taste.
What would Miss Berry say, I wonder?

Sir Ralph Woodford's son has just arrived here
from Egypt, where he has been with Major Byng,
who was reported dead after the battle of Hohenlinden. Mr. Windham wrote to my brother about
the major, who is his nephew, and took the opportunity of giving him a strong dash of his politics.
To-morrow we all go to St. Germain, a few miles
from Paris, to see " Esthère," one of Racine's plays,

acted by the young ladies of a famous boarding
school kept by a Madame Campan. She was
a bed-chamber woman of the poor Queen Marie
Antoinette, and has, by her cleverness and character,
been able to keep up her school during the whole of
the revolution upon the same footing.

12*th*.—The strange intelligence with which Dorant
was primed, when so inopportunely stopped on his
voyage to France, he has found a way of conveying to my brother, and Lord Cornwallis has received
some hints, of which it is supposed he might make
some advantageous use. But hints, it is thought,
are not readily taken in that quarter. There has
been much delay for some days in the transmission of
the reports of the proceedings at Amiens. Perhaps
it would be almost high treason to say that the dis-
cussions are protracted unnecessarily by the English
Negotiator; but the very *merry* letters that find
their way hither from the seat of Congress give such
amusing details of the "pottering old woman's" leisurely mode of transacting business, that one cannot
refrain from hearty laughter *sous cape*, while the
object of it is, of course, cried up as a sort of British
Solomon. He is, indeed, looked upon as a fine old
boy, and as conscientiously desirous to do the work he
has been charged with, in the best manner. But, as if
aware that he is not qualified for it, he cannot move a
step without reference to England. This, my brother
says, is much to be regretted, as it affords the French
Government a pretext, they are only too glad to avail
themselves of, for their complaints against England.

15*th.*—Public attention is wholly absorbed by the delay in the signing of the Definitive Treaty. It is commented upon in every society, and, in some instances, with expressions so disrespectful towards the English Government that it has been found necessary to take notice of them. Serious doubts prevail as to the final issue of the Congress, and it is suspected that the idea of a rupture of the negotiation is now floating in the mind of Bonaparte.

In the Official "Moniteur" it is unequivocally asserted that the signature is retarded solely by His Majesty's Government. This statement ends with an appeal to the British nation, by which the First Consul, who is himself the author of it, seems to wish by anticipation to throw off the odium which a renewal of the war might bring upon him. It is made to appear, also, that the principal powers of Europe concur in his plans and operations.

Yet it is believed that, owing to the internal state of the country, and the situation of the armament of St. Domingo, the First Consul, himself, will not desire to renew the war; but that from the jumble of interests that exists here, and which must be taken into consideration, he experiences as much difficulty from the approach of peace as he ever met with in the conduct of the war.

Difficulties press upon him, and they are of a nature which his temper and frame of mind are ill-suited to overcome, and seem to put him off his guard against the danger that menaces him.

War, then, may serve his object better than peace,

as it would enable him to employ many of his bitterest enemies in distant situations, where their thirst of military glory and military plunder would be gratified, which for a time would stifle all feeling of resentment against him.

18*th*.—A whole batch of presentations awaits the signing of the Treaty. Mrs. Damer and Miss Berry, who arrived the other day, will be of the number. *En attendant* they are fully employed, and highly delighted with the spoils of war with which this gay city is enriched. The weather is become so mild and fine that we can now go the round of sights again with some pleasure. It is high spring in the garden of this house, flowers are peeping forth, and the ground is so well laid out that, if the Treaty should remain much longer unsigned, and war not be the consequence, I foresee that we shall have some pleasant al fresco entertainments. The last two mild evenings our foreign visitors took their coffee in the garden, and smoked there.

19*th*.—Some connoisseurs, who had been inspecting the pictures, condemned much the retouching by French artists, which some of the finest works of the old Italian masters have undergone since their arrival. They ought, they contended, to have been exhibited in the condition in which they were received. But it appears they were so much injured in their transport, that some of the most valuable paintings could not have been shown without the restoration of the defaced portions. But the wreck of the original works, connoisseurs say, would have

given, all true lovers of art more pleasure than
the renovations and botchings, as they are termed,
of incompetent artists. However, the most skilful
painters have been employed on them, and time will
efface the traces of the modern brush.

20th.—M. Talleyrand had a long conversation
with my brother yesterday on the " inexplicable conduct of the English Government." All the principal
articles of the Treaty having been agreed to, eight or
ten days ago, he finds it difficult to understand the
delay in signing it. Nothing could exceed, he says,
the surprise of the First Consul when he learned that
Lord Cornwallis had received fresh instructions,
which directed him to reject what he had already
consented to sign.

Notwithstanding these remonstrances and their
profession of anxiety for the conclusion of peace, my
brother declares that he can observe in the conduct
of the French Government nothing that bears an
appearance of the cordiality and good faith so liberally
observed by England towards France, but, on the
contrary, deep duplicity and an eager desire to take
every possible unfair advantage to increase their own
power and influence, and to separate England from
the rest of the world.

22nd.—It was remarked in conversation yesterday,
how large a number of Generals of inferior note had
latterly been appointed to the Sénat Conservatem, and
it was explained that it was a means adopted by the
First Consul for dissolving, without *éclat*, the military confederacy formed against him, it being, while

doing so, a great object with him also to impress the
world with a belief that his government is carried on
without any opposition or extraordinary exertion of
authority.

26th.—At last! A French courier has brought the
Treaty. He made the journey with such unusual
speed that he has reached Paris from Amiens in nine
hours and a half!

Letters—March 27*th.*—By the time this reaches
England our business here, I imagine, will be settled,
and your guns be firing, and bells ringing. Yesterday a French courier, who made a wonderfully quick
journey from Amiens, brought the Definitive Treaty,
signed on the 24th. As soon as M. Talleyrand
received it, he carried it to the First Consul, although he was then engaged in the council of state.
Immediately he read it to the assembled members,
and informed them there were no secret articles.

At about five o'clock, the guns of Paris thundered·
forth to the inhabitants the glad tidings of peace.
The news was communicated officially at the theatres.
Between eight and nine the Treaty was published in
a special edition of the "Moniteur," and the palace of
the Tuileries was illuminated.

In the course of the afternoon notice was sent to
the foreign ministers that the First Consul would
receive their congratulations this morning, after they
had paid their respects to Madame Bonaparte on this
auspicious occasion. This is quite an innovation. It
is the first time she has formally received the whole
of the *corps diplomatique.* However, she acquitted

herself in her new *rôle*, as I am told, with her accustomed ease of manner.

She was seated on a *canapé*, most exquisitely
dressed, when the foreign ministers entered her
apartment — a spacious and elegantly arranged
boudoir looking on the gardens;—throughout the
reception she remained seated, and addressed to each
of her visitors a few well-chosen words of felicitation
on the great and happy work just completed. It has
been remarked since, and by one who is not disposed
to flatter her, that her bearing was graceful and
becoming, and not wanting in proper dignity.

On taking leave of Madame Bonaparte, the
corps diplomatique were conducted to the audience-
chamber of the First Consul. He, as usual, received
them standing; on either side the Second and Third
Consuls, and the accustomed surrounding of ministers,
officers of state, &c. But he had laid aside his
military dress, and wore that of a Councillor of State.
Apparently he was in his most gracious mood, and
expressed himself much gratified at the happy event
which was the cause of his meeting that day the
representatives of those foreign Courts who had
so cordially combined with him to bring about the
pacification of Europe; adding, with especial reference
to England, "as far as the peace just concluded
depends on me it will be permanent; for no motive,
but that of honour, shall induce me to break it."

Diaries—March 28th.—In the course of some conversation that followed, my brother observed, "How
much it surprised him that it had been found possible

to prepare the Treaty for signature so soon after the articles had been agreed upon."

The First Consul and M. Talleyrand both acquiesced in his observation, but the former said that " upon such an occasion some extraordinary exertion was to be expected."

29th.--A messenger from Lord Cornwallis brought yesterday the information that the Treaty was signed only on the 27th, and soon after my brother was told that what had been published on Friday was the paper that had been agreed to in the protocol of the conference between the respective plenipotentiaries. In the course of the day he happened to meet M. Talleyrand, and some allusion being made to the premature publication of the Treaty, the latter intimated that its object had been to prevent stock-jobbing. But if this was in any way the cause of it, it may be inferred, from some transactions that took place on the *Bourse* a fortnight ago, that it was to afford an opportunity to make good a considerable deficiency in the money matters of some persons connected with the government, in consequence of the Treaty not having been signed, as was expected, ten days sooner. But however this may be, it is certain that as little time as possible was lost between the arrival of the courier and the communication of the Treaty.

31st.--As a sort of prelude to the publication of the *Concordatum*, orders were given on Saturday for a *Te Deum* to be sung, and high mass to be celebrated the next day, by Cardinal Caprera, at the Cathedral

of Notre Dame. Notice was sent to the Cardinal to
be ready for the ceremony, which was to be conducted
with great pomp and magnificence. But early on
Sunday morning he was informed that it was not to
take place. This change of intention is supposed to
be owing to the difficulty of so soon displacing the
constitutional clergy, who now have possession of
Notre Dame, and to the impossibility of fitly preparing the church, at so short a notice, for so solemn an
event as the restoration of divine worship in France.
For Notre Dame, like other sacred edifices, was
pillaged and defaced at the time of the revolution,
and has since fallen, from neglect, into a dirty,
ruinous condition.

The public reception of the cardinal as the Pope's
legate will take place with the publication of the
Concordatum.

Report says that the offices of Second and Third
Consul will be abolished about the same time, and
that Bonaparte will take exclusively to himself the
nominal as well as the real direction of affairs.

The hereditary Prince of Orange speaks in terms of
much regret of a title different from that his family
has usually borne being now to be adopted by it.

Letters—April 2nd.—We do not yet know when
we shall leave Paris, but until we leave we are
gentlemen at large, with little to do but to amuse
ourselves.

It is strange, that the anxious interest which the
people generally seemed to take in the Congress at
Amiens, during the early stage of its deliberations,

has subsided into utter indifference since the final result was known. The First Consul is greatly mortified at the apathy of the people, and did not conceal his displeasure from the trade deputations, when they presented themselves to congratulate him on the re-establishment of peace.

He received them with great coldness, and gave them clearly to understand that, as he had diligently laboured to secure for the French nation an advantageous peace, he looked for some more decided manifestation of thankfulness, than he had hitherto received, from those who were most to be benefited by his patriotic efforts.

The poorer classes still clamour for the cheap bread they are, unfortunately, not likely to get; and the commercial people who looked for a great revival of trade, as soon as only the preliminaries were ratified, are of course still disappointed. However, all the hotels are overflowing with English; for we have an inundation from our shores since the signature of the Treaty, and the flood increases daily, and will no doubt go on increasing. The Parisians take every possible advantage of this, treating all our countrymen as "les riches milors." Those who find their way to this house complain loudly; extortion, they say, is the rule with the shopkeepers in their dealings with their visitors, and on all sides they fleece them most thoroughly.

6th.—Perhaps this will be the last letter I shall send you from Paris, for my brother has received his letter of recall, and waits only for an audience to

deliver it.   He reckons on setting out in a fortnight.
Although established so short a time, there are a
great many things to do, and many people to take
leave of, before setting off.   Nothing is said to him
from Downing Street of his future destination; but
he still preserves the hope of not leaving Europe.

8*th.* — M. Talleyrand informed my brother, on
his requesting permission to take leave of the First
Consul, that it would be informal, and inconsistent
with the rules of etiquette established here, to take
leave so abruptly.   He reminded him that his orders
were to return immediately; Mr. Merry, who had
conducted the business at Amiens, being fixed on
by His Majesty's Government as the proper person to
exchange the Treaties, and succeed him as minister
until the arrival of an ambassador.   No day is however yet fixed for his audience.

General Berthier, the minister of war, is spoken of
as likely to have the London embassy.   No doubt he
would be glad to accept it, as he is displeased with
some retrenchments lately made in his department
by the First Consul, and has, besides, *liaisons* which
he would be glad, *on dit*, to escape from; not being
able to carry off those affairs with so high a hand as
his colleague, M. Talleyrand.

Diaries—April 11*th.*—The *Concordatum* between
this government and the Church of Rome, and the
different articles by which it provides for a Church
Establishment in France, received the sanction of
the *corps legislatif* on the 8th.   On the following
day Cardinal Caprera was admitted to an audience

of the First Consul as *legate à latere,* from his Holiness the pope.

It is reported that the ceremony was conducted in a manner in every respect similar to that which was customary under the former government.

12*th.*—The First Consul has finally fixed on Easter Sunday for the festivities in honour of the general peace.

13*th.*—All is bustle, activity, and animation; and if the peace itself is disregarded, the keenest anxiety is yet shown, by all classes of this *peuple mobile,* to celebrate it with the utmost *éclat.*   .

16*th.*—As the 18th approaches, Paris becomes fuller, and nothing seems to interest any one which has not some reference to the forthcoming fêtes. Many visitors flock in daily from the provinces, where Bonaparte is said to be very popular; and where, generally, the inhabitants consider themselves indebted to him for the tranquillity of the last two years. They seem to have no particular motive for dissatisfaction with the present order of things— which, if not perfect, they think is as good as any they have yet known—but such as may arise from an unextinguished sentiment of attachment to their legitimate sovereign, and to the religion of their fathers. These feelings are said to be most prevalent in the south of France; they are not, however, strong enough to induce any active exertion.

19*th.*—Easter morning was ushered in by some passing showers, but the whole city was in motion very early. Throngs of sight-seers—some not a

little bespattered—picked their way through the
muddy pools of the Paris streets, avoiding, as best
they could, the crazy *fiacres* that dodged about in
greater numbers, and caused greater confusion than
ever.

The First Consul gave an early audience to the
corps diplomatique before going in procession to Notre
Dame.

The *Concordatum* was published to the sound of
trumpets and the thunder of artillery, and the joy of
the populace seemed unbounded; for with many the
religious part of the ceremony was the principal
attraction. The Pope's legate was, therefore, the
object of profound veneration, and fairly divided the
honours of the day with the " nation's great bene-
factor," by whom this happy change, " peace on
earth, peace with the Church and with Heaven," has
been brought about.

Admission to Notre Dame was by tickets, for all
who were not present officially; yet the cathedral
was in every part crowded to excess, so numerous
and urgent had the applicants been.

So short a time had been allowed for decorating
and embellishing the interior of the building, that we
were the more struck, on entering, with the change
from the dirt and desolation of the other day to the
pomp and splendour of yesterday.

The *Te Deum* was sung magnificently, and with
deep feeling; many persons found it difficult to restrain their emotion, while not a few were over-
powered by it. For this first solemn celebration of

high mass necessarily awakened the saddest feelings, and the most painful memories, in the greater part of the congregation.

The carriages of the First Consul and his colleagues, and the green, gold-embroidered, liveries of their attendants, were exceedingly rich. Some of the principal officers, and the foreign ministers generally, made a respectable part of the show in that way; but, although Spartan simplicity is no longer the order of the day, a decent private vehicle is still a rarity, and citizen coachmen are still unliveried.

At the audience of the morning, my brother took leave of the First Consul. In reply to the assurance that it was "His Majesty's desire to cement the union and good understanding now happily re-established between the French Republic and England," he requested that the king might be informed that it was "equally his sincere determination to employ every means in his power to render the peace durable, and productive of mutual satisfaction and advantage."

He then noticed the circumstance of my brother having been the first minister appointed to this country after the cessation of hostilities, and expressed in very obliging terms the recollection which he said he should retain of his having been here, and his wish that his future destination might be in every respect satisfactory to him. Later, my brother made his final bow to Madame; and to-day he takes leave of the Second and Third Consuls and M. Talleyrand.

We had a dinner in celebration of the great events that were fêted yesterday, and afterwards we went to look at the illuminations, in which the French are said to excel.

That of the British mission represented a temple—the closed temple of Janus, I believe—with many columns, round which thousands of coloured lamps were wreathed. It was a very effective display, and was greatly admired.

The streets were thronged with a very orderly mob of sight-seers, and, for the general convenience and safety, no *fiacres* were allowed to be out that evening.

The public buildings, the residences of the members of the government, and those of the foreign ministers, were all brilliantly lighted up. The Place Vendôme, Place de la Revolution, &c., glowed with colour from the many-tinted lamps.

The Palais du Corps Législatif—once the Palais Bourbon—was compared to a palace of jewels, so thickly was it covered with gleaming lamps, and their colours so harmoniously intermixed. The entire length of the Tuileries was marked by lines of fire, and festooned with flowers and variegated lamps, and draped with numerous flags; those of all nations intermingling with the *drapeau republicain*. A portion of the gardens was illuminated; in the vicinity was a display of fireworks, and another on the river; while a concert of military bands enlivened the scene.

Outside the grounds, and near the palace, a temporary fountain had been erected. Last evening it streamed with bright Bourdeaux, and many a bumper was quaffed there in honour of "La paix et le pacificateur!" and in one instance we heard: "Le héros! qui veut se faire aimer en *vin!*— *en vain.*"

Whatever the peace itself may prove to be, the brilliant *fête de nuit* with which it has been celebrated was an undoubted success; and I am glad we have had the opportunity of witnessing that, as well as the solemn ceremonies of the morning.

20th.—All our arrangements are completed; and to-morrow morning, early, we shall be *en route* for Old England. We have lived for five months in a perfect maze of plots, Jacobin, military, and royalist; surrounded by spies, noting every act, and reporting every word; yet I, at least, leave the gay capital with regret. And gay, indeed, it is, for notwithstanding the undercurrent of stratagem and intrigue, in general society a genial tone lies on the surface, and a lively *sans façon* mode of life prevails that is irresistibly pleasing and attractive.

Mr. F. J. Jackson to Mrs. Jackson.

Royal Hotel, Pall Mall,
24th April, 1802.

MY DEAR MOTHER,

I take up the first pen and piece of paper I find to tell you that we arrived again in this great town between ten and eleven this morning, after a good and prosperous journey, having left Paris on Wednesday morning last.

We landed yesterday at Dover between nine and

ten, but had to wait there so long to have the
carriage brought on shore that I could only reach
Dartford last night.

I have been fortunate in catching Mr. Addington
and Lord Hawkesbury before they leave town for
the week's end, and have met with such a reception
as convinces me my labours have not been in vain.

I am not quite sure whether before you last heard
from us, Merry had received an intimation that he
might go as minister to America; which, as that
post was offered me, corroborates the information I
had received of my being destined to Berlin.

Lord Hawkesbury has appointed me to meet him
on Thursday, when I may obtain some light on the
subject if I do not receive any positive information. I have, however, little or no doubt, as there
is in fact nothing else in the line worth my acceptance, and they do not probably mean to turn me
out of it.

I see all the town is prepared for an illumination,
which will probably take place on Monday. I did
not bring the Ratifications, as the papers announced,
because my time of couriership is past, and I certainly should have no inclination to recommence it
upon this occasion. I imagine they will arrive to-
night or to-morrow, and then you may illuminate or
not, as you please.

I see nothing here that equals my illumination
last Sunday, when we had been in procession to
Notre Dame to celebrate the re-establisment of
religious worship. They tell me Otto's is very fine,

and the *badeaux* are driving about all day to see
only the preparations. I just lay my hand on the
drawing of mine, and send it you for your amusement. Imagine six thousand lamps on the columns
of my temple.

Adieu ! I have a thousand people to see, and
things to do.

Ever your dutiful son,

F. J. J.

P.S. Everybody says to me, " How fat you are
grown !" and, in fact, my clothes are getting too
small ; so, you see, that frogs and sour wine have
done more for me than roast beef and port. I leave
George to tell his own story.

Mr. Francis Jackson's appointment to Berlin did
not take place so soon after his return from Paris as
he had been led to expect. On the 1st of May he
writes to Mrs. Jackson, his mother : " The business
—that is the actual appointment—is still kept in
suspense, for reasons which I do not quite understand, as Lord Hawkesbury himself said he should
send either Frere or me to Berlin. And as F. is all
but gazetted *i.e.*—approved of by the king— for
Madrid, the conclusion with regard to me ought to
follow of course."

" The only conjecture I can form, is that the
hesitation may proceed from the Court of Spain
having, without waiting for any opinion or appointment from us, named an ambassador—the Duke of

Frias—to London, and I imagine they will hardly give Frere that character."

On the 30th of June no positive conclusion had been come to ; but Mr. Addington, who was then going to Devizes to be elected, appointed a meeting for the 8th of July.

Under that date, Mr. Jackson says, " Mr. Addington told me he had agreed with Lord Hawkesbury that all the king's ministers should go immediately to their respective posts; that, having got over the elections, they should proceed to carry this resolution into effect, and hoped that he should soon be able to tell me the precise time when I may make my arrangements for setting out. All this, you see, is general, but so far satisfactory that it would be the height of duplicity, as well as of injustice, to go on talking to me of a thing as settled which they meant afterwards to overturn.

" Everybody is talking of the balloons and the elections, and the latter seem to go off more quietly than the former.

" It is really certain that Sir John Warren is to be metamorphosed from an admiral to an ambassador, and will replace Lord St. Helens.

" Lord Whitworth will not go until Andreossi comes—probably about the beginning of October. I suspect—though I know no reason why it should be so—that the rest of us will stay in England till that time, when the great and general arrangement will take place. The extraordinary feature of it will be Sir J. Warren's appointment to St. Petersburg."

July 23*rd.*—I have heard nothing more of my future destination, but imagine we shall all be called upon to wake up together.

I dined on Sunday with the Speaker, and we talked the matter over. Abbot agreed with me that everything was in as satisfactory a state as could be, short of the appointment being officially announced. Indeed, I consider that ministers are so pledged to me, in various ways, that I am very easy on the subject; not being at all anxious as to Berlin in particular.

Abbot met with a curious opposition at Woodstock from an Irishman who wished to prevent his being chosen Speaker in the new parliament, and offered himself as a candidate, only that he might petition against him. For this reason Abbot was returned for another of the Duke of Marlborough's boroughs, Heytesbury, which keeps out Charles Moore—who is to sit for that place—till A. has made his election.

The delay that occurs in my business is rather a serious consideration, as far as George is concerned. He must not be idling with you at Bath. He must study; his Latin and Greek must not be neglected, and, if needful, a private tutor must be engaged to keep him to it. I am the more anxious about this, because I have often repented that I did not regularly follow up my classical studies, as I might have done after leaving Erlang. While on the subject, I may say that I think you and some of his Bath friends are in error, to encourage him in the

idea that he is equal to, and ought to have, the
appointment of secretary. It cannot be ; and, were
it even possible, I should, for his sake, object to it for
the present. He may be anxious and assiduous, but
has not had sufficient training in the general routine
of business; and, besides, I wish him to pursue his
education further. He will, with me, have greater
opportunities for self-improvement, and for gaining a
certain kind of knowledge of mankind, which is
indispensable for success in our line, than would
probably be afforded him under another chief; but
Mr. George must abate his pretensions for awhile,
and be content, if he goes with me, to be first *student*
in my *pépinière.*

August 21*st.* —You see the newspapers have settled
my appointment, and have given me young Rolleston—who was to have gone with Wickham—as
secretary. But Lord Hawkesbury told me last week
that, although he was to the full as anxious as
myself that we should all be at our posts, and hoped
very shortly to assign to me mine, which he did
not doubt would be the one I wished, yet a
particular circumstance prevented him from pro-
nouncing at this moment. Although he did not
explain this particular circumstance, I know it to be
no other than the uncertainty that still exists as to
the Court of Spain. After all, an ambassador may
be sent there, and some arrangement made in consequence, by which my destination will be altered.
This will be no cause of dissatisfaction to me, if I
get, as I am undoubtedly entitled to, a situation of

equal emolument; for Berlin, in itself, has no charms for me.

Tell George he must wait patiently. Were I to reply in volumes to his volumes, I could say no more than I did in my last. I beg you to inculcate that again and again. It is creditable to desire to earn an independence by his own talents and assiduity, and he is, I hope, fitting himself to do so, either under me or elsewhere; but in all trades an apprenticeship must be passed through.

September 8*th.*—I was thinking of joining you at Bath, when two circumstances decided against it —Frere's appointment to Madrid in last night's "Gazette," and an invitation to dinner from the Princess of Wales, which, as I fear she thinks I have been already somewhat deficient in not calling upon her, I did not like to refuse.

As soon as it is known that Andreossi is on the move, Lord Whitworth will set out. Sir. J. Warren will weigh anchor on Monday or Tuesday; Arbuthnot left town to-day, and the rest have received orders to start.

10*th.*—As the superscription of the letter sent to Bath, under the idea that I had gone down there, indicated its contents, I hope you may have been induced to open it.

I saw both Lord Hawkesbury and Mr. Addington at the levée; but neither gave me grounds for supposing my fate would be so soon decided. Lord H. must have taken the king's pleasure after the levée, and desired Rolleston to write immediately.

15*th.*—The thing is done at last, and done hand-somely—1,500*l.* equipage-money, and 5,000*l.* per annum, commencing from the 5th of July.

Lord Hawkesbury desires me to kiss hands at the levée to be held this day week, and I must of course go to the drawing-room to-morrow week. After that, I shall spend a few days with you; but for a variety of very weighty reasons it is thought desirable that I should be gone as soon as possible.   .

A plan will be brought forward in the ensuing session of parliament to regulate the payment of the civil list, so as in future to prevent arrears, and, *perhaps*, to give us *net* the nominal amount of our salaries. I know this is intended, but I doubt the execution of the latter part of the plan.

I am, however, at present well pleased with my prospects, and I think those of the public have mended of late, though there is a great talk of war; because many people wish for war on principle, and many others from motives of interest.

I am of opinion that *just now* we shall have no war. If it be deferred for a year or two, we shall be better able to renew the contest with vigour, and with a chance of being better supported, than at present, by the rest of Europe.

I have seen young Robert Stevens several times of late, and for hours together. I like him well thus far. His brother-in-law and his uncle wish me to take him as my private secretary, and he is himself anxious to go to Berlin with me. But my idea is that he is qualified to act rather as a companion-tutor to George for a year or so. I shall observe, before deciding how they would be likely to get on together, and whether Stevens, though clever and well-informed, is not of too retiring and reserved a disposition to prevent G. from taking the lead, and acting for himself.

Drake gets Munich; he and family will cross to Havre, and take Paris on their way to his residence.

It occurs to me that I never answered your question of "How I returned from Broadstairs?" As the wind was fair, and the Canterbury races made it probable that I should be stopped for horses on the road, I embarked on the Thursday in the Margate Hoy, where I was much better accommodated than I expected. A hundred and twenty passengers offered, to be sure, a motley crew, and a good deal of amusement to observers. We had a very pleasant sail on Thursday as far as the Hop, and reached Billingsgate between six and seven on Saturday morning. As for the rest of your queries, you must wait for the answers until we meet.

Adieu, &c.,

F. J. J.

Letters—October 26*th.*—This, my dear M., is our last day in London—we shall certainly leave to-morrow—everything is ready; all visits paid; all business done.

The new coach is very handsome, but your needle-work hammercloth will be used but for second best; for gala, my brother has a bearskin. It was with

difficulty he could get skins enough for the purpose—
they are so much the rage now, as well for hammer-
cloths as for muffs and tippets. The king sent him a
very gracious message by Lord Hawkesbury, with
permission to wear the Windsor uniform.

The Duchess of York has not yet sent us the letters
she said she would háve for her relations and
old friends at Berlin; but I understand she does
not now trouble herself much about them. ·Their
Majesties, however, and other members of the royal
family, have charged my brother with letters to
their relatives at Hanover and Brunswick, which will
oblige us to make a little *détour* from the direct line
of our journey.

We wish to reach Harwich as early as possible on
the 28th, to take the chance of being able to sail
immediately, and to proceed without a stop—wind
and weather permitting—to Hamburg.

As ships of war cannot go up the Elbe, the offer
of a frigate to Cuxhaven has been declined, and one
of the packets is now waiting our arrival at Harwich.

Harwich, 28th.—We left town yesterday at twelve,
and got to Witham about half-past five. Dined and
slept at the Blue Posts inn; were off this morning
between seven and eight; breakfasted at Colchester,
and arrived here about one. Notice had been sent
to the agent of my brother's intention to embark
immediately, but the captain, for some reason, has a
fancy to put off the voyage till to-morrow, and has
thrown so many difficulties in the way of our going,
that he has at last got his own way, and we take the

chance of the wind remaining as fair to-morrow as it is to-day.

29th, Noon.—We are just going on board with rather more wind than seems pleasant. Adieu my dear M., &c.

Diaries—Hamburg, Nov. 6th.—We were three hours beating out of the harbour against a stiff and unfavourable breeze. On the evening of the 2nd, we anchored in the roads before Cuxhaven. A boat was sent off for a pilot, and a fresh supply of provisions. At daybreak, on the 3rd, we weighed anchor, and by ten-at night got up to Altona, but as the gates of the town are closed at six, we were obliged to sleep on board. The next morning we rose early, and walked into Hamburg; breakfasted at an inn, then took a coach—which the inn provides, as also a *laquais de place*—and went to call on Sir George Rumbold, the British Chargé d'Affaires. We dined with him, and afterwards he took us to a supper to which he had been invited, which appears to be the fashionable entertainment here.

They handed us tea as we went in, then at once set us down to whist and casino; at eleven the supper was announced. It consisted of every imaginable variety of fish, meat, poultry, sweets, &c., with wines of all sorts, and champagne in abundance. One by one this endless array of dishes was carried from the table, carved, and handed round; which ceremony detained us at the hospitable board of the wealthy merchant at whose house it took place, until two A.M. This fatiguing business ended, we followed

the example of others—took leave of the master and
mistress in the eating-room, gave the servant a
gratuity, and retired. Nothing but French was
spoken. Yesterday we went to see the church of
St. Michael, which is higher than St. Paul's. It has
an immense flight of steps, of which we mounted about
two-thirds—five or six hundred—and were rewarded
with a most magnificent view of the Elbe, the adjacent
and distant country; the villas on the banks of the
river, the fortifications and intrenchments; indeed, a
perfect panorama of the town, the river, and suburbs.
Nearer the top, the tower is surrounded by a lead
terrace, where a guard is stationed, whose sole
business is to walk round it every quarter of an hour
through the day and night, in order to give instant
notice of any outbreak of fire. When this occurs
a peculiar kind of trumpet is blown, and a flag hung
out, pointing towards that quarter of the town where
fire is seen—if it happens in the night, a lantern is
suspended at the end of the flag-staff. At the foot of
the tower another guard is stationed, to answer the
signals made above, and to take the necessary steps
for extinguishing the fire.

By all accounts Hamburg *was* a very interesting
and a very gay place. If so, what a change! Two
bad theatres, French and German—at which Mr.
Stevens and I looked in—and a round of those ever-
lasting heavy suppers now constitute the gaieties.
We did a two o'clock dinner yesterday, and at night
another supper at the house of *Count* Cobourn, as
they call the English consul here. " La belle et

riche comtesse," his wife, from whom I believe he
derives his title, and who has, of course, endowed
him with her riches, is a remarkably pretty woman,
and entertained us in a manner worthy of her great
reputation here. These and many other civilities my
brother returns to night by a grand supper at our
hotel, and to-morrow we shall once more be *en
route*.

Hanover, Nov. 10*th.*—What with the supper and the
leave-takings of our hospitable friends, we did not get
to roost till near three next morning. However, we
were ready for the boat between seven and eight,
and had rather a pleasant sail down a branch of the
Elbe to Harbourg, where the carriages had been
sent the night before, and were then waiting for us
to step into ; we four filled the old travelling carriage
my brother brought over for the journey, and the
servants, a coach bought in Hamburg. Off we
started, without further delay, at the rate of about
two, or two and a half miles per hour, and without
stopping—except when the postilions chose it—until
we reached a miserable place where we were to dine.
If we had not all been as hungry as hunters, we
might perhaps have quarrelled with our dinner ; as it
was, we ate what was set before us, asking no
questions, and returned quickly to the coaches; for
we had to travel through the night, and had no time
to spare if we were to reach Celle, as was proposed,
for breakfast.

What we saw of the country was deplorably
wretched, and the roads were more execrable than

can be imagined. A courier had been sent on to provide relays of horses, but the operation of changing them was never got through under half an hour. But Celle was reached by seven o'clock, and, by much urging of the postilions, we managed to get to Hanover that afternoon. My brother went to the palace in the evening, for he intended to resume the journey next day. The duke, however, invited him to dinner, which happened also not to be at the usual hour—two o'clock—but at six; for his royal highness was going out shooting that morning, and asked him to join the party. It was a very large one, and attended by a great many " beaters," as they are called, whose business is to beat about the woods while the *sportsmen* stand at the entrance of the avenues, and pop at the birds as fast as they can load. By this means an almost inconceivable number is in one day killed by each person, who kills, in fact, for the sake of killing. I confess that I cannot look on this as sport, or as anything more than wanton cruelty, which disgusts me whenever I think of it.

We shall get off this afternoon, and should have been some way already on our journey, but that his royal highness sent his aide-de-camp, Major Decken, to take *us* to see an old palace just outside the town, called Herren Hausen. There is really nothing remarkable in it. They say it was kept up in good style in George the First's time; now, some people of the Court reside in it, and the gardens—which are extensive, and are laid out in the formal manner of those of Versailles—are its only attraction.

Hanover is certainly a fine old town, and the theatre is pretty; but there is a certain sort of sleepy air about everything and everybody in it.

We got into Berlin last evening the 15th, and in very high spirits, from the mere fact that our tedious journey was ended at last. We made a very short stay at Brunswick—for the duke was away—and I saw little of the town ; but it seemed as dozy and easy going as Hanover. We have since jogged and jolted on with no more serious casualties by the way than a carriage-wheel coming off, and getting two or three times stuck in the mud. But the nights were bitterly cold, and the first snow of the season fell last evening—unusually early, they say—and it now lies thick on the ground.

BERLIN.

Letters—Nov. 18*th.*—My brother had his first conference with the Prussian minister yesterday, and will enter on the duties of his mission without loss of time ; but as the Court is at Potzdam, and the king somewhat indisposed, he cannot immediately have his audience. He has, therefore, more time for what is almost as important—looking after, and securing a suitable house.

We dined yesterday with Mr. Casamajor, Secretary of Legation and Chargé d'Affaires. He is very pleasant and gentlemanlike, and gave us quite a sumptuous repast. Besides ourselves, there was no one but Mr. Rose, a son of the famous Treasury

man. Not approving of the present administration,
yet not wishing to go into opposition, he has come
abroad with his wife and family, and a whole train
of servants, amounting to a suite of eighteen persons,
and, having spent the summer in travelling about,
proposes to winter in Berlin. I am told that Mrs.
Rose answers fully to her name, being as beautiful
as the queen of flowers herself.

After dinner we went to the French play. The
theatre forms part of Mr. Casamajor's house, and
was the private theatre of Prince Henry. Since
his death, his company of actors have taken it on
a speculation—for hitherto there have been none
but German theatres—and propose to give twelve
representations; playing twice a week. This new
idea seems to have met with much favour in Berlin,
for the house was crowded. It is, however, extremely
small, but beautifully decorated. There are only
four boxes, and ladies of the first rank crowd into the
parterre, where those who have not engaged a chair
before the performance commences, are obliged to
stand the whole evening. I know nothing more of
Berlin at present, than that it seems empty and dull.
During the war, many English families made it
their residence, and the city, they say, was then
lively and busy, from the constant influx of travellers.
But our compatriots have all flocked off to Paris,
which gay capital is now the centre of attraction;
while, until royalty leaves Potzdam, the Prussian
beau monde will not return to Berlin—perhaps I
should rather say, *la haute noblesse*—society being

divided and subdivided into quite distinct classes.
First, *la haute*; then, *la petite noblesse*. *La colonie
Française* stands third on the list, and consists of
a pleasant set of people, whose ancestors settled
in this city in the time of the great Frederick.
Each of those three classes is divided into different
sets, at the head of which is one of the foreign
ministers' wives, or one of the first ladies of the
place. The number of these sets is indefinite, and is
added to as disputes of etiquette, and similar reasons,
occur to separate their members.

22*nd.*—The weather has been so abominable, that
I have not been able to see much of the town of
Berlin. As to the buildings, it may be placed as the
first in Europe, according to the testimony of
travellers; but in many other respects, it is undoubtedly very inferior. The small number of
inhabitants, in proportion to the size of it, renders its
long straight streets very dull and dreary. Like those
of Paris, they have no *trottoirs*, and are more offen-
sively dirty than even the black mud-begrimed streets
of that lively capital. The snow having disappeared,
and the clouds somewhat dispersed, Mr. Stevens and
I took a long walk in what they call here a park—a
small place thickly covered with trees, and close on
the skirts of the town. The river Spree runs by one
side of it; on the bank is a palace, that looks like
a large manufactory, and which belongs to Prince
Ferdinand.

To this park all the fashionables repair in the
evening to promenade, to drink coffee or beer, and

smoke pipes; just as the common people in England
go to Hammersmith tea-gardens. Many ladies may
be seen amongst the company; frequently there are
balls, and on these occasions no smoking is allowed.
But, by-and-by, I shall be more *au fait* on these
matters; just now they are, of course, going, or
gone out of season.

There are some rather pretty houses built round
the park, and most families, who can afford it, engage
one for the summer, and fancy they are living in the
country. They are small, a good deal in the style of
the houses in the King's Road, with all the dust of
a sandy drive immediately upon them. Yet they
are so much in vogue, that Lord Carysfort gave 100*l.*
for one of them, for three months.

When we returned, we found that my brother had
been informed that the king had named Tuesday for
his audience. We are to accompany him, and we
set out for Potzdam at seven this evening; for His
Majesty has appointed to receive him at the early
hour of half-past nine.

24*th.*—It was eleven o'clock before our sixteen
miles were accomplished; but as a courier had been
sent on before us, our beds were prepared, and we
turned in at once, having to turn out pretty early
next morning, that my brother might have time to
dress for the king, and we time to see a little of
the lions.

Before he was ready for his business, we were
setting out on ours, with a *laquais de place,* when
the rain came pelting down heavily, and, as Sans

Souci is some little way out of Potzdam, we determined to hire a coach. The only one we could get
was a vile sort of tumbledown four-wheeled chaise, far
too bad for any old dowager, for the use of which
they made us pay two dollars an hour.

There is nothing remarkable in Sans Souci, as
regards the house itself—it is a small villa, a
little snuggery, nothing more—but one cannot
but be greatly interested in this favourite retreat
of the great Frederick. We were shown the
room in which he died, and the library where his
voluminous works were composed. His books on
the art of war, and on matters connected with
military life, were lying on the reading desk, just as
he had left them. Another time I shall examine the
library more minutely. We saw a large monument,
sacred to the canine species. A number of small
English dogs are buried along the sides of it, and
flat stones are laid over them, on which the names
of the deceased animals are inscribed. I think I
saw as many as ten or twelve of them. The great
man was fond of these creatures, and used to be
much diverted with the tricks and antics they were
taught to perform. Whether the four-footed culprit
that, by the upsetting of a lighted candle, was the
cause of the destruction of the whole of the MS. of
the original History of the Seven Years' War, lies
under one of these stones, I know not. His grave
ought certainly to have been a marked, if not a dis-
honoured one; for the history he destroyed, written
during the campaigns, was doubtless more trustworthy

than the mendacious one, hurriedly composed in 1769;
when the hero of it, annoyed that his most brilliant
successes should not be fully made known to posterity,
sent for the records from the public archives, copied
from them the dates and headings, and filled in the
details from memory, aided by imagination.

The gardens of Sans Souci are said to be fine, but
we let them stand over for more favourable weather.

The marble palace gives you more the idea of a
palace in a fairy play, or one of those described in
the Arabian nights, than what it was intended to pass
for—a structure of elegant Grecian architecture.

You enter by a fine hall, with pillars of Silesian
marble, of a reddish hue, on pedestals of a different
colour. Antique statues are ranged along the sides;
the rooms, none of which are very large, are
decorated with lustres; glasses all of one piece; tables
of variegated marbles, and chimey-pieces ornamented
with mosaic work. The ceilings contain all the gods
and goddesses that ever were heard of; the walls are
hung with embroidered silk; the grand-staircase is
of marble, and the wall appears to be; but it is of
composition, which they have brought to such a
degree of perfection here, that it is hardly to be
distinguished from marble. There is an immense
deal of gilding; the pillars before the doors on one
side of the house are gilded; the broad cornices are
gilded; there are gilded figures of Apollo, Diana,
Cupid, and other deities, and indeed everything, upon
which gold-leaf could be stuck, has received it. The
general effect is gaudy, rather than grand, and

although you perceive that there has been lavish
expenditure, you are none the less impressed by the
prevalence of bad taste.

25th.—I was employed for some hours yesterday
in copying my brother's account of his audience.
The reception he met with from their Majesties has
been very gratifying to him. The interview was a
long one, and the king talked much of old times,
and inquired what he had been doing since he left
Berlin, saying amongst other obliging things, that
" His Majesty could not have made choice of a
minister who would be more agreeable to him than
one whom he looked upon as an old acquaintance."

He spoke much of our king, and inquired with
solicitude respecting the actual state of his health.
He ended the conversation by saying, " Je vous
repète que je suis bien aise de renouveller connoissance avec vous, et je serai charmé que vous
ayez quelque plaisir à vous trouver de nouveau à
Berlin."

Immediately afterwards he was introduced to the
queen, who received him in the same apartment;
attended by her *grande .maîtresse,* three *dames
d'honneur,* and a chamberlain. She was extremely
gracious, and desired that my brother would convey
to their Majesties the expression of her constant affection, and solicitude for their welfare and happiness.

He says the queen is really a beauty, and would
be thought so even if she did not sit upon a throne.
You know she is our queen's niece. She is so fond
of dancing, that the Court comes to town that the

Carnival may begin a week earlier than usual, and Her Majesty go down a few country dances previous to her confinement, which is to happen some time towards the end of January.

27th.—My brother will now get through his first introductions at the other Courts — the Queen-Dowager, Prince Henry, and the other members of the royal family, to all of whom a separate presentation is necessary—and then we shall endeavour to get speedily settled.

Stevens and I get on very well together. He is pleasant and sensible, but my brother has to un-stiffen his joints a little, which he thinks, after a year or two more of college life, would have been impracticable. However, he is well satisfied, and I think him a good sort of fellow.

29th.—At last the British Mission has a " local habitation," and one large enough to cover the half of your Lansdowne Crescent. It is the late residence of Lord Carysfort, and the right wing of a palace, the centre of which is occupied by Mr. Rose and his numerous train, and the left wing by another foreign mission.

Our portion contains upwards of twenty large rooms, some forty and fifty feet in length, besides a magnificent ball-room, in which the ladies tell my brother they expect him to give them many nice balls, for, following the queen's example, dancing is now all the rage.

There are marble pillars and statues in abundance, and the rent of this part of the palace is 300*l.* a-year,

furnished most elegantly, and with every requisite
but beds; it being the custom here for the tenants of
furnished houses to supply themselves with those
necessary articles. In this instance, however, there
is a single exception to the general rule. It is a
magnificent state bed, with hangings of crimson
velvet, embroidered and fringed with gold. The
state room in which it is placed is richly decorated,
and the furniture corresponds with the bed. This is
not quite so modern, but certainly as handsome, as
the one I saw at Burleigh, and for which his
lordship gave 3000*l*.

You will be curious to know to whom this palace
belongs. It did belong to no less a personage than
the late king, who gave it, superbly furnished, to his
chère amie, Madame de Lichtenau. And it is still
called Lichtenau House, though Madame de L. has
been sentenced—but privately, because the character
of the late king was implicated in the charges
brought against her—to banishment to Colberg, on a
pension of 4000 thalers a-year. The greater part
of her property was confiscated, but this palace yet
belongs to her. It is said that the present king
wishes to buy it for his-sister, the Princess of
Orange Fulda, but that Madame declines to part
with it, except on terms so enormous that they have
been rejected.

The palace is situated *Unter den Linden*, the
fashionable promenade, and the pleasantest part of
Berlin. We hope to take possession within a fortnight, but the non-arrival of the baggage begins to

look serious; the ship that brings it has at last, we
hear, got up to within a few miles of Hamburg, but
there sticks for want of water.

30th.—My brother goes on renewing his old
acquaintances, many of whom are only now returning from the country. Some pleasant houses
are open to us in the evening, and on the arrival of
the royal family we shall begin, I hope, to have a
little life and gaiety.

Diaries—Dec. 10*th.*—" *Il est dans l'intérêt de chaque
Pouvoir de faire tous les efforts possible de remettre
l'Europe dans son assiette.*" Such were the concluding words of a discussion, or rather a conversation to which I was, last evening an attentive
listener. They were spoken by Count Haugwitz,
after having said, " Our ideas of the balance of
power are completely destroyed, and we cannot be
too earnest in our endeavours to replace it by some
equivalent system." The Russian minister, and two
or three of the ministers from the German courts,
were present ; but Count Haugwitz probably then
paraded the independent action, as he termed it, of
the Prussian Government in the present state of
European affairs, with the intention of impressing
my brother with a belief that this country is not so
totally dependent on the will of the First Consul as
the capricious and venal policy pursued by the
government would seem to indicate. If so, it was
labour in vain, for not only he, but all the world,
knows that Prussia acts only in subservience to
France. It is said, that the king feels most forcibly

the painful predicament into which the country is brought. Yet he allows himself to be swayed and guided by the opinions of persons in the French interest, and it is with them that the principal acts of the government originate.

I could not but notice the difference of manner—a sort of steadiness and composure—that characterized these German politicians, from that of the vivacious *intrigants* whose disputations I had sometimes listened to last winter, and which seemed to be ever on the point of becoming altercations, until a sudden relapse brought them down to a friendly understanding. My brother says the national character is more sterling and solid. I was going to write stolid—thus, by accident, I have expressed my own idea of it, if not a correct one.

11*th*.—Bonaparte, it is said, has appointed the term of three years for the reconstruction of the French navy, and great exertions are making at Toulon to bring into activity the commerce which France has obtained the privilege of carrying on in the Black Sea; the extensive woods, hitherto untouched, of the provinces bordering on that sea, affording excellent timber for naval purposes. Canals are also being cut, which are to communicate with one another, or with navigable rivers, throughout the northern provinces of France. All this is supposed to be done with a view to the invasion of England, when, in the judgment of Bonaparte, a favourable opportunity shall offer for the attempt.

12*th*.—I have just seen a curious and interesting

relic of the olden times—the scarf which, from the time of Charlemagne, had been used at the coronation of the emperors of Germany. It was discovered at Paderborn by a Prussian commissary, while searching the public offices of that town. It is supposed to have been carried away at the time of the French invasion, but how or by whom it was left at Paderborn is not known. Count Haugwitz has communicated this circumstance to M. de Stadion, the Austrian minister, who expects to be invested with a full power to receive back this article of the imperial insignia, with all due form and solemnity.

Letters—Dec. 13th.—Although we have very few English here at present, we have yet what is called the fashionable English lounge, where you go on certain evenings, at seven o'clock, to cards, tea, and supper. It is all over by eleven, for they keep very early hours in Berlin. This lounge is at the house of Doctor Brown, the Court physician. I cannot say I care much for the entertainment. Doctor Brown and his wife are not very pleasant people, and are inclined to give themselves insufferable airs. He has been a lucky fellow this Dr. Brown : some twelve or thirteen years ago he held a subordinate appointment as one of the medical advisers of the royal family, when he was called upon to perform the operation of innoculating the prince royal with the cow-pox. He succeeded perfectly, and the king was so well satisfied with him, that when the prince—the present king— recovered, His Majesty not only thanked Dr. Brown in the most gracious and condescending manner, but

wrote him a very handsome letter and requested his
acceptance of 2000 louis of this country, about 1500*l.*
sterling; added a hundred a-year to his salary;
appointed him sole physician to the king and his
court, and gave him the title of privy councillor,
with the promise of a house, as soon as it could be
built and got ready for him. His Majesty could
hardly have shown more gratitude and generosity
had Jenner himself performed the operation. I
believe he intended by it to show also his sense of
the value of Jenner's discovery, and to encourage
his subjects to avail themselves of it. Dr. Brown has,
of course, since become eminent, influential, and rich.

22*nd.*—We have not had a messenger from
England since we came here, but have been busy all
the day despatching one that arrived from St.
Petersburg. That Court is much dissatisfied with
the King of Sweden, of whose occasional eccentricities
you have heard before. He has recently *christened*
his son by the title of the Duke of Finland. His
Swedish Majesty also intends, it is rumoured, to
destroy the remainder of the Swedish navy. His
minister at this Court has, in private conversation,
acknowledged that such an intention was entertained
by His Majesty, but he hoped he might yet be
persuaded to let his ships rot at their moorings
rather than burn them.

We see by the newspapers that the appointment of
the gallant admiral to St. Petersburg has been
noticed in the House, and his fitness for it called in
question. Mr. Dundas contrived to lug the distin-

guished seaman into the debate on the Bill for the
appointment of commissioners to inquire into the
existing abuses of the navy department. Upon
which Mr. Addington rose and extolled his colleague,
Lord Hawkesbury, for having chosen men of the
first talent to fill such missions, and the one in
question among the rest. We know here, that Sir
John's pen has not been idle since he arrived at his
destination, and as his long yarns all travel to us
under flying seal, we have an opportunity of knowing
that the admiral is quite sure no wily Russian
diplomatist will ever get to the windward of him.

27*th.*—We celebrated Christmas in our new abode,
and divine service was read for the first time. The
congregation, including ourselves, amounted to seventeen. Mr. Stevens read the whole service, except
those portions which, being only in deacon's orders,
he is not allowed to read. Sunday the service was
repeated to the same congregation, and we are to
have it every Sunday at eleven.

The grand doings we had in Paris last year were
to have been repeated in Berlin this Christmas, but
the non-arrival of the baggage made it impossible.
It is now transhipped, and has three weeks of inland
navigation, but we are in fear and trembling lest
it should be frozen up for the winter. Mr. Rose,
Mr. Stevens, and I, were on our skates yesterday,
just to try the ice. But we hear that it is not *bon ton*
to *patiner* in Berlin, though there are places most
convenient for it. It is an amusement, they say, fit
only for blackguards and street boys; but as soon as

the ice is a little firmer we mean to clear their thick
pates of that notion. The king, queen, and royal
family are now all in town. I doff my hat to the
king almost daily, for he is constantly walking about
Berlin, and is no more noticed than any other
person, except by the civility of a passing salute from
those who chance to recognize him. He wears always
the uniform of an officer of the *gendarmes*, and is
accompanied by one of his aides-de-camp; but the
people, though the greater part of them know who he
is, show no anxiety to see him; he is allowed to pass
on like the rest of the world, which I think far more
polite than the sort of thing that takes place with us.

There has been a fair in Berlin for fifteen days,
but owing to the miserable weather and the absence
of foreign visitors it interfered very little with the
usual quietude and monotony of the place. It
ended on Christmas Day, when it is customary with
the Germans to have family parties, to which all who
are invited are expected to go laden with fairings,
as presents for the children of the family.

I was allowed to see a Christmas fairing, which
had not been bought at the fair, but had been
prepared for one of the princesses, who had devised
it, as a gift to the queen. You were shown a framed
drawing of a group of little children playing on a
grass-plot. This vanished, on a string being touched
at the back, and the figures of the little royalties
appeared; very like them too—and they are beautiful children—and dressed as they usually are. This
Christmas offering was dedicated *à une tendre mère*,

and was greatly admired by the ladies, especially by Mrs. Rose, who has a bunch of tiny rosebuds of her own, and who might almost dispute the palm of beauty with her Prussian Majesty herself.

By-the-by, this reminds me that Stevens attempts to rally me on what he calls my " ardent worship at the shrine of beauty," saying what is, I suppose, the right thing for a sage of twenty-five to say to a youth in his eighteenth year, that " the qualities of the heart and mind are of higher import in woman than beauty of person." I, of course, agree in this, but tell him that I also think beauty of person no despicable gift—adieu, *chère mère*, &c.

1803.

Letters— January 4th.—I was to have made my *début* in the *beau monde* of Berlin at the commencement of this year, by sending round my cards with my brother's, and I had promised myself a great deal of pleasure from the round of festivities which the Berlinois engage in at this season.

However, my brother and I had a long conversation on New Year's morning, as we had last year at Paris, the result of which was that I took his advice, and gave up the idea of going into general society this year. I devote it, on the contrary, to study and business, and commence to-morrow a course of private lectures on history, statistics, &c., with Professor Ancillon—a distinguished man, in his line, here—and on the following day a course of French and general literature, with another professor. This will occupy me every day for two or three hours, which, with quill driving for my brother, for never less than six or seven hours daily, will be all I can manage. This arrangement releases me from Stevens, which I am not at all sorry for, though, on the other hand, as it will give him more work as a secretary, I am not so well satisfied with it. Stevens, I find, would not be unwilling to throw off the clerical character, and take to *our line*. And I know that since it has been hinted that Mr. Casamajor, the secretary of legation to this mission, who went to England on leave soon after our arrival, is endeavouring to get an independent appointment, therefore, may probably not return, Mr. Stevens's friends have been exerting themselves in London to obtain for him the promise of the secretaryship, should it become vacant. Their applications have not been very favourably responded to, and I believe he will be obliged to do what I think he ought to do, stick to the profession he has entered, and which he is most fitted for. He is a very good sort of fellow, a little odd sometimes ; but we are very well together, though I could not help looking upon him lately in the light of an impediment to me.

When we get our goods and chattels, which are now frozen up in the river about twenty miles from this, we shall have plenty of company at home ; but you will see that I am not going to live quite the life of a hermit when I tell you how I have begun the year.

I was at a ball at M. de Löwenstern's, on the 31st.

M. de L. and his eldest son, Otto, are connected with the Russian mission. They are Livonians; the whole of the family reside in Berlin, and a very charming one it is. Otto and I are sworn friends. His sister is charming.

Our ball was a very gay one, for the 31st of December is a day of great festivity in Berlin. When the hands of the clock marked midnight, and we were all engaged in a country dance, the music suddenly ceased; each musician snatched up a French horn, and blew in the new year in such a sonorous manner that one would have thought *Æolus's* bag was, *de nouveau*, rent asunder.

The first blast brought the dancing to an end, *pro tempore* only; and there ensued such a chaos of hugging, kissing, congratulating, shaking of hands, as I never before witnessed. Of course I followed the general example, and saluted all the pretty girls present. When we had thus ushered in the new year, dancing was resumed, and with supper occupied us until three in the morning.

The next evening we went to another ball, at the Swedish minister's; a very grand affair, very fully attended, and kept up with more spirit than I gave the Germans credit for, until as late as the preceding one.

7th.—Last night I was at the opera, which is conducted on a plan entirely different from that of either England or France. There are but twelve representations in the year; eight are free, the remaining four must be paid for. But the king

defrays the expense of both, the money received on
the pay nights being reserved for charitable purposes.
The house is larger than Covent Garden, and very
handsome, as far as one can see it, for nearly all the
light is thrown on the stage.. The king and queen
and all their family were there in the state box,
which is an immense room, in the shape of the shell
at Westminster. Indeed, all the boxes are large, and
going to the opera is like going to an evening party,
from the style in which the boxes, or rooms, are
fitted up, and the number of people that are visiting
in and out; everybody one knows is to be found
there—for no one thinks of missing the opera. It
begins at five, and ends before ten.

The singing was not bad, but the ballet that
followed the opera was anything but entertaining,
being nothing more than groups of dancing imps,
devils, and bears; a sort of bad pantomime. It is
fortunate that there should be so many entertainments during the carnival, as the loss of my brother's
house as a place of resort—owing to the predicament
the frost has placed us in—is the less felt. It is
lucky, too, that Prince William of Gloucester, who
had accepted my brother's proposal to reside in his
house during his visit to Berlin, has changed his
plan. He has written from Stockholm to say he will
not be here until April.

Our latest news from England is, that Mr. Pitt
has discovered the mysterious secret of the " Invisible girl."

Diaries—Jan. 10*th.*—Letters received here from

Paris state that a violent scene of altercation between Count Cobenzl and Talleyrand preceded the signing of the convention between Austria and France. The threats of the French minister, however, prevailed over the difficulties which the Imperial ambassador's instructions threw in the way of further concession to France.

17*th*.—The French agents are very diligent in circulating reports of the non-fulfilment by England of the treaty of Amiens, and there is a very general expectation here of an approaching rupture between France and England; this is further strengthened by the report, set about by the same individuals, since the last messenger came from St. Petersburg, that France has agreed to the proposals of that Court, relative to Malta, and that England is the sole cause of any differences between the two countries.

25*th*. — The intelligence, whether well or ill-founded, of the French troops marching to Naples, has been received without causing any surprise, it being regarded as only a necessary preliminary to Bonaparte's intended attack upon the Morea.

From England, they have sent us only a number of copies of Mr. Addington's speech of the 10th of December last, on the subject of finance, which is said to have produced a most favourable effect on the public funds, and to have given general satisfaction throughout the country.

Letters—Jan. 26*th*.—The extraordinary severity of the weather has caused a gap in our correspondence. All the ports of Holland are frozen, and unless a

messenger is sent by way of Calais, it seems likely
that we shall still be some time without letters public
or private. Except in one or two remarkable instances, such a winter has never been known here.
Fahrenheit's thermometer has stood at 34° below
zero, and for several days at 25°. Two of our
servants have fallen ill from cold, and one lies dan-
gerously so, attended by Dr. Brown. It is seldom
colder in Russia, and there have been several
instances of travellers being frost-bitten.

Their Serene Highnesses Prince William of Brunswick, and his bride—the Princess of Baden—are staying at the palace, and will be here ten days longer,
when they go to Prenzlow, where the prince's regiment is in garrison. On their account there have
been some addition to the usual gaieties of this season.

27th.—Last Sunday the glass, which on the previous day had marked 30° below freezing point, ran
up to within only 4°, and there was a clear sky and a
bright sun. All the world at once went out walking,
riding, and driving *Unter den Linden.* I never saw a
more cheerful scene. To day it is as cold, or colder,
than ever. Yet with all this I have been but three
or four times on my skates; for this intensely severe
frost has been accompanied by a still severer wind,
that has made it impossible to stir out of the house.
With the renewed vigour of the frost we have the
redoubled fury of the wind, so that I cannot avail
myself of the finest ice both for quality and quantity
I ever saw. We have skated from Berlin to
Charlottenberg, five miles, in ten minutes, which is

not bad travelling, especially here, where with a carriage and eight horses you could not get so far under an hour.

No couriers or messengers arrive but those despatched from St. Petersburg by the gallant admiral. Nevertheless, we are scribbling all day, and dancing all night. I must tell you what occurred at a ball at the Russian minister's, to Miss Jennings, Mrs. Rose's aunt. She was introduced to a Polish lady of rank—I need not tell you her name—who knew a few words of English, and was anxious to try a conversation. They did not get on very well, but Miss J., willing to say something she thought the lady would understand, inquired partly by words, partly by gesture, the name of another lady who was present. *Madame la princesse* answered, " Damn eyes, I not know !" Miss Jennings said she opened *her* eyes pretty wide with astonishment, and looked round, hoping no one was near enough to hear it. *La grande dame* taking this for doubt, repeated the words several times with still greater emphasis. " I knew not which way to look," said Miss Jennings; " some one must wickedly have told her it was a familiar English way of asserting a thing, and I could not attempt to explain her error to her, poor lady."

Diaries—Feb. 5th.—We have a traveller arrived from Pera, who has had good opportunities of observing the conduct of the French ambassador at that place, and who describes it as that of a man desiring to *faire effet.* For that purpose he makes as

many visits to the great personages of the country
—both those in and those out of office—as he can
possibly devise the slightest means of justifying.
During these visits he talks a great deal of himself
and of his campaigns; of the wealth, power, and
resources of France. Of the interests of the Ottoman
empire, and those of the French republic running in
the same channel. Of the possibility of the Sultan
recovering the Crimea, provided he trusts to the
friendship of the First Consul, whose sincerity he
maintains, cannot reasonably be called in question,
and who would, he is sure, willingly assist the
Porte, with a corps of French troops to reduce Ali
Pacha, of Janina, to that state of obedience which
the general welfare of the Turkish empire, and
more particularly the prosperity of the neighbouring
provinces, seems to require.

The Turks are said to be well aware of the tendency
of these insinuations, and by no means inclined to
put the complaisance of their friend, the First Consul,
to the test.

10*th*.—Their Majesties intend taking a journey to
visit the Westphalian acquisitions of this crown,
directly after the spring reviews. Thence they go to
Anspach, where the king will review the regiments
stationed in the Margraviate. It is said that the queen
will avail herself of this journey to obtain permission
for the Princess Solms to return to Berlin.

Several of the Chapters, situated in these newly
acquired Prussian provinces, have sent deputies to
Berlin to solicit His Majesty's favour for their

respective institutions. No determination has yet been come to on the subject, but it is supposed that one or two of the principal Chapters will be retained as a resource for the younger branches of noble families who do not adopt the military profession.

Letters—Feb. 16*th.—* We go on sighing in vain for the end of the frost, which gave signs of breaking up, but returned yesterday in full vigour. Our frozen-up goods will, I fear, arrive in sad plight.—*En atten-dant* the advent of the *state coach*, my brother has bought four fine coach horses—splendid dapple greys, with cropped ears. Our coachman and the English part of the establishment that came with us, think they have been rather outrageously bamboozled by being brought to such a climate as this; but they are getting round a little now. We are not sorry that the saddle horses were detained in England, for there would have been no one to look after them, and, besides, we have not had three riding days since our arrival.

You inquire after Mrs. L.—she is at Dresden, with a French emigrant as her avowed cicisbeo. Society, both English and German, from all accounts, is rather oddly composed at that residence, and there are frequent explosions of indignation, on the part of the ladies, on questions of precedence and etiquette.

Elliot, the envoy, who is now going to Naples, you may, perhaps, remember. He married his cook, my brother says. She is a good sort of a woman I believe, and has presented her lord and master with a fine family of nine children. The secretary of legation, *selon ce qu'on dit*, also took his wife from the servants' hall. She is, however, as I know, a pretty and clever woman ; and probably both these ladies owe their transplantation to the drawing-room as much to personal merit as good looks; though some of the members of the Dresden *coterie* are not willing to see the matter in that light.

24*th*.—There was a court-ball last night, on the occasion of the Princess Henry's birthday. The queen was present, but left the ball-room soon after nine. Just before eleven the *grande maitresse*, Comtesse Voss, re-entered the room, and announced to His Majesty the queen's safe *accouchement* of a daughter.

This happy event is considered by some who were present, and many who were not, as having occurred rather *mal à propos*—a few days too soon, in fact—as the queen had promised to attend a grand *fête* and masquerade on the 1st of March, given by nine gentlemen, who have subscribed fifty louis each to defray the expenses.

That Her Majesty cannot be present is a terrible· disappointment to everybody, and the announcement that the queen dowager will be her representative at the *fête* is but a sorry consolation. The queen, we are assured, regrets her enforced absence as much as her devoted subjects and admirers regret it. This is saying a great deal, for in society, amongst the younger men especially, there prevails a feeling of chivalrous devotion towards her ; and a sunny smile, or glance of her bright laughing eyes, is a mark of

favour eagerly sought for. Such loveliness as hers,
few women are endowed with; and she is as amiable
and gracious as she is beautiful; full of vivacity, and
enters with so much spirit, and such apparent enjoyment, into every amusement. But I must·stop
here, or you will think my head is turned, as many
heads have already been, by the beauty and grace of
Queen Louise of Prussia.

March 2nd.— My brother says, the hours we
expend on our pleasures are to be deducted from
those we give to sleep, and not from those sacred to
business. Therefore, before Ancillon comes, I sit
down to tell you of the doings that have kept us up
half the night.

Our masquerade took place, and was as successful as
it could be, minus the presence of the queen. There
were between six and seven hundred tickets issued,
and, to prevent confusion, the masks were obliged to
declare themselves before they were admitted.

The company began to assemble at seven, and at
nine, the *fête* commenced with a sham fight on horse-
back, between eight young men, dressed very richly,
as ancient knights. The combat was accompanied
by spirited martial music.

When this was ended, trumpets, and drums, and
all kinds of wild music announced the approach of
the procession, called the first quadrille. It was
preceded by a good and evil genius ; four magicians
and four fairies followed, then water gods, sala-
manders, and dwarfs, with a variety of nondescripts
bringing up the rear.

As soon as they all were ranged before the cano-
pied chair of state that had been provided for the
queen—then occupied by her *locum tenens*, the queen
mother—the genii began a dialogue, in which the
evil one got the worst of the argument.   The magicians then stepped forward—their office was somewhat
shorn of its importance by the recent event in the
royal family; for it had been intended that they
should foretell the sex and the destiny of the expected
little royalty, confirm all gifts bestowed by benignant
fairies, and annul those of malignant ones.   The
question of the sex of the unborn infant was,
naturally, a perplexing one, and was still undecided
when—fortunately for the reputation of the sooth-
sayers, for they inclined to a prince—it was settled
for them by the *accouchement* of the queen.

Several royal personages and others of the first
distinction took part in this famous quadrille, to the
number of about sixty.

The fairies, were the Princess Louise, the Princess
of Orange, Mde. d'Engeström, and Comtesse Blumen-
thal.   The four magicians, were two of the foreign
ministers, Mr. Rose, and my brother.

The dialogues and incantations were composed by
M. de Bynon, the French Chargé d'Affaires, and in
them, the baby princess was promised a very pro-
minent place in the court of Venus, should she possess
but a tithe of her mother's beauty.

The whole concluded with what was termed in the
programme, a beautiful *danse à l'opéra*, by seven of
the prettiest young ladies of Berlin, lightly arrayed

in skirts and scarfs of pink and blue gossamer, and led by Mrs. Rose, herself the prettiest of them all.

After this the general company began dancing and quizzing and flirting.

For myself I assumed the disguise of a pedlar, and went about with a box full of beads, rings, and chains, and some especially prepared pretty things, enclosed in papers of very flattering verses, for certain ladies who were there, and who did not discover who the donor was; though they hunted me up and down and quizzed me unmercifully.

Diaries—March 4th.—It has transpired that some time before the death of Prince Henry of Prussia an intimate correspondence was carried on between him and the Queen of Sweden, in which the characters of the late and present King of Prussia were very freely criticized and treated with considerable severity. At the death of Prince Henry the king ordered his papers, which by his will were to be given to a French officer, to be taken possession of, and it was given out that the prince had directed a certain portion of them to be burnt. As the correspondence in question formed no part of that handed over to the French officer, the King and Queen of Sweden have since been exceedingly anxious to ascertain how it was disposed of, and at last M. d'Engeström has succeeded in obtaining, for their Majesties' satisfaction, a written assurance from Count Haugwitz that the whole has been burnt; though with a verbal hint that the subject of it was not unknown to the person whom it most concerned.

This circumstance is not calculated to diminish the coldness and reserve which this Court assumes in its communications with that of Stockholm. The King of Sweden has ordered his minister to discover in what manner Bonaparte's notification of his intention to take the title of Consular Majesty would be received at Berlin. It is, however, likely that no attention will be paid to this insinuation of His Swedish Majesty's wish to oppose the acknowledgment of the title.

It is known that the intention existed to adopt such a title, but it is thought that if Bonaparte should assume a new one, it is far more likely to be that of Emperor than Consular Majesty.

8th.—Within these few days Bonaparte has written to the king to announce the death of General Le Clair. The letter was delivered to Count Haugwitz by the French Chargé d'Affaires. The answer will be returned through M. de Lucchesini. The King of Prussia, in writing to Bonaparte, addresses him " Great and dear friend!"

He has expressed a wish to meet the king at Wesel, when he visits his Westphalian dominions; but His Majesty is averse from it, and wishes if possible to avoid the meeting. However, nothing positive is yet decided upon.

10th.—We hear that a great stir has been created in England by the new armament, and agitation has also become general on the Continent, but we hope the affair may yet blow over without the calamity of a fresh war.

15th.—We have the king's message by an *estafette* just arrived. It seems to be a mere toss up between peace and war. Meanwhile Boney gives us a super-abundance of quill-driving. For the last two days we have been at it from six in the morning till eight at night, with little or no intermission.

Messengers from Sir J. Borlase Warren also come thick upon us. Northern blasts we call them, since a lady, speaking of the gallant admiral one evening lately at Dr. Brown's, named him Sir John Boreas, and was much disconcerted when everybody laughed, and it was explained to her that, although somewhat of a blusterer, he was only entitled to the name of the furious northern god with a slight difference.

21st.—Yesterday morning the sudden and un-expected appearance of General Duroc occasioned a great sensation in Berlin. He was accompanied by a young man named Ségur, who is attached to Bona-parte's staff. They left Paris on the 12th, and must have used extraordinary diligence on their journey, as they mention having been delayed on the road by more than one accident. Some hours after, the English mails were received, when the state of the negotiation at Paris, and the measures adopted by the British Government became known, and it was at once generally believed that Duroc's mission was connected with them.

22nd.—The General brought a letter from Bona-parte to the king, of which a great mystery is made; Count Haugwitz declaring that he is ignorant of its contents, and Duroc asserting that they are equally unknown to him.

23rd.—At the same time, an approaching rupture between England and France is confidently alluded to, and it is publicly said that this Court sees with regret a prospect of the renewal of war, and is greatly embarrassed by it. Some persons justly attribute the impending evil to Bonaparte's offensive irritability and destructive ambition ; while the French party ascribe it to England's non-fulfilment of her Treaty obligations.

25th.—To-day all the world has passed from apprehension that immediate war was inevitable, and that Prussia would be obliged to join France against England, to confidence in an amicable and speedy arrangement of matters. For it has been allowed to ooze out that "the king has it in his power to render an essential service to humanity;" and, as General Duroc's language is extremely pacific, it is inferred that His Prussian Majesty is urged to undertake the office of mediator between the aggrieved ruler of France and the evasive government of England. This is a proposal very congenial to the king, who, not only without reluctance or hesitation but willingly would lend himself to any measure that should contribute to the promotion of peace.

Bonaparte is reported to have written to the king, "For fifteen years I have made war against England, for fifteen more I am ready to continue the contest; but I wish for peace."

27th.—Duroc left Berlin this morning with the king's answer. He is said to be much satisfied with the result of his mission, which is doubtless correct, as the direction of foreign affairs is, in fact, wholly in the hands of the cabinet secretary, M. Lombard, who, himself a Frenchman, is entirely devoted to French interests, and exercises great influence over the king.

31st.—Duroc, while here, spoke constantly and in very strong terms, respecting the negotiation going on in Paris, and of the perfidy of the British Government in violating the Treaty of Amiens; and it is now sought to disseminate opinions unfavourable to England and her present measures, by means of insidious and scurrilous articles in the French, German, and Dutch papers that circulate in Berlin.

Letters—April 3rd.—Of course, everybody is now become a politician, and people in England have probably looked a little in this direction lately, where anxiety is as great, to know the result of the busy scene transacting between London and Paris. My brother says he is not at all surprised at the account you give us of his colleague in that capital. A Russian friend writes us thence, " The fact is, his lordship has very little in him, and makes up for the deficiency by a great display of pomposity, for which he always had a *penchant,* although it is not altogether reconcilable with his having spent six or seven thousand a year at St. Petersburg that came out of the pocket of one of

the rich women with whom our country abounds."
The lady referred to had reached this city on her
way to London to join him, when she learnt the
news of his marriage to the duchess.   My brother
does not believe that there is any foundation for the
report that he behaves very ill to her Grace.   He
seemed most attentive to her in England, though it
is true she would never let him go from her side,
and it was clear that the difference of a Paris life
would occasion her many an uneasy moment.

6*th*.—That the invasion fever should have set in
so early, and at Bath too, is diverting.   One old
lady has really died of nervous terror, you say.
Now I should like to know what *she* especially
feared.   We have heard of another who has had a
suit of men's clothes made for her daughter, and
seventy guineas sewn up in the waistband of her
pantaloons or breeches.   Others are ready for a
start, they say, but whither they are bound is not
mentioned.   It would seem that the Great Man
would have an easy conquest could he but once
make good his footing on the shores of the tight
little island, instead of finding, as he has been
assured, that not only every man, but every woman
and child would be ready to shoulder a musket to
oppose him.

9*th*.—A great sensation has been caused here by
the arrival of M. and Madame Garnier, and has
entirely diverted the minds of the Berliners from the
prospect of war.   Monsieur has promised them to
make an ascent, in the course of a few days, in his

"Grand Aerial Ark," the name he gives to his balloon. The people are all crazy about it. The king has given Garnier fifty louis towards his expenses, and tickets, at about six shillings each, are being sold in great numbers. One of the *savants* of this place purposed to accompany Garnier; but, as only two persons can ascend at a time, G. said his wife should go up first, and he would, at a certain time and place named by him, change his cargo. Whether he could do this is doubted by some; but Garnier announced in the papers that, *by means of his wonderful ark*, he could draw blood from the eyes, nose, and head. This so terrified the poor *savant* that he now positively declines to pay his proposed visit to the clouds.

Garnier is likely to gain much more by his ark in Germany than he did in England. As soon as his entertainments come to an end, the queen, who is quite well and blooming again, goes into the country, as does the king, to prepare for the reviews that take place next month.

12th.—At last, all our baggage is arrived, and, considering how many months it has been frozen up, in very tolerable condition. The new coach, about which we were very anxious, has escaped with a few scratches only. My brother made his first appearance in it yesterday, to go to the last Court of this season. To give you an instance of the stupid curiosity which the people of this town are famed for, there was such a crowd to look at the new equipage, that my brother had some difficulty in making

his way to it. It is certainly very handsome ; and
the bearskin and dappled greys will, I fancy, throw
even Mrs. Rose's carriage — which daily attracts a
gaping multitude—into the shade.

18*th*.—Garnier's attempt at an ascent was a
failure ; the aerial ark would not rise to any height.
G. was in a great fuss ; said proper arrangements had
not been made for him ; and appeared to think his
failure the result of some secret cabal. He is gone
off to St. Petersburg, where he expects to be better
received ; though he made a great deal of money
here, and had he really been a grand seigneur, the
attentions paid him could hardly have been exceeded.

20*th*.—Prince William has written to my brother,
to announce his arrival here the beginning of May.
He accepts the offer of quarters in our house, though
an apartment will be prepared for him in the king's
palace, should he choose to occupy it. But there are
certain heavy expenses attending that piece of
hospitality which he will be very glad, I believe, to
avoid.

Diaries—April 26*th*.—The king has felt greatly the
loss of Major Holtzman, his adjutant-general, who
died about a fortnight ago. He was much es-
teemed by His Majesty, and was considered a man
of talent and high principle, but of little or no
personal ambition. The king's confidential advisers
have felt some difficulty in suggesting a suitable
successor for an office so immediately connected with
the person of the sovereign. But, to the annoyance
of Messrs. Beym and Lombard, while they were

consulting on the matter, the king, unknown to them, sent to Posen to General Zastrow, who had formerly filled the appointment, but resigned it for the command of a regiment, owing to his dislike of the restraints put upon him by the secret influence of the above-named secretaries. General Zastrow recommended to His Majesty M. de Kleist, a former aide-de-camp of Field-Marshal Möllendorff; and he— a thorough anti-Gallican, they say—will be named to the vacant office.

30th.—Two gentlemen, *en courier,* I hear, are announced—from the north, of course. I was just sitting down to write, but all hands are called up to re-despatch the said gentlemen before night.

This Court, it appears, is dissatisfied with the inaction of that of St. Petersburg. It is thought that a more decided interest in the affairs of the north of Germany ought to be shown in that quarter, and complaints are made of the want of energy in the councils of Russia. These complaints come, strangely enough, from a power that has no system of its own, save that of doing nothing.

May 4th.—The king has lately shown such evident symptoms of dejection, that the least observant of those about him have remarked his great depression of spirits. He is said to have expressed himself, if not indeed energetically, at least most feelingly, respecting the unfortunate predicament he is placed in, and in terms bespeaking a resolution to resist the evil; or, if that be not possible, to bear himself manfully under the pressure

of it. But there is no doubt that he would most
thankfully welcome the hand that should assist him,
or the voice that should give him courage to extricate
himself from it. The king's chief happiness, say
those who know him well, consists in the absence of
all trouble. His disposition is slothful; he is guided
by his fears, and distrusts his own powers. Therefore, he desires to show no opposition to France, and
might, perhaps, be disposed to yield everything to
her, if not restrained by the urgent representations
of his ministers, of the danger to his commercial
interests which a misunderstanding with England
might expose him to.

Letters—May 10*th.*—My brother went yesterday
to Potzdam, to meet Prince William of Gloucester;
his royal highness will come to Berlin to-morrow.
He will take up his quarters in *our* palace, and on
Friday we shall have a grand dinner. Then follow
the reviews, and we enter on our second carnival.
Balls and galas every night; a sudden return to
gaiety, to render the subsequent dulness of the
Berlin summer more dull by contrast, unless we
should be kept lively by war's alarms.

Many young Englishmen have come over to
attend the reviews, amongst others one who promises
to be a very pleasant addition to our society, Mr.
Cavendish, the eldest son of Lord George Cavendish.
He has just left Cambridge. His aunt, the Duchess
of Devonshire, wrote to my brother, recommending
her nephew to his good offices, and saying he was a
most amiable young man. I should say he answers

completely to his introduction, and that we shall probably be a good deal together during his stay.

14th.—Most of the military and naval men we had here are ordered home; and Prince William—who had intended to remain until he went to Hanover on the 4th of June—has thought it right to make the best of his way home also.

I cannot say that I think him any loss; but, as he really seemed cordial and sincere, and like an old friend in his manner towards my brother, I am sorry he could not stay out his visit.

19th.—I have attended two of the reviews. On the first day it rained so hard that, as the enemy was not at the gates of Berlin, I thought it as well to keep my coat and myself dry. The next day proved favourable. There were thirty-five thousand men, infantry and cavalry, in the field. The whole representation of an attack and defence was gone through. The manœuvres were executed with the most perfect precision and exactness, and everything was conducted with the greatest order. The king was attended by a numerous and brilliant staff, and looked remarkably well, if not quite so dauntless as the great little man and his staff of dashing officers I saw last year in the court of the Tuileries, and who is probably destined to give us all a good deal of trouble before he is finally put down. In the evening we had a ball at Count Haugwitz's.

Diaries—May 21*st to* 23*rd.*—The Prussians are desirous of preventing the French from entering Hanover; for once there the French army would command at Hamburg, and probably extend its influence to Denmark, by means of the operations it would command at Holstein. Military men and others are, therefore, greatly opposed to allowing the French to establish themselves in the centre of the kingdom of Prussia ; but the king is setting out for Magdeburg without having consented to adopt the necessary vigorous line of conduct that has been urged upon him, and to which he almost pledged himself to Colonel Decken. The secret influence of his cabinet secretaries, and the artful conduct of the French, combined with his own natural timidity, have weighed too heavily against it.

24th.—Reports have come in of Lord Whitworth having left Paris. There is much excited discussion respecting it, and great agitation prevails.

27th.—The king went to Magdeburg to consult the Duke of Brunswick, whose counsels have confirmed him in maintaining the submissive line of conduct he is inclined to observe towards France.

28th.—We have just received our " Declaration." It is a pity, my brother says, that those who penned it had not learned to write better French. It reaches us just as we have concluded our gaieties. We have been dancing all night at Count Schulenberg's. Two or three Englishmen are setting off to-day in alarm, lest they should not be able to reach home if they delay their journey for twenty four hours. Mr. Cavendish elects to stay with us for the present.

June 2nd.—The French have behaved with great

rigour in Holland; some reports say, with great inhumanity. At all events, our communications with the Hague are entirely cut off, and probably so by Cuxhaven. Our agent has been thrown into prison; a messenger also, and his despatches taken from him. We are waiting anxiously for what is to follow. Some enthusiasts still hope that the king, from considerations of his own and his country's interests, may even yet be roused to take some vigorous and immediate steps to check the advance of the French.

7th.—By *estafette* we learn that the French army entered Hanover on the 5th.

11th.—The arrangements for the occupation of the town seem to have been made very leisurely, and domestic comfort thoughtfully attended to. The report says, " On the evening of the 4th of June, some French officers and *commis de commissariat* rode into the town to choose quarters for the staff and commissariat. Early on the 5th, General Mathieu, the commissary-general, with several assistants, arrived at the house of the provincial States, to confer with the members and to make requisitions, which were granted to the extent of three millions sterling. He then examined the electoral chest, and locked it up. Shortly after, the General-in-chief, Mortier, accompanied by several Generals, and a numerous staff, entered Hanover, and occupied the house of H.R.H. the Duke of Cambridge. General Berthier took possession of the palace; General Chinnez—in quality of commandant of the town—the house of

F.M. Count Walmoden ; General Lalois, that of the minister, Von der Decken.

" All royal arms and ciphers were effaced. Two cannon, two vedettes of hussars, and two of grenadiers were stationed before the duke's palace.

" About noon the entry of the French troops commenced, and was conducted with the greatest order. A profound silence reigned, as well on the part of the troops as of the spectators.

" The Generals and staff-officers dined that day with General Mortier, who, before they rose from table, proposed the health of the First Consul. It was drunk with enthusiastic acclamation.

" In the evening, General Mortier gave audience to a deputation, and remitted half a million of the three millions demanded by General Mathieu, taking bills of exchange on Hamburg at forty days' sight for the remaining two and a half. He arranged for the serving of a certain number of covers daily, for the tables of all the Generals, at the king's expense ; also for the rations of the troops. He complained of the insufficiency and style of the furniture of the palace, and ordered that it should be newly furnished. Great discontent was expressed at the sending away of the royal equipages and the royal stud ; and it was insisted that six carriages and sets of horses, with thirty saddle horses, should be kept in readiness the whole day, for the use of the Generals and staff-officers. The magistracy has charged itself with this duty, and has, in consequence, to purchase horses from private individuals.

" The king's stables have been turned into barracks, and the apartments of the Master of the Horse arranged to serve as a hospital. Great burdens are laid upon the nobility, and upon all classes as much as possible. General Mortier has also desired a French theatre to be prepared immediately.

" M. M. Von Ramdohr and Von Henüber have set out for Paris, to make representations to the First Consul.

" The disturbances occasioned by the populace, a few days before the entry of the French, were carried to a great height; even the arsenal was pillaged, and the orders of the magistrates were not regarded. Commotions still prevail throughout the country, the subjects refusing to pay the public taxes.

" The lower classes, who express loudly their discontent against the government, console themselves with the hope that the French army will detach the Electorate of Hanover from England. The actual state of the country is, indeed, in the highest degree distressing ; long time has it sighed under the burden of taxes scarcely supportable, added to which are the enormous contributions, &c., &c. What will the end of it be ?"

14*th.*—The London mails, of the 24th and 27th ult., were seized by the French commander in Holland, and sent to Paris for Boney's amusement. Many private letters, even to Englishmen, were allowed to pass, and have reached their destination in this city; but those addressed to my brother, M. Simonville, at the Hague, directed to be burnt—a

very friendly act in one who used to dine with us
continually in Paris. At that time I thought he and
my brother great cronies, yet we learn that mere
private spite was the cause of this *auto-da-fé*.

16th.—The French have bled the inhabitants of
Celle pretty copiously. The country is to pay three
millions of louis, in bills of exchange on Paris; two
hundred thousand in ready money, for re-clothing the
French troops, besides providing horses for the
cavalry, and without including the requisitions for
provisions. A correspondent writes, " Celle is ruined,
to a certainty, for the next half century."

The French have not yet entered Göttingen.
General Mortier, it seems, waits for more precise
orders from Bonaparte, to whom the university has
sent a deputation, entreating him to except entirely
the town of Göttingen from receiving troops.
Mortier has been waited on for the same object. He
is reported to have said in a jocular manner, " Cannot
you receive one hundred, two hundred, three—"
" Count no further, General," interrupted Professor
Martins. " Well," replied Mortier, " the city of
Göttingen shall have only a small garrison, and you
may assure all the members of the university, that
they shall not be in any way molested."

The First Consul's answer is expected to be favourable; the French students continue to pursue their
studies at Göttingen, and apartments are taken for
the son of the ex-minister, La Croix. The English
students have left. The public chests have been seques-
tered for the use of the Republic; those of the univer-

sity and other learned institutions are to be appro-
priated as before. In consequence, "the noble and
generous character of General Mortier" has been
highly extolled at Göttingen!

17th.—At the surrender of the fortress of Hameln,
the French were astonished at the number and
beauty of the artillery, and its furniture. Many
pieces were found there which the Hanoverians had
taken from the French during the Seven Years' War.
They are to be sent off at once to France.

19th.—A corps of French has taken possession of
Cuxhaven, and the senate of Hamburg has been
requested to lay an embargo on the British shipping
in that port.

21st.—The French find themselves so well provided
for at Hanover, that those officers who have wives
and families have sent for them. General Leopold
Berthier was to be married there last week; the
expense of the extra festivities to be defrayed by the
country. The people complain greatly of their
increased and increasing burden, the expensive
tables of the Generals, the free subsistence of all other
officers, and the large allowances to the troops.

24th.—Certain classes of the people are said to be
animated by a feeling of antipathy and detestation
of Prussia, so violent as to be scarcely credible. The
indignation excited by the burdensome exactions of
the French is slight compared with it, though the
arrangements now making throughout the Electorate seem to indicate that they reckon on a
lengthened occupation of it. A letter just received

says,—" The army of reserve, under the orders of
General Dessolles, is being reinforced by small
detachments. A contract, renewable in forty days,
has just been made for provisioning them. Several
engineers have arrived at General Mortier's army,
and are ordered to examine the places on the Elbe
that can be put into a state of defence, as well as to
take steps for extending the fortifications of Stade,
Minburg, and Hameln, and strengthening the existing
ones. Timber for the purpose has already been
allotted, and further sums of money will be demanded.
But this the country can by no possibility furnish;
its coffers are empty, and credit cannot be had.

" If the project of Bonaparte be, in fact, what these
measures seem to point to, we shall soon see a French
colony firmly established in the heart of Germany,
whence by degrees it will extend itself like the spot
of oil that, in the end, covers the whole of the
material on which it was dropped."

This private communication concludes thus : " Woe
to Prussia and her neighbours, if they allow the
Electorate of Hanover to become, in the hands of
France, an immense *place d'armes*; for she will not
fail, thence, imperiously to dictate the law to them."

25*th.*—It is reported here that Bonaparte has
offered Hamburg to Denmark, on condition that her
ports shall be closed, and that she will endeavour to
shut the Sound against the British navy. He takes
great offence at the armaments of Russia ; those of
Denmark are, however, likely to affect him much
more.

27*th.*—The king is not returned, and the delay is supposed to be intentional, that he may put off giving an answer to the pressing demands of Russia, as to whether he will continue to see with indifference the progress of the French in the north of Germany. Count Haugwitz asserts that he urges the king to adopt a more becoming line of conduct, but that his efforts are paralyzed by the secret counsels of those who serve French interests. It is the practice of these persons to extenuate every enormity committed by France, and to place in the most unfavourable point of view every step which England is obliged to take for the purpose of self-defence, or in the ordinary precaution of her maritime policy. Then, the king has so habituated himself to a retired, quiet mode of life that, as well in that respect, as from disposition, the idea of a war is utterly distasteful to him, and repugnant to his feelings.

The French have formed a camp at Lüneberg, called *un camp de plaisance.*

Letters—July 8*th.*—Our correspondence is now very irregular, many of our letters fall into the hands of the French, but we are about to despatch this messenger by the Copenhagen route.

The weather has become so excessively hot that there is a great falling off in our society. But we do not feel it, for these are not idle times with us; not only have we the pen pretty constantly in hand, but we are also beginning to be overwhelmed with the influx of affrighted travellers who are seeking Berlin

L 2

as a city of refuge, to await a safe opportunity of returning to England.

Many of our countrymen were at Geneva when the order was received to put all Englishmen under arrest. A precipitate flight was the consequence; some of them have found their way to Berlin, they scarcely know how, assuming any disguise they could obtain, and travelling part of the way on foot.

The French lately discovered that His Majesty's fine stud—the removal of which so annoyed them when they took possession of Hanover—was at Böitzenberg. A peremptory order was immediately issued to bring all the horses back; and it has been obeyed, without the slightest attempt to evade or oppose it.

Diaries—July 16*th.*—The blockade of the Elbe causes much anxiety here, as great losses must fall on the Embden Herring Company, should their fishing vessels not be allowed to enter the river at the proper season for curing the fish and bringing them to market. M. Lombard has been despatched on a mission to Bonaparte, who is now at Brussels, the object of which is to obtain the withdrawal of the French troops from the banks of the Elbe.

19*th to* 22*nd.*—Notwithstanding Bonaparte's flattering assurances that he " commits with confidence the interests of France to the wise and impartial judgment of the Emperor of Russia," His Imperial Majesty has so strongly urged the king not to be ensnared by the artifices of France, but to adopt more energetic measures, that military preparations have actually been set on foot. They are carried on, however, with all possible secrecy, it being desired that this bold step should not come to the knowledge of the French minister, though it seems extraordinary he should be supposed to be ignorant of a circumstance that is everywhere the subject of conversation, and in some circles of much congratulation.

No doubt the king sees, as well as others, the danger surrounding him, and drawing nearer every day; but he sees it as one in a dream who is withheld from making the necessary efforts to save himself.

24*th.*—The Hanoverian troops, who so lately resolved not to lay down their arms, not to repass the Elbe, not to surrender themselves prisoners to be marched to France, but to defend, to the last drop of their blood, the honour of their monarch and their own well-earned reputation, have a second time capitulated, and are disbanded. I fear this failure in their resolution will have a bad effect on the King of Prussia, who, when he heard of their resolve, expressed great admiration of the noble spirit and sentiments that dictated it. But some of the regiments mutinied, when facing French troops and shedding blood seemed likely to become realities. It is mentioned, however, in extenuation of their dastardly conduct, that those regiments repented, and begged to be led against the enemy. There is also this unfortunate fact in their favour—their commander, F.M. Count Walmoden, is worn out by age and infirmities, which may serve also to excuse his own miserable want of energy, and his wish rather to negotiate than to fight.

26th.—The French are felling timber in Hanover in large quantities, and are preparing, by Bonaparte's orders, to build ships in the little port of Vegesack.

31st.—It is reported that Bonaparte means to leave on foot some Hanoverian regiments, in the manner the French formerly had the Swiss regiments, the Royal Allemands, and the Royal Suédois, in order the more easily to seduce the Hanoverians from their allegiance to the king. The old uniform is to be retained, the officers 'to hold the same rank as before; and that this plan may occasion no.jealousy, Prussia, Holland, and Spain are to be allowed to recruit from our late army.

Of the horses delivered over to the French by the Hanoverian cavalry, two thousand are destined for the army of the Rhine. Large numbers of troops are assembling between Cologne and Cleves, and on the Batavian frontiers.

A recent letter from Hanover says, " To the already melancholy statement of our misfortunes must be added that of the fresh demands made by the French on this unfortunate Electorate. They ask us for seven million two hundred thousand livres, as a contribution for three months, ending with the month of October. Of this sum two million livres only can be found. Besides this, we have the war taxes, made more oppressive by the troops being képt constantly in movement. Detachments are marched backwards and forwards; troops of cavalry are sent from place to place; the incomplete battalions are being increased by twenty-seven men per company, and the burden of this miserable country is made more insupportable day by day by heavier and more oppressive exactions. The representations that have been made on this subject have hitherto produced nothing but the assurance that, should a loan become necessary, France herself will assist us in the negotiation of it." It is a slight consolation to learn that the very strictest discipline is observed amongst the troops, and that a few days ago three men who had been marauding during their march were shot.

M. Talleyrand, a nephew of the minister, arrived in Berlin, *en courier*, yesterday evening from St. Petersburg. The passage of French couriers has not been so frequent, it is said, since the time of the Directory and Sièyes' mission.

Aug. 5th.—The movements of Bonaparte afford an unfailing subject for conversation and discussion. The motive for his sudden journey from Brussels to Paris is very variously explained, though the true one is probably known only to himself. It is most generally conjectured that great disturbances had been fomented in Paris, by his enemies, during his absence.

11th.—M. Lombard has returned from his—in every sense—extraordinary mission. He is highly gratified with his reception at Brussels, and the flattering compliments paid him by the First Consul.

This Court also affects to derive great satisfaction and security, from the general assurances M. Lombard has been desired to convey to the king of Bonaparte's friendly dispositions.

As to the special object of the mission—the withdrawal of the French troops from the banks of the Elbe—the precise answer that has been given has not been allowed to become known ; but it is evident that it is of a nature to ensure the continuance of the king's favourite policy of inaction, and his acquiescence in the views of France.

In society, M. Lombard everywhere talks of the candour and frankness of Bonaparte's explanations ; his great friendship for the King of Prussia; his wish to establish a general peace and to spend the remainder of his life in quietude; occupied only in promoting the happiness and prosperity of the nation whose interests have been committed to his charge. England alone, it appears, opposes a barrier to the realization of his views. But, M. Lombard allows it to be inferred, though he does not in plain terms say so, that the preparations for bringing this perfidious foe to her senses are well advanced, and success in the attempt not despaired of.

M. Lombard has also Bonaparte's picture to display, very richly set in diamonds ; a present from the great man as a special mark of his favour. Besides this, he brought with him two large boxes of millinery and dresses of great value ; a present from Madame Bonaparte to the queen of beauty, and accompanied by a letter, signed Josephine.

Letters—August 12*th.*—I get confused with the details of ladies' laces; but, as this part of M. Lombard's mission will greatly interest my mother and sisters, I have sought enlightenment on the subject from Mademoiselle de D., a very competent authority. There are three dresses, I learn, one of the finest Brussels point; another of white satin, woven with a pattern in gold thread, and ornamented with Alençon lace; the third is of a pale grey satin, magnificently embroidered with steel. Her Majesty pronounces them " *superbes ;*" whether they will *faire effet* in the way intended or expected remains to be seen.

You write in very low spirits, but we do not find that the same despondency is general in our country. It would, indeed, be unfortunate if it were so at a time like the present, when great spirit, exertion, and unanimity are so urgently needed.

People in general, on the continent, look forward with certain expectation to an invasion ; but nobody thinks that it can or ought to succeed. My brother and the English we have here, are convinced that we have nothing to fear in the end. But to justify such security we must act, they say, as if we had everything to fear, and must take such precautions against an attempt that may very likely be made, as alone can render it abortive should it really take place.

16*th.*—A messenger arrived this morning with the mail of the 5th. We are delighted with the additional proofs you daily give of your spirit, and with the complete dressing Sir Francis Burdett has at last received. It cannot fail, I should say, to give pleasure to the heart of every true, honest John Bull. If I could ever envy any man his feelings, it would be Mr. Byng on that glorious occasion.

What do you say to my "pretensions," now you know who is to be our new envoy at Dresden? The official people here are as much, or perhaps more, surprised than we are, for they all knew Wynn when he was at Berlin three years ago—and about my age—with his uncle, Mr. T. Grenville.

Many of our unfortunate countrymen have lately passed through Berlin, amongst others two gentlemen, one the son of Sir G. Burrel, who had been refused passports to leave Italy, but escaped by making their servant their master, he passing for an American, and they for his valet and courier. We have also a letter from a lady, who, with her maid, has really suffered much fatigue and privation before reaching neutral ground. All the money she had with her—one hundred and fifty louis, which she had concealed in her hat—was taken from her when she was searched at the *barrière* on leaving Geneva; her remonstrances being silenced by threats of imprisonment. She complains bitterly of the Misses Berry, who were then on their travels. "When they arrived at their hotel at Geneva, before leaving their carriage, a private letter," she says, "was put into their hands, informing them of the intended arrest of the English. Without an instant's delay they returned to Lausanne, forgetting in their selfish terror, to give notice of what was about to happen to their countrymen and countrywomen—many of whom were well known to them--who filled the Hotel Secherin, which they passed as they drove out of Geneva." But I suppose the Misses Berry were not more selfishly alive to their own danger than were the rest of the world ; *sauve qui peut* seems to have been the order of the day.

The great press of business does not allow of our going into, what is called here, the country, which, for my own part, I am glad of ; for our palace *Unter den Linden* is a far more desirable abode, even during the great heats, than a New Road or Paddington villa in the midst of the Brandenburg sands. We, however, went to a dinner the other day, given by the Prussian minister, Count H., at his country-house, to several of the *corps diplomatique* and the principal foreigners staying here. I accompanied my brother and Mr. Cavendish. The company assembled at one o'clock at a house, which would be called in England a farm-house, being surrounded by barns and out-houses, and having, almost under its windows, an excellent farm-yard, well stocked with poultry of different sorts, the usual animals, &c. The originality of the whole entertainment was very amusing. Count H.—dressed in a russet-brown coat, and black cloth boots—might have been taken, but for his ribands and stars, for a well-to-do farmer.

As the dinner was not to be served until two, the Count proposed a walk to his guests, and took us into a fine piece of Luzern, the merits of which he

entered into, and described its various qualities. In
the next field we saw some very fine wheat, just
ready to cut; for the harvest, though wonderfully
abundant this year throughout Germany, is yet, we
learnt, somewhat later than usual. The Count
seemed remarkably proud of this wheat, and cried
out every moment, " Voilà! Messieurs, voilà!" and,
turning to my brother repeatedly, said, " Dites donc,
Monsieur; en avez vous de meilleur en Angleterre?"

He then took us to the cattle-stalls, where he had
eighty of the finest oxen in the country. They are
of a very large sort, and are sent for, he told us,
when lean, from Poland to be fattened here; just as
we do with Welsh heifers. It was rather diverting
to see all the red, blue, and yellow ribands and
stars going through the rows of oxen, and scratching
their polls; then listening gravely to the agri-
cultural teaching of their host, as he led the way to
some new wonder, they following on tiptoe to avoid
the dirt.   One of the company was so much
impressed by the information he had acquired on
farming affairs that, on leaving the oxen-sheds, he
called out, " Mais, les fumiers, Monsieur le comte!—
Les fumiers doivent former un grand objet ici!" This
remark caused a general laugh, though it was less
pleasant than apt, as each one felt when he looked
down at his own and his neighbour's shoes.

After this, some machines for cutting hay and
straw together, in an easy and effective manner,
were shown and explained to us; also two rooms full
of silkworms, from which silk of great fineness has

been produced, and has been manufactured for Her Majesty's use.

When we had got thus far, dinner was announced; and when this heavy German business was concluded, you may readily suppose we were pretty well knocked up for the day.

Sept. 10*th.*—As there really was nobody in Berlin, and war and diplomacy alike were at a stand-still, my brother, for the sake of a stag-hunt, resolved on a ten days' trip to the little principality of Dessau in Upper Saxony; and Cavendish, who likes Berlin so well that he will remain some time longer, went with us. As severe weather sets in here earlier than in England, hunting begins as soon as the harvest is over. There are not more than three or four packs of hounds in all Germany, for the spirit of the thing is not much felt; the country is not always adapted for it, and there are few private fortunes that can support the expense, although it is a mere trifle compared with that of a kennel in England. The Prince of Dessau, who acquired the taste for hunting during the several journeys he made in England, lives very much like a country gentleman of the old stamp, of four or five thousand per annum, preferring the enjoyments and freedom of private life to the confinement and *gêne* of a court. He is very hospitable, and is particularly pleased when strangers, especially Englishmen, go to see his country and his hunt. The former is beautiful—a good soil, well cultivated, rich in oak woods and meadows, and watered by the Elbe. In the prince's house at Wörlitz, and in the gardens surrounding it, as much taste is displayed as at Stowe or at Blenheim. We stayed three hunting days, and were then obliged to hasten back to Berlin; for the king, having at last bought Lichtenau House for his sister, the Princess of Orange, we have been obliged to seek another abode.

My brother has secured, for the term of his residence here, the smaller, but more compact house of the former imperial minister.

Diaries—Sept. 14*th.*—No news has arrived in my brother's absence, except that contained in letters from the East, which report that the Turkish empire is falling rapidly to pieces; that Roumalia, Roumania, and even Wallachia are overrun by rebels; the whole of Egypt, with the exception of Alexandria, in the hands of the Beys; and, by the last accounts from Arabia, Mecca and Medina in the possession of Abdul Wahibi and his followers.

26*th.*—Bonaparte has sent agents from Paris to endeavour to sell all the royal domains in the Electorate of Hanover. No purchasers have hitherto come forward.

27*th.*—Permission has been given to General Mortier to march a brigade of infantry through Hildesheim, on its way to Arnhem.

Letters—Nov. 7*th.*—During the recent lull in politics and diplomacy—at least, so far as anything has occurred or reached us in Berlin—we have been most busily engaged with the new arrangements and changes in our home. We have furnished and taken possession of our house, and my brother has placed a mistress at the head of it. He was married yesterday to Mlle. de Dorville. After the ceremony, he and his bride, contrary to the Prussian custom —which ordains that the newly· married couple should, on the morning after the wedding, give a breakfast, to which their friends and acquaintance repair · to offer their congratulations—set out for Freienwalde, the Tunbridge Wells of this neighbourhood, but now even more deserted than that place is at this season. The queen dowager has a country-house there; my sister-in-law will be presented to her in her new character of the wife of the British minister, and I suppose they · will not find another soul at Freienwalde besides themselves.

16*th.*—The happy pair returned, after a honeymoon of five days, to commence a round of dinners, suppers, and balls, to be given and received in honour of the auspicious event. Their first grand dinner took place yesterday. The Duke of Brunswick, the Princess of Orange, the Duchess of Courland, the foreign ministers now in town, with other grandees, native and foreign, to the number of thirty-five, were present. Mr. Cavendish, and Mr. Wynn, our young Envoy to Dresden, were, besides ourselves, the only Englishmen present. The marriage feasts and festivities—which on our side are to conclude with a ball and supper to about two hundred persons—will be got over, it is hoped, by the time the king and queen leave Potzdam, when the bride will go through her presentations, and we shall return to

our usual sober routine. Our present doings would
furnish many edifying columns to the "Morning
Post," if it had but an efficient reporter in Berlin to
record them.

Diaries—Nov. 18*th.*—This Court is much embarrassed, and the general sensation is great, respecting
the recent proposals submitted by Bonaparte to
Russia and Prussia on the subject of Hanover. He
wishes it to be arranged by the three powers, that
France should retain undisturbed possession of the
Electorate, engaging himself not to increase the
number of troops there, and not to penetrate
further into Germany ; that Russia and Prussia
should, conjointly, set on foot an army of neutrality,
and Vienna be engaged not to interfere with the
measures of France.

The emperor refused to accede to these propositions, and insisted that the immediate evacuation
of Hanover was indispensable to the safety of the
north of Germany. "Prussia," he said, "must be left
entirely to herself if she persisted in seconding the
views of France." To add to the embarrassment of
the Prussian Court, the Duke of Mecklenberg
Schwerin has complained of the violation of his
territory by French troops. The king professes
great indignation at this conduct of Bonaparte, yet
shudders at the idea of entering into a contest
with him. Even Beym is loud in invective against
him, and Lombard thinks himself personally affected
by the deceit put upon him at Brussels, and his own
too great credulity on that occasion.

The king has proposed to guarantee France from any and every continental attack, if she consents to leave the north of Germany in tranquillity, and will withdraw her army from the Electorate of Hanover —a feeble and hopeless attempt to avert a threatened danger, made without due thought, or apprehension of the many serious considerations with which such an act abounds.

Complaints of the increasingly oppressive exactions of the French in Hanover reach us almost daily. It would seem that they are so familiarized with acts of plunder and extortion, that those in power consider the contributions they demand need know scarcely any other limits than those of their own wants, and the resources of the countries they ransack in rotation.

Conspiracies to overthrow Bonaparte and his government are forming by both royalists and republicans, and the union of these parties is said to be not only possible but probable. "If it really be so, the sentiments and principles of Louis XVIII. must have undergone a very considerable change," say those who are tolerably well acquainted with the character of that prince, and who believe that it would be almost impossible to induce him to bend to such concessions as appear to form the groundwork of the plan the republican plotters would propose to him.

It is also thought, with respect to the dispositions of the interior of France, that the government of Bonaparte would be preferred to that of the pure republicans, who, although they may be numerous, would find their efforts to overthrow the existing state of things not only not seconded to the extent they expect, but on the contrary opposed.

Several letters have lately been received here, through the ordinary post from Frankfort, from a man who signs himself, sometimes, "Saint Alexander," at others, "Count Pagowski," and who says he belonged to the Polish Legion, proposing to carry off Bonaparte, dead or alive, from St. Omer. For this purpose he has demanded 2000*l.* In one letter he announced that he had drawn a bill on my brother for an advance of 150*l.* No notice was taken of his letters, and his draft, which was duly presented, was protested. This person has since made his appearance in Berlin, and has informed M. de Bruges— himself connected with the plots of the royalist Georges—that if he heard of Bonaparte's arrival at St. Omer he must conclude that the execution of his plan was suspended, as it would be impossible to strike the blow when Bonaparte was in the midst of his army.

It was believed by this person that Bonaparte would not leave Paris till the 15th of December ; and so great is the confidence he professes to place in the dispositions of parties, and in the means organized, as he says, *with the assistance of a powerful government*, that the only difficulty he seems to foresee is that of fixing upon a suitable state of things when Bonaparte *shall be no more.* M. de Haugwitz says, however, that Bonaparte is daily expected at Mayence, as he intends to make a tour in the four new departments, in his way to St. Omer.

21*st.*—Numerous copies of "A letter to Bonaparte," written by the Berne correspondent for the promotion of one of the royalist plots now in agitation, have been sent here from Munich for distribution. It will also appear in all the considerable towns of every country in Europe, except Spain and Portugal, which are too difficult of access. It will be received at Constantinople, and in every department of the interior of France ; for which latter purpose measures have been taken to elude the vigilance of the French Government. This letter is expected to produce an effect very favourable to the royalist schemes.

There are persons, however, who doubt this result, who even regret that such futile measures should be resorted to ; who consider the policy of the government that countenances such schemes, and affords aid to the schemers, as deficient in wisdom and dignity.

Hints are thrown out—and by no means obscure ones—showing plainly that the quarter whence the ample supplies are derived, for the carrying on of this dirty work, is no secret. That the ever watchful vigilance of the French police should have failed to discover it is, therefore, not likely. It is probable, even, that the persons who take an active part in these plots are themselves agents of the French Government. But, at all events, they are, as in former instances of this kind others have been found to be, mere needy unprincipled adventurers, seeking to enrich themselves, by means of the credulity of those who lend an ear to their vain projects, and who supply the large sums—over the expenditure of which no control whatever can be exercised—which they represent to be needful for their realization.

Whatever may be thought of the despotic rule and restless ambition of Bonaparte, it is firmly believed they are not so intolerable to the French, that his overthrow can be accomplished by the intrigues of a few hot-headed royalists, and two or three discontented military men.   But, that while the spirit to resist him by force of arms is wanting in that quarter especially interested in opposing him, we can look only to time, and that "vaulting ambition" which will eventually overleap itself, for the final downfall of the present ruler of France.

Letters—December 1st.—Wynn has just left us for Dresden.   He is a pleasant young fellow, only two or three years older than myself, and apparently not that.   It has been remarked here that in the present state of continental affairs, how extraordinary it is that mere boys should be appointed to such responsible posts.   Wynn, himself, seemed to be rather embarrassed when introduced, as His Majesty's envoy, to some shrewd old diplomats in Berlin.   It is rather hard, he owns, on Mr. Grey, the secretary of legation, to have one so much his junior placed over him, but, as the government has chosen to appoint him, he says, he cannot be supposed to be very sorry for it.   His appointment is a proof that it is no bad thing to have a violent "opposionist" for a patron.

Wynn says that Casamajor will not return here,

and that it was thought my brother would ask for the vacant secretaryship for me. He advised me to urge him to do so ; but I shall not.

We are expecting Lord Aberdeen, who was with us in Paris, and some anxiety is felt at the delay in his arrival. He was last heard of in the Morea, whence he was to pass to Zante, to Venice, Vienna, &c.

5th.—We hear that such preparations are making in England to receive the invaders as will put to shame some of the powers of Europe, for the extreme pusillanimity of their behaviour, and that Mr. Pitt does not intend to be much in town this winter, as both he and Lord Grenville are greatly occupied with their military commands. They are doing incalculable good, and with a just confidence are awaiting the threatened attack. That it will cer- tainly be made seems to be the general expectation in our country. A contrary opinion is held here.

Diaries—December 17*th.*—We learn that a mes- senger who was on his way to England, in company with another person, was driven by the postilion to Ratzberg instead of Schwerin, and to an hotel occupied by several French officers. The travellers were in great alarm on discovering that they had thus fallen into the clutches of the French, and expected to be searched or otherwise molested. But, instead of the treatment they looked for, they met with the greatest politeness, and were pressed to partake of dinner, which was about to be served. They did so, and afterwards were allowed, without hindrance, to proceed on their journey. That they thus escaped can only be accounted for from the circumstance of the messenger, who was Mr. Stuart's own servant, not travelling with courier horses.

22nd.—The foreign ministers last evening paid their respects to their Majesties, at an assembly given by the Duke of Brunswick Oels. The king took occasion to say to the British minister, that " should Bonaparte, contrary to the general expectation, succeed in landing any part of his army in England, it was his hope and firm persuasion that he would be repulsed with that energy which had ever characterized the British nation." " But," added the king, " the ardour of Bonaparte to attempt the invasion has lately, I think, considerably abated." Her Majesty, also, was graciously complimentary. A few evenings ago, my brother and his wife being at a ball, and feeling a little tired, left just as supper was announced. This remarkable fact, which was attributed to the lady being in an interesting situation, was communicated, it appears, to the queen, and Her Majesty, with many gracious smiles of approbation, openly made it a special subject of congratulation to my sister-in-law and brother at the Duke of Brunswick's assembly! This was thought a great compliment.

1804.

Letters—January 2nd.—Besides actual business, I am now in the midst of preparations for my presentation next week, and am in a perplexing state of uncertainty as to the fate of a uniform which should

ere this have arrived from London. It is the same
as that worn by my friend Cavendish, red, faced with
yellow, and silver epaulettes—the uniform of his
father's regiment, which he has obtained leave for
me to wear. We are afraid that it is gone, together
with a Windsor uniform for my brother, to grace the
carnival at Paris. If so, it will be a sorry commencement of my Court career, and I shall be obliged—
en attendant better success next time—to put up with
the work of a Berlin tailor. To-morrow, I begin my
round of visits to all the old ladies, and the invitations
to the Princess Henry's and the Ferdinand court will
probably follow next week. Not that this is a very
pleasant part of the business, for although it is not,
of course, the fashion to say so, the princess is as stiff
as a poker.

Our time will probably be much engaged throughout the month with courtly business; for the king's
brother, Prince William, is to be married on Thursday
the 12th, and on Tuesday his bride makes her public
entry into Berlin. Balls and suppers without end
will follow.

The etiquette of this Court requires that the queen,
and the bride, should dance a minuet with all the
princes, the ministers of the country, and the foreign
ministers. Rather fatiguing for the illustrious ladies,
and embarassing to some of the gentlemen who are
to be thus honoured, and who " now must dance that
never danced before." Many are taking lessons of a
dancing master.

6th.—I was presented to their Majesties last night,

at the Duke of Brunswick Oels, and in rather a
singular manner—in plain clothes. The duke gives
a weekly ball, at which the Court generally assists ;
but it had been signified that the king and queen
would not be present last evening, and, consequently,
everybody went in undress. However, on entering
the ante-room, the first person we saw was the
grand maréchal to announce their Majesties' change
of plan. We were, of course, about to take wing
immediately, when we were informed that the king,
very graciously, had said he would be happy to see
me, dressed as I was. Thus, for the first time since
the Prussian monarchy has existed, has the honour of
being presented in plain clothes been conferred.

The Frenchmen were a little *estomaqués* at this,
and wished, I am convinced, that they had had somebody in the same predicament to present.

8th.—The foreign ministers who had been informed that they would be invited to dance minuets
with the queen and princess, at the forthcoming
royal marriage, have received notice that this part of
the programme will be omitted. It has been ascertained that no instance is on record of a queen of
Prussia having danced with ministers of the second
order. But it is supposed that this expedient has
been adopted with a view to preclude the possibility
of difficulties arising on the subject of precedence
amongst the foreign ministers, and to settle also a
doubtful point of etiquette.

11th.—The king and queen went to Potzdam on
Monday, to meet the Princess Amelia of Hesse

Homberg; yesterday she made her public entry into Berlin, in the midst of an immense concourse of people, and escorted by the different guilds of armed burghers. In the evening their Majesties, accompanied by the young princess, appeared most unexpectedly at a ball given by the tradesmen of the city. Their intention was, no doubt, to make some acknowledgment to the burghers for the part they had voluntarily taken in the morning's procession, and the enthusiastic greeting they had given the princess. But the circumstance has been much commented upon in Berlin to-day, and has been pronounced *infra dig.* by some persons, gracious condescension by others.

13*th*.—Yesterday, the marriage of Prince William and the Princess Amelia took place at the palace. The royal diadem was placed on the head of the bride by the queen mother, in the presence of the royal family. They then went in procession to the state rooms, fitted up by Frederick I., and where all royal marriages are performed.

The prince, in the uniform of a Prussian general, with the princess, dressed in white satin and silver— four maids of honour bearing her train—walked first; the king, with the queen mother; the queen, with Prince Henry, and eight other royal couples followed. Each was preceded by gentlemen of their respective courts, and followed by their chief officers, with the maids of honour attending the royal ladies.

The procession passed through the old court chapel and the gallery—two hundred feet in length—to the

White Hall, in which are the statues, in white marble, of the old electors.

Here the Court chaplain, M. Sack, was waiting, under a canopy of red velvet, to perform the marriage ceremony. All the royal family, with the exception of the queen mother—for whom a velvet-covered chair was provided—stood in a half circle round the bride and bridegroom; the rest of the company formed a second half circle outside the royal one.

At the moment when the rings were exchanged, a signal was given, and the twenty-four cannon before the palace were fired in succession three times.

The Court then proceeded to the card-room, where the newly-married couple sat down to whist with the king and the queen mother. The Queen, Prince Henry, the bride's mother—the Landgravine of Hesse—and the Prince of Orange, formed another table; the rest of the company made up four others. When they had finished their rubber, they adjourned to the state-room, and the royal party took supper; which was served on gold plate, and under a canopy of red velvet. During the repast a band of music was stationed in the silver orchestra. This orchestra is, in fact, only plated; the original one was of solid silver, but at the commencement of the Seven Years' War, the Great Frederick, finding his coffers rather empty, melted it down for crowns, and supplied its place with the present one.

The meats served to the royal table were cut up by Generals Elsna and Beville—standing—and were afterwards distributed, or handed round, by the marshal, and officers of the Court, *les grandes maîtresses*, and maids of honour. These menial offices are performed by them only on such exceptional occasions, and their duties end when the royal party have drunk their first glass, ·which, according to court etiquette, is always immediately after the first course is served. Their distinguished attendants then retire to take supper also, with the rest of the company, at adjoining tables. There were five of those extra tables, each presided over by a person of high rank.

Supper ended, they returned to the White Hall, and the ministers of state, each with a fourfold burning torch of white wax in his hand, assembled near the throne to await the arrival of the Court to commence the Fackel dance, with which the marriage ceremony concludes; a custom observed only at this Court, and supposed to have been originally intended to represent the Court of Hymen conducting the new-married pair to the nuptial chamber.

As soon as the royal party entered, the trumpets and kettle-drums of the king's Garde du Corps, and the regiment of Gendarmes, struck up a sort of polonaise. The grand marshal, with his long black wand, led off first. The ministers, with their flaming torches, followed. Then came the prince and his wife, and the four maids of honour bearing the train. Slowly marching towards the royalties, ranged in a circle round the throne, the princess left the arm of her husband, and advancing towards the king, curtseyed profoundly, thus inviting him to make the first *tour* with her. This over, the same ceremony was gone through with all the princes, according to the order observed in the marriage procession. The prince then commenced his *tours*, first with the queen mother, then the queen, and all the princesses in succession; the ministers, with their hymeneal torches, preceding each couple. To some of the festive torch-bearers these numerous *tours* seemed to be *tours de force* they were hardly equal to; and they must surely have succumbed if Providence had not spared them the minuets with which they at first were threatened. But at length the *tours* were ended; and the royal bride and bridegroom were then escorted to their apartments to undress; the former by the queen mother and the other royal ladies, the latter by the king and princes.

When the princess was supposed to be in bed, the company assembled in the ante-room to receive from her *grande maîtresse* small pieces of embroidered riband, representing her royal highness's garter.

Thus ended this royal wedding, which put me in mind of an old drama, got up with new scenery, dresses, processions, banquets, trumpets, kettle-drums, &c., &c.

We take our share of the general fuss, and celebrate the happy event by a ball on the 18th.

Diaries—Jan. 15th.—Notwithstanding the deep plunge into gaiety and pleasure which all classes in Berlin have lately taken, there has been, at times, great anxiety evinced to know whether Bonaparte would accede to the king's proposal of guarantee, and would evacuate Hanover.

17th.—Yesterday morning the arrival of a French courier momentarily raised the hopes of two or three of the statesmen of this country; but it soon became known that the only news he had brought was that the First Consul had left Paris on a certain day—which proves to have been that he had named for declaring his intentions to the king—and that no communication whatever on the subject had been sent to this government. The courier, however, was the bearer of a magnificent lace dress for the queen, a new year's present from Madame Bonaparte. A break in the frost has also brought us news from home. There, too, they are waiting with some anxiety to know Bonaparte's pleasure as to the threatened invasion. Here, the opinion is that the Dutch may be soon ordered to push out, but that nothing further will be attempted until he has, at least, made a previous trial of our strength. Mr. Pitt, we learn, still continues highly displeased and very hostile, yet not induced to enter into the systematic opposition recommended by his adherents, who have even wished him to unite with Mr. Fox, but have as yet failed in their endeavour.

The tacit refusal of Bonaparte to accede to the King of Prussia's proposal of guarantee, has since been confirmed by the verbal declaration of his minister, and is the subject of great embarrassment and annoyance to this Government. The Prussians would submit to their present disappointment, with only a suppressed murmur, were it not that they are compelled to communicate their situation to the Court of St. Petersburg. Their situation is, in fact, that of a man who would quietly put up with an insult if it were not overheard. The king is, therefore ill-humoured and disgusted. " When," said a Prussian officer, to-day, speaking bitterly of the present state of things, " when will the irresistible course of events prove strong enough to overcome the *vis inertia* of our king !"

It is said that the king does not intend to hold the reviews, as has been customary during the summer in different districts of the country. General Köchritz, in allusion to this report, said it was in contemplation to form a camp of forty thousand men *near Spandau*, in order to instruct in the business of a campaign the many young officers now in the army who had not seen service.

23*rd.*—It is asserted here that the King of Sweden, who is at Carlsruhe, is courting Bonaparte—after taking all the money he could get from England— with a view to have Norway ceded to him by Denmark; that power to be offered Bremen and Verden as a compensation, with, *perhaps*, Swedish Pomerania to Prussia. This being made known to General Köchritz, his answer is thus reported, " the king found himself already too deeply engaged in plans of partition and indemnity that he could not recede from, and otherwise, they were too repugnant to his character to form them." It is thought that His Swedish Majesty would be glad to find a favourable opportunity of joining in a war against Prussia. It is, however, likely that all this is the mere invention of the King of Sweden's enemies; for the feeling towards him at this Court is by no means cordial. He is said to have a mania for imitating the conduct of Gustavus Adolphus, without possessing his abilities. However, it is certain that, although somewhat eccentric at times, he displays an independence of character that is wanting here, and that the freedom of his remarks on the policy of this Court, and the occasional remonstrances he has made to the king are the chief causes of the little favour he meets with from the Prussian Government.

Feb. 1st to 12th.—The rumour that the king does not intend to hold the Berlin spring reviews this year, that those also of Königsberg and Warsaw will not take place, and that the exercises of the troops will be postponed till the formation of the camps, has formed the subject of general conversation, and latterly had supplanted that of the long-talked-of invasion of England. But Bonaparte's recent arrangements, and the powers conferred on Murat, as Governor of Paris, seem to denote that he purposes to absent himself for some time, and the invasion is, therefore, again become an interesting theme. The Elector of Hesse Cassel has also furnished us with another, by adopting the extraordinary resolution of ordering all his subjects in the Prussian service—and there are about sixty officers of different grades—to return home on pain of confiscation of their property.

18*th.*—We have the English mails in, through Holland, to the 2nd. The papers speak of the Prince of Wales's *illness.* A private letter explains that his royal highness and the Duke of N. had for three successive days been so completely drunk, that the former at last fell like a pig, and lay for several hours to all appearance dead ; bleeding, they say, relieved him. A subject of greater interest than the drunken bouts of this royal *débauché* is, the plan we see Mr. Addington has brought forward for the settlement of the Civil List. It is to be hoped that the servants of the crown will receive from it a permanent benefit in the regular payment of their respective salaries. It seems extraordinary, to say no more, that England, the richest country in the world, should be the only one that leaves the numerous dependents of its government so long without reaping the fruit of their labour.

21*st.*—Another royal marriage is on the *tapis,* between Prince Henry, the king's eldest brother, and the eldest daughter of the hereditary Prince of Denmark. The princess's picture has already been received, and an interview between the illustrious personages will take place in the summer, at the baths of Neudorff.

25*th.*—Very startling intelligence has been received from Paris—that of the arrest of General Moreau, and several other persons, in Paris and different parts of France. The King of Prussia gave the first intimation of the General's arrest at a court-ball; amongst other persons to M. Laforêt, the French minister, who treated it as a groundless rumour. But when the king said he had positive intelligence of the fact, he replied that " General Moreau, with very great military talents, had always been deficient in the qualities that form a good citizen." Speaking on. the subject to Count Du-moustier—the last minister of Louis XVI. to this Court—the king observed, that " he began to think those emigrants were in the right who had not returned to France."

The public show an eager curiosity on the subject, and consider these arrests as a symptom of the in-stability of Bonaparte's government. The immediate conclusion drawn from them, by my brother, is, that Bonaparte will be more desirous than before of engaging in a continental war. The reports of reinforcements being sent to the army in Hanover, and of the intention of the French to occupy the Hanse Towns, seem to strengthen this inference.

March 2nd.—We are all on the tiptoe of expecta-tion ; and the anxiety on the part of the public is not a little increased by a report, just received from the Hague, of the death of Bonaparte. No credit, how-ever, is given to it in well-informed quarters. Some indications among the people of a disposition to rejoice openly at the event were speedily repressed by a public contradiction of the report.

6th.—The result of Moreau's trial is awaited with inconceivable anxiety. The general persuasion is, that he will be sacrificed to the personal enmity of Bonaparte, and to the necessity of withdrawing the

attention of the French nation from the loss of St.
Domingo and the abandonment of the expedition
against England.

7th.—The Emperor of Russia has announced to
this Court that he intends to march his army through
the Prussian territory, and expects it will meet with
no obstacle, as the king had not refused a passage
to the French on their way to Hanover.

Letters—March 8th.—Notwithstanding the sensation created here by what has occurred in Paris, all
this great town is now completely taken up with
preparations for a grand *fête* at the opera house, to
celebrate the queen's birthday on the 12th, and the
pretty girls of Berlin have been practising dances
and marches these three weeks past with the ballet
masters of the opera. The queen herself is to take
the part of Statyra, the daughter of Darius, in the
quadrille called " Alexander's return from his Indian
Victories." Statyra makes a conquest of the conqueror at first sight, which no doubt our queen of
beauty would have done, had the hero had the happiness of seeing her.

The Court has determined to exclude the *corps
diplomatique* from their quadrille, that there may be
no questions of precedence to settle. They are all
quite content to be excluded, and, in white dominos,
to be spectators only.

With reference to this *fête* I must tell you a story
of an Englishman we have here, who supplies the
place of all other foreigners. He is a Colonel Pollen,
who once, my brother tells me, attempted to play

a part in the House of Commons, and did distinguish himself as effectually there, as elsewhere, by
his most consummate effrontery. For some time he
has been travelling about the Continent, because it is
not very convenient to him to remain in England; and
last year he married a Miss Gascoigne, at St. Petersburg, after a few days' acquaintance. He came to
Berlin about a month ago, and has contrived to push
himself so forward as to have the opportunity of
doing a thing unheard of in the annals of this or
any other Court. There had been a consultation
about the dresses to be worn at the *fête* of the 12th,
in the queen's quadrille. Pollen went off in search
of some prints, and returned with them while the king
and royal family were at dinner. Without any
ceremony, he walked into the dining-room, and fami-
liarly commenced his conversation with their Majesties,
who were so good as not to order him to be turned
out. In fact, they appeared to feel less on the occasion than the persons of their Court, who cry out
vehemently at this great breach of decorum.

He is one of that sort of travellers who bring
discredit on our national character.

An Englishman of another stamp, Mr. Drummond,
our ambassador at the Porte, has been with us for the
last three weeks, and is likely to remain some time
longer. He waits partly on account of the unfavourable state of the weather, but still more on account
of the pleasure he finds in the society of Madame de
Staël, who favours us at times with invitations to her
readings of her own works. Those who can best

N 2

flatter her, and pay the most servile homage, not only to the intellect she has, but to the beauty she has not, are her most welcome guests.

Mr. Drummond is decorated with the Order of the Crescent, instituted in honour of Lord Nelson, and which, with the one exception of the present Russian ambassador, has been conferred on Englishmen only. " The great value and beauty of the insignia make up for the newness of the order," he says. This and the service of plate he got, as ambassador, will compensate him, it is to be hoped, for what he calls the many " disagreeablenesses " of his embassy; which has lasted but six months, and he does not intend to return.

10*th.*—A report has reached us, said to be brought to Holland by a fishing boat, of the king having died on the 28th ult. We have five mails due, and are therefore much in the dark, as regards English news; but, from a variety of circumstances, we are inclined to hope and believe that the report of His Majesty's death is a fabrication of our enemies, who look, though I trust in vain, to that melancholy event as the source of dissensions amongst our leaders which may be turned by them to profitable account.

Diaries—March 14*th.*—Notwithstanding the armaments of Russia, it is fully understood here that she will continue at peace unless Bonaparte should make any further attacks on the north of Europe, or should attempt to realize his ambitious views on the side of Turkey. The emperor has been advised to treat the King of Prussia *civilly*, lest he should throw himself into the arms of France; but to place no further confidence in him, and to arm, for the purpose of being ready for any events that may arise. His Imperial Majesty is said to be much displeased with M. Alopeus, who has been represented to him, somewhat unjustly, as a determined *Berlinois.* He is to be left, we are told, at his post for the present only, because the emperor has determined to have no longer any intimate relations with the king. At the same time the poor king—for it is impossible not to like and to pity him ; " bon bourgeois, et bon père de famille," as nature has made him, though fate, for his own and his country's misfortune, most perversely has placed him in a position for which far sterner stuff than he is made of is needed—the poor king, I must repeat, is sorely distressed at the isolated position in which he now finds himself. He professes the same horror, as before, of Bonaparte's acts, and shows the same disposition to upbraid him as the cause of his embarrassments, yet he retains the same unvarying inclination to listen to the temporizing counsels of subordinate and irresponsible ministers as has hitherto been, and seems likely to continue to be, the leading feature of the King of Prussia's Government.

20th.—We have the "Moniteur" of the 10th. It announces the arrest of Georges; but in a manner that leaves it doubtful whether he was taken alive or not. He killed, it appears, one police officer, and wounded another.

The letters from Paris state that public opinion was so strongly pronounced in favour of General Moreau, that it was thought the First Consul would not venture to proceed to extremities against him; more especially as no sufficient proof of his connection with Georges, or with General Pichegru, was forthcoming, to satisfy even the tribunal by which he would be judged.

M. Baykoff attached to the Russian mission at Paris, and passing through Berlin on his way to St. Petersburg, describes the state of terror that prevailed in that capital, when he came away, as resembling that which oppressed the inhabitants of St. Petersburg under the reign of the Emperor Paul. The arrest of Georges, it was hoped, would cause some relaxation in the rigorous conduct of the police; but imprisonments continued to be made up to the time of his departure. The number of persons already apprehended in Paris, on suspicion, amounts to nearly two thousand.

24th.—Returning home at near five this morning, after having supped, and danced all night, at Baron Hardenberg's, we encountered the messenger with mails from England to the 9th. We have the happiness of receiving favourable intelligence of the king's health. The alarm has been very great respecting it, but we are assured that his faculties are, at this time, perfectly restored, and that the country has escaped the frightful danger to which a continuance of his illness must necessarily have exposed it.

Home politics are as unsettled as ever. Mr. Fox and Lord Grenville have coalesced, or co-operated—which is their word—for the purpose of turning out the present Administration.

Mr. Pitt, on the contrary, stands aloof from any

systematic opposition. He intends, we are told, to
endeavour to do all the good in his power by giving
his advice, and by answering likewise, when occasion
may seem to require it; but further than this he is
not inclined to go. He is however, in his mind, most
decidedly hostile to Mr. Addington, and nothing, it is
believed, would tempt him to join his Administration.

The country, in the meanwhile, is looking towards
Mr. Pitt with an anxious eye, and it is asserted that
no measure, whatever, would make the king half so
popular, as that of recalling to his councils the only
man who is looked up to, in this hour of danger,
with perfect confidence. It is generally felt, that if
Mr. Pitt were prime minister, the internal defence of
the country would be still more secure; that the war,
which we shall probably ere long be engaged in, would
be carried on with far greater vigour; that those
continental powers who must, from the nature of
things, be well disposed towards us, would be inspired
with greater confidence; in short, the idea strongly
prevails, that, had the country such a man as Mr.
Pitt to guide it, it would be better prepared for the
active operations of war, and better able to negotiate
with security when the fit hour arrives. However,
as it is said, the impulse must come from the sovereign.
The country is too well disposed to attempt to
produce any change in the government by clamorous
interposition, and to attempt to give any notions
respecting His Majesty's present or future intentions
would, as our informant says, be entering into too
wide a field of conjecture and surmise. We have

only, then, to thank the Almighty that our sovereign is again fully able to judge for himself what course is most advisable. He has not yet, it seems, attended to any kind of business, but this, we are assured in the strongest terms, is more from precaution than incapacity.

Of the invasion, they know no more than we do; but it is naturally inferred, from the recent events in Paris, that it is likely to be postponed. Bonaparte's attention, it is presumed, must in great part be directed towards the preservation of tranquillity in the interior of France. It is, however, delightful to see the spirit that animates the whole people of England, and which is so unanimously directed to one and the same object. It gives us confidence that the country will defend itself, whether the government be vigilant and vigorous, or as supine and inert as its enemies represent it to be.

25th.—My brother, in answer to my question whether he did not think it would have been good policy in our Government to have made greater attempts for bringing Russia over to our side, said that "*possibly* it might have been; but, on the other hand, as it was certain that the propositions advanced by the emperor in his late mediation were, to the full, as advantageous to our enemy as they could have been to us, there was no ground for imagining, that, until the war had assumed a different aspect, any such interference could be expected from Russia as might be of beneficial consequence to our interests. But, were the interests of Russia herself in any way

endangered by the mad projects of Bonaparte ; were
Greece attacked, or were the invasion of England to
be unsuccessfully attempted, then, and then, perhaps,
only, might we be offered such assistance by Russia
as we should now seek in vain." Sir J. B. Warren,
we know, has been much disappointed that the
government have not turned their thoughts to St.
Petersburg with the earnestness he expected. For
the numerous couriers he has despatched, rarely has
one been sent back to him. However, we have one
piece of news to forward on to him which may,
perhaps, make him bear up under disappointments in
his political expectations—the salary of his embassy
is increased to 10,000*l.* a-year, net, and regularly
paid. Some other missions have also an increase.
Berlin, it was expected, would have come in for a
share, as her pretensions were urged by Mr. Arbuthnot, the present under-secretary, who is fully aware
how desirable it is that foreign ministers should be
enabled to live in honourable style ; but Lord Hawkesbury and Mr. Addington were both of opinion that
the Berlin mission was sufficiently paid, at the
present rate of 5000*l.* a-year. With regard to the
charge of pusillanimity, which the emperor and his
ministers have brought against this Court, it is the
feeling in England, that the policy of the Court of
St. Petersburg has been marked by extreme short-
sightedness and inactivity, and has been in every
degree utterly unworthy of a mighty empire, which
ought to rescue the Continent from the bondage that
France has imposed on it. It is known here, that

after the unsuccessful attempt made last year by
Russia to stir up the king to vigorous measures
against France, the Chancellor Woronzow drew up
and laid before the emperor a long paper, in which
he detailed the whole interested policy of the
government of Prussia for the last half century, and
concluded by recommending a permanent alliance
with Austria.

27th.—Deep grief and resentment have been
produced amongst all classes of people, by the
information, just received, of an arbitrary and violent
act, and a most flagrant violation of neutral territory,
on the part of the French Government. On the
14th, the First Consul's adjutant, Caulincourt, arrived
at Strasburg, with an order to arrest several persons
in that city and in Offenburg, amongst them five ladies
—widows and sisters of emigrants. On the following
night, Caulincourt, with a considerable detachment
of troops, passed the Rhine, and halted at Kehl.
Another detachment, commanded by a General, crossed
at Coppel, and at five the next morning arrived
at Ettenheim, the residence of the Duc d'Enghien.

His highness's house was then forcibly entered,
and he was dragged from his bed, and taken to a
mill, at some distance. There he was allowed to
dress, and thence was conducted to the citadel of
Strasburg. The duke's adjutant, the Abbé Weinborn,
and his *valet-de-chambre* were also seized and taken
thither. The Princess de Rohan Rochefort, who
resided in the duke's house, followed him to Strasburg,
but was not arrested. The duke is represented to

have borne these indignities with great calmness, and when informed that he was charged with conspiring against the French Government, answered, " Qu'un prince de la Maison de Bourbon ne trempérait jamais dans une conspiration obscure ; mais qu'il n'avait pas peur de se déclarer, ouvertement, l'ennemi du gouvernement actuel de la France."

The " Strasburg Gazette," of the 17th, gives a very singular reason for these arrests, viz., that information had been received that a large number of emigrants had assembled on the right bank of the Rhine, with the intention of getting possession of the citadel of Strasburg.

Ettenheim was formerly the residence of the Bishops of Strasburg. In the late plan of indemnity it was allotted to the Elector of Baden, who, in addition to this attack on his territory, has been made to suffer the mockery of the French agents; who, after they had seized and carried off the duke, sent a requisition to the Elector to deliver him up to them. Such an act never occurred in the wildest days of French anarchy. People are overwhelmed with astonishment at the audacity of the undertaking, and lost in conjecture as to the consequences that may result from it; or perhaps one should say, rather, that would have resulted, in times when the great powers of Europe were united in a common bond to resent outrages on the independence of sovereigns.

30th.—By letters from Frankfort, we learn that the commandant at Mayence had sent to that city a detachment of *gendarmes*, who made domiciliary visits in all the inns, and in many private houses, in search of persons connected with the late counter-revolutionary movements in France.

Some persons are sanguine enough to see in this violent conduct of the French Government, the certainty of a continental war; but few who are well acquainted with the actual state of affairs here, believe that there exists sufficient spirit, or enough of self-respect, dignity, and independence of character, where alone they could be effectual, to resent with becoming vigour the repeated outrages to which Germany is exposed.

31st.—The Elector of Baden has ordered all emigrants to leave his territory within three days.

The French agents are circulating a story of the discovery of a correspondence between Louis XVIII. and the Duc d'Enghien, amongst the papers of the latter, for counter-revolutionary purposes. It is, however, perfectly well known that the political interests of the family were not at all entrusted to the duke, and that it was entirely from private personal motives that he continued to reside so near the French frontier, and in opposition to the advice of the Duc de Condé.

Moreau's confidential friend, General Lahorie, was at Frankfort about a fortnight ago, and, it is supposed, it was with a view to secure his person, that the domiciliary incursions were made.

Paris letters say arrests continue to be frequent, and that the prisons are so full, that numbers of prisoners are conveyed almost every night to some place of confinement in the country. *

April 1st.—A Prussian officer, passing lately through Hanover, called, according to the military etiquette, upon the French commander-in-chief. Before being admitted to the General, he was told that he must take off his sword! On remonstrating against a proceeding so unmilitary, and so contrary to his sense of propriety, he learnt that the regulation was general throughout the service, and that no French commander-in-chief would now receive, even a French officer, with a sword by his side. A traveller, who arrived here yesterday, met the Duc d'Enghien on the road between Strasburg and Paris. He was escorted by a detachment of *gendarmes*, and there was a guard of several persons in the carriage.

The King of Prussia, his ministers and confidential advisers, are, of course, vehement in their reprobation of this infamous act, and the recent violation of German territory.

Letters—April 2nd.—We have little time now for anything but official business, and the quill is seldom out of my fingers. Mr. Stevens left us ten days ago, *en courier* with important despatches from St. Petersburg and Berlin. It was rather unexpected, and he will not return. He is a good-hearted fellow, I believe, but one of the oddest I ever met with. However, he has made an excellent courier, as far as we have heard of him, and gained great credit for it here. Mr. Drummond left us yesterday ; he is a loss to us, being a most pleasant man, full of information, and possessing 'a fund of anecdote. He has been upon *the go* for some weeks; but the charms of Madame de Stäel — with whom he was deeply smitten—detained him till now. The roads furnished him with an excellent excuse for lengthening his stay; however, hero like, he tore himself from the chains, which were binding him closer every day, lest by longer delay he should find them too firmly riveted to be broken. *Le voilà donc parti.* Cavendish, to our great regret, follows to-morrow.

Ask Mr. Stevens about Madame de Stäel; she is a very curious personage, I assure you. Naturally good-humoured, I should think, but overwhelmingly self-sufficient, and having the highest contempt for everything she meets with in Berlin. Her daughter, a child of nine or ten years, has imbibed her mother's ideas in this respect, as the following little anecdotes tend to prove.

At a children's ball, at Prince Ferdinand's, she met with another little girl whom she seemed to think very pleasant, and said she liked very much; finding, however, *in the course of conversation* that her new acquaintance was German, mademoiselle pushed the child away, and in an angry tone said, " Allez vous-en! Vous êtes Allemande, allez vous-en! Les Allemands sont tous des sots!" This, though consi- dered *assez fort*, is nothing to the other, which almost amounts to infantine *lèse-majesté*. Being at another juvenile re-union at the palace, and taking offence at something the prince royal said, or did to her, she

very coolly gave him a swingeing box on the ear;
upon which he rushed to his mother, hid his face in
her dress, and cried; the young lady herself, when
remonstrated with, remaining calm and unmoved.
It is said that Madame de Stäel has been desired to
keep her at home until she has learned better manners;
and Madame herself will soon find, if she is not more
careful, that *les bons Berlinois*, whose civilities she
returns with contempt, are beginning to think they
have borne rudeness enough, even from *tant d'esprit
et de réputation*. As to the child, it is clear to every
one that she must be, at least tacitly, encouraged in
her impertinence by her mother.

At this moment we have a curious set, of our
own countrywomen, at the Court of Berlin. Two
new arrivals are Lady Musgrave, and the Dowager
Countess of Kingston, the latter, by all accounts, half
crazy. She has been especially recommended to my
brother by the Electress of Würtemberg. She was
travelling with two daughters, but has married them
both at Stutgard to Germans, one of whom bears the
singular name of *Vingt-cinq gros*. The countess
does so many odd things that I am anxious to make
her acquaintance; I shall be gratified to-day as she
dines with us on her return from Hanover. She set
off for that place, almost as soon as she reached Berlin,
with only an old servant to accompany her. Being
warned that she ran great danger of being taken
prisoner, she laughed at the idea, and said, the French,
she was sure, would not take her, she merely wanted
to see the town of Hanover, and should tell them so.

Nothing would stop her, so away she went, and has returned, as she predicted, safe and sound.

She told my sister that she announced herself to the commander-in-chief, who received her most politely, directed that she should be shown all she wished to see in Hanover, and, when her curiosity was gratified, sent an escort with her two miles out of the town. Accordingly, she is delighted with the French and the attentions she received from them. Cavendish, who dines with us for the last time to-day, expects, as I do, to be much entertained with her ladyship's account of the French occupation. Many persons are surprised at her return, for it was thought, in these days of plots and arrests, that any one running into the lion's mouth could expect nothing less than to be detained there.

Diaries—April 3rd.—It being reported, and believed, that the Emperor of Germany has ordered his ambassador at Paris to congratulate the First Consul on the discovery of the late conspiracy, a person yesterday took occasion to ask M. de Haugwitz whether similar instructions had been sent to M. de Lucchesini. He answered most positively in the negative; but added that there was no necessity for giving such instructions to M. de L., as he was always ready to compliment Bonaparte.

The Chevalier de Bray called on my brother yesterday, to say, that information had been received from Paris of the French Government having intercepted a correspondence between Mr. Drake and some agents employed by him in France. That the corre-

spondence, together with the report of the grand
judge to the First Consul concerning it, was printed,
and had been communicated by M. Talleyrand, to all
the foreign ministers at Paris.   It had been sent by
a courier to Munich, and there was reason to believe
that Bonaparte would require the Elector to demand
the recall of Mr. Drake.   "It would be very desirable," said M. de Bray, as if offering a suggestion
of his own, " for the British Government to find some
pretext for recalling him, and thus spare the Elector
the disagreeable necessity of applying to them for
that purpose ; which his friendly relations with, and
personal regard for, Mr. Drake would render doubly
painful to him."

This was not a pleasant communication to receive,
and still less was it a pleasant one to reply to.   M.
de Bray was told that, after the numerous occasions
in which the French Government had exercised
its utmost malignity in forging and propagating
calumnies against the British Government, the
present proceeding could only be considered as a
fresh instance of its desire to conceal its own unjusti-
fiable acts under the flimsy pretext of supposed
grievances against Great Britain.   That it was for
the Elector to consider how best to defend his own
dignity and independence, menaced in common with
that of other sovereigns, by the unheard of outrages
practised by the First Consul, and by his contempt of
all rights save that of force, which, unhappily, he
had it in his power to employ for the misery of
Europe.   That, if his electoral highness complained

that Mr. Drake had failed in his ministerial functions, doubtless, suitable attention would be paid to
his complaint. But it was to be apprehended that
no disposition would be found in His Majesty's
Government to listen to any frivolous story, originating in the personal feeling of a man whose enmity
must be considered an honour by every subject of the
British empire, or to be accessory to any act of
unbecoming submission to an unjust decision.

4th.—M. Laforêt and the French party are on the
qui vive to know what steps will be taken as regards
Mr. Drake. Public opinion here is very strong
against England ; for the judge's report and the
transcripts of Drake's letters, ten in number, have
been generally read, and fully discussed. It is a
miserable business, to say the least of it, and for my
part I pity poor Drake. The judge's report contains
remarks only upon the most striking passages of the
correspondence. The letters appear to have been
delivered to the French police by the person to whom
they were addressed. To one of them a note is
appended, which says, that the agent employed by
Mr. Drake will shortly publish the particulars of his
conversation with that gentleman, and with one of
the British ministers in London, to prove, amongst
other things, that the *General*, to whom frequent
allusion is made, is only an imaginary person.
Perhaps he will tell us what became of the thousands
he received from his dupes, for the purpose of carrying out the projects from which such great results
were expected. It is likely that this affair will not

excite the attention and disapprobation it would have done, had the Ettenheim outrage ended less tragically. A letter from M. Oubril states that the unfortunate prince was shot five hours after his arrival at the Chateau de Vincennes. His highness, after being carried to Strasburg, was left twenty-four hours in the citadel. He was then taken to Vincennes, where already a military commission was assembled to begin his *trial.* The prince, it seems, had no suspicion of their intention to proceed immediately to extremities against him ; but when the sentence of death was announced to him, he heard it with much composure, requesting only that a confessor might have access to him. This was denied him, and he was at once led out to execution. He refused to have his eyes bandaged, saying " he had never been afraid to look death in the face." He requested the officer of the guard to deliver his watch and a ring to the Princess de Rohan Rochefort; then, with an air of dignity, and in a firm and resolute tone, he said. " Soldats Français! Faites votre devoir, et ne me manquez pas."

This is indeed an execrable act, and seems to justify the employment of any means to deprive Bonaparte of the power he so cruelly misuses. Many have said so, since this fatal news reached us. Sensations of grief and indignation are universal, and strongly expressed by all classes of people in this city. By no one is the melancholy event more feelingly deplored than by the king.

6th.—When the King of Sweden heard of the

arrest of the Duc d'Enghien, he instantly despatched a courier to his minister at Paris with orders to intercede with the French Government on his highness's behalf, and to request the ministers of other foreign powers to join with him for that purpose. But it is believed that the prince was already executed when His Majesty's orders reached Paris.

About two months ago a M. de Bülow, an officer formerly in the Russian service, who resided on a small estate near Berlin, went from home with a Russian passport, and shortly after it was reported that he had been arrested by the French, and shot as a spy. They accused him of collecting intelligence for the purpose of carrying it to England. It has, however, lately transpired that the unfortunate individual arrested by the French, and executed within twenty-four hours, was not M. Bülow, that gentleman having himself communicated the fact to his family.

7th.—The Elector has informed Mr. Drake that he must no longer appear at his Court, and has submitted to the British Government the expediency of recalling him. Bonaparte insisted upon this step being taken, leaving the Elector, however, the alternative of seeing Munich occupied by a French force. The king has given the Red Eagle to the Bavarian minister, M. de Bray. He has just left Berlin for Munich on some private business of his own, he gives out, and will return in as short a time as possible ; but the real object of his journey, there is reason to believe, is, at the king's suggestion, to advise his electoral highness, with reference to the representations he proposes to make to England, to put a little water in his wine.

9th.—The emperor has refused the King of Prussia the privilege he desired to obtain of purchasing in Russia about three hundred horses, yearly, for the use of the light cavalry. In consequence, the king has declined to ratify an arrangement that has long been on foot for the exchange of deserters between Russia and Prussia; the advantage of which is almost entirely on the side of Russia, both as regards civil and military runaways. The Russian peasants who are in bondage, have, of late years, it seems, deserted in large numbers to the Prussian provinces, where the lot of the peasant is less hard than in Russia.

12th.—The letters from Carlsruhe inform us that the King of Sweden, on learning the fate of the Duc d'Enghien, expressed himself in such strong terms of indignation to the French Chargé d'Affaires, that that gentleman declared to the Elector of Baden's minister that he should not again appear at court in the presence of His Swedish Majesty. As soon as this was reported at Paris, Talleyrand sent for Baron Ehrenschwärd, and told him, that, in order not to break off all intercourse between the two countries, the First Consul " voulait bien regarder la conduite du roi son maître à Carlsruhe, ainsi que la démonstration qu'il avait fait faire à Paris, comme non avenue." Since that M. Ehrenschwärd has informed M. Talleyrand that he was about to avail himself of a leave of absence, to quit Paris for some time.

19th.—The mail from Warsaw to Berlin has been

several times robbed of late ; it is supposed by agents
of the French, and that their object is to possess themselves of the letters of Louis XVIII. It is expected
that Bonaparte will apply to the king for the expul-
sion of His most Christian Majesty, and that an old
regulation, that no Frenchman who is not under the
protection of some foreign minister shall be admitted
into the Prussian dominions, will be revived.

21*st.*—A great sensation has been made throughout Germany by a pamphlet lately published, entitled
" Napoleon Bonaparte and the French Nation under
his Consulate." It has given much offence to the
great man, and its prohibition is demanded. It is
already suppressed in several of the small states, but
can still be obtained of Berlin booksellers.

23*rd.*—It is announced that the office of First
Consul is about to be made hereditary in the family
of Bonaparte, who desires that this new dignity
should be recognized by the King of Prussia. His
Majesty is said to have replied that he will not be the
first or the last to acknowledge any new title the
First Consul may assume.

The long talked of coronation of Bonaparte at
Aix-la-Chapelle, as Emperor of the Gauls, is to take
place, *on dit*, very shortly.

25*th.*—The dismissal of another British minister is
demanded, Mr. Spencer Smith, Chargé d'Affaires at
Stutgard. And the German newspapers, with reference to Drake's affair, are allowed to publish with
impunity the most outrageous and indecent attacks on
the British Government, and even on His Britannic

Majesty himself. The papers under Prussian control
are certainly more cautious than others in the language they employ ; but the " Hamburg Gazette,"
under .pretence of giving the official articles from
the French papers, is become the vehicle by which
the First Consul and his agents promulgate the most
atrocious calumnies, against every person, and everything dear and sacred to British feelings. An
unfavourable impression is thus made on the public
mind, to the great prejudice of the British cause.

28*th*.—It is decided that the king will not hold his
annual spring reviews ; and as Bonaparte has expressed some apprehensions respecting the assembling
of the Westphalian garrisons, it is not unlikely that
even that review may be countermanded. The
Elector of Hesse had issued orders for assembling his
troops as usual, but no sooner heard that this had
given umbrage to the French minister than he sent
off expresses to the distant regiments to desire they
would remain in their quarters, as only that part
of his army which forms the garrison of Cassel would
be reviewed.

30*th*.—The Warsaw mail from this city has again
been robbed, by eight men, wearing masks. All
letters addressed to Louis XVIII. and his suite were
taken, but the money and bills of exchange were left
untouched. The king has sent an autograph letter
to His most Christian Majesty, to assure him of the
continuance of his protection, and that he need not
apprehend the effects of any attempt to disturb him in
his present retreat. He has also advised the French

king to hold no intercourse with any persons who
were implicated in the late conspiracy at Paris.

May 1st.—Again, there is a report in circulation
that the Electorate of Hanover is to be divided
between the Elector of Hesse and the Dukes of
Brunswick and Mecklenburg Schwerin; the largest
share to the Duke of Brunswick, and the reversion of
the electoral dignity to *Prince William, the King of
Prussia's second son.**

4th.—The fate of the unfortunate Duc d'Enghien
has caused the profoundest sorrow at St. Petersburg.
All accounts concur in representing the feelings of
both the Court and the people as those of horror and
indignation towards the perpetrator of the vile act.
But so great is the abject fear entertained at Vienna
of Bonaparte, that the Austrian minister, Count
Cobenzl, went so far as to say that a strong proof of
His Imperial Majesty's friendly sentiments towards
the First Consul, and of the interest he took in all
that personally concerned him, might be found in the
silence he had observed respecting the late events in
the Electorate of Baden; events which had ended in
a catastrophe, occasioned, no doubt, by imperious
necessity, and indispensable considerations of personal
safety on the part of the First Consul; and that as
to the violation of German territory, His Imperial
Majesty attributed it to the indiscreet zeal of a few
gendarmes, acting without orders.

Letters—May 6th.—We are not surprised to hear
that Drake's business has caused some sensation in

* The present Emperor-King.

England, and increased the unpopularity of the present Administration, and that both Drake and the ministers are roundly abused for their "ignorance and weakness." Drake's friends, however, need have no fear, we imagine, for his safety. He and his family are at present at, or near, Dresden. No instructions have reached him from the Government since the discovery was made—which is difficult to account for—and he has not wished to return without orders, lest his presence should embarrass ministers in the defence they will make. He leaves them at liberty to choose their own ground, and to make the most of it. His present plan, I believe, is to leave his family at Carlsbad, and to come to Berlin *incog.*, before returning to England. My brother advises him not to assume any disguise.

The Court of St. Petersburg goes into mourning for a fortnight for the Duc d'Enghien. I hoped that our Court would have done likewise, but am told that the duke was too far removed from the crown, even had the monarchy still existed. Prince Naritzkin was to give a ball to the Court a few days after the news of the duke's fate reached St. Petersburg; but the emperor, on receiving the sad intelligence, immediately sent his excuses, and, when the reason was known, the ball was put off. The Court mourning was of course notified to the *corps diplomatique;* but as General Hédonville, the French minister, could not appear in mourning, he found the doors of the principal houses at which he had been accustomed to visit shut against him.

9*th.*—The long-lost Lord Aberdeen, for whose safety we were all very anxious, arrived here about a week since; a tantalizing visit, for he left us again yesterday, being naturally desirous of getting back to England. He has traversed the whole of the Mórea, and is now as well stored with what he calls " the active knowledge of Homer," as he already was with the passive one. He regrets having missed Mr. Drummond and Madame de Stäel. The latter was called away unexpectedly by the sudden illness of her father, who has since died at Coppet. She is not expected to return, as she has allowed it to be generally known that her *accueil*—flattering as most persons would have thought it—had not been so cordial as she had expected.

Extract of a letter from Mr. Francis Jackson
to Mrs. Jackson.

May 8th, 1804.

My thoughts of late have been very much engaged homewards, and I am looking forward anxiously to the events that may follow the debate of the 23rd. Persons recently come from England, and who ought to know the state of things, assure us that it does not seem posssible that Addington can stand his ground much longer, and that there certainly will be a change. No conjecture can yet be made as to the persons who may form a future Administration, but as the universal cry is for Pitt, it is fairly probable that he will be the leader, and before this may reach you. If the united talents of the first statesmen of the

country are necessary to enable us to resist successfully the designs of our enemy, and to bring confusion
upon him, I am persuaded that Mr. Addington will
be the first to wish for such an union.

Stevens's letter was written under the unfortunate
impression of the sad news that met him on his arrival
in England. You say that he has learned, at least,
enough of diplomacy to have become very reserved,
and cautious of giving a direct answer. I know not
why he should be so, as you could only wish to learn
from him our way of life, and other principal particulars with which he is of course fully acquainted,
though I never could succeed, as I wished at first, in
making a companion of him. From the nature of
his college life his ideas are confined, and he is slow
in receiving new ones. He has so much—almost
childish—simplicity that I was forced to employ him
as a mere machine, and could not produce him in the
world as I would otherwise have done. I believe he
did once catch at a suggestion I chanced to throw
out, without attaching any serious meaning to it, and
for awhile turned his thoughts from the church to
diplomacy ; but he has not the sort of quickness and
brightness that form very desirable qualifications in
our business. I had brought him, however, to be a
most excellent copying secretary, and he could not,
of course, live as he did here for a year and a half
without improving very much in manners, &c. This,
added to a very admirable disposition, and a most
respectable character, made up for his natural indo-
lence and want of energy.

As for George, he derived very little, if any, benefit from him, for Stevens was so totally incapable of commanding respect, that George soon felt his own superiority in quickness of comprehension, and had so frequently occasion to laugh at the rustic and primitive notions of the collegian, that I was obliged, even at the first, to be continually at their heels to make them read or do anything together, and afterwards to keep a good watch to prevent them from quarrelling. Never having been able to assume the control that I wished, and constantly represented to him as necessary, Stevens was at length hurt at the airs which George, as he gained ground, would every now and then give himself, and especially upon finding how well he was received in society, and the greater attention with which, as my brother, naturally he was everywhere treated. I must say that George works hard ; he is fond of business, and, since the great press which recent events have brought on us, his journeymanship has been a severe one. He answers perfectly well all the practical purposes of a secretary, and wants only a little more experience and knowledge of the world to qualify him for any appointment we may be able to procure for him. I know not yet who will succeed Casamajor, as secretary of legation. But I do not encourage G. in looking to that, for Lord Hawkesbury, I understand, is averse from those appointments ; the young men who obtain them being too soon anxious to become ministers.

F. J. J.

Diaries—May 13*th.*—M. Messias, the French Chargé
d'Affaires at Baden, has represented to the Elector's
chief minister, M. d'Edelheim, that the First Consul
cannot see with indifference the residence of the King
of Sweden so near the French frontier, after his late
extraordinary conduct, and the undisguised sentiments of hostility he had expressed towards France.
He has strongly urged M. d'Edelheim to recommend
the Elector to prevail on the King to return to his
own dominions.

14*th.*—From the reports in the French papers, it
seems that the great Liliputian will shortly assume the
imperial dignity.—Carnot, and another member of
the tribunate, Lamprecht, said that if a sovereign was
deemed necessary for France, it would be better to
choose one from the royal house that had so long
governed it.

16*th.*—Drake came here yesterday morning, and
is lodged in our house. He looks older by several
years than when we last saw him. His wife and
family are gone down the Elbe from Dresden. He
has not determined which route *he* will take; but
his stay will be short here, as my brother has received
an intimation from the Government that he will not
be allowed to remain in Berlin. Of course he has
remonstrated, and endeavoured to *faire bonne mine à
mauvais jeu.* But public opinion runs strongly against
England in this matter.

20*th.*—Drake leaves us in a great fright about his
journey home. His wife has more courage than he
has, for he fears to take the same route, which has

some conveniences in point of distance, &c. ; however he will continue, we trust, to keep out of the claws of the French. It is droll enough that, in his journey from Munich, he should have been closely followed by a Sir Francis and Lady Drake, who were everywhere taken for the envoy and his wife.

24th.—We were very anxious to see how the new ministry would be formed, and my brother has now received the usual notification from the Foreign office. His new chief, Lord Harrowby, is known to him only by sight. Copies have also come in to-day of the Senatus Consultem, addressed to the French senate, respecting the establishment of the imperial dignity in the family of Bonaparte. It is expected that it will receive the sanction of the senate without any material alteration.

Bonaparte, in default of male issue, is to have the faculty of choosing his successer from the families of Joseph and Louis.* In the oath taken upon accession—for it is doubted whether there will be a coronation—he is to promise, amongst other things, to guarantee to the purchasers of national and church property the full and perpetual enjoyment of it. There are to be six or eight great officers of state. Talleyrand is to be Chancellor of State, with a salary of 40,000 livres.

Some persons are sanguine enough to hope that, under the new order of things, Bonaparte himself may be more disposed to enjoy, and to allow others to enjoy, that peace and tranquillity which have been hitherto incompatible with his system of government.

* See Appendix, No. 1.

27th.—We have the announcement of Bonaparte having been proclaimed Emperor of the French.

It is remarkable that at the time of the murder of the Duc d'Enghien, the French ministers at foreign courts were instructed to enter into a spontaneous justification of that atrocious act. M. Laforêt commenced a conversation for this purpose with M. de Haugwitz, but the latter begged him to drop the subject, saying that the king was so deeply afflicted by the intelligence, that he would not wish to make any communication to him respecting it. It is pretended, that the internal tranquillity of France called for decisive measures, one of which was, the arrest and execution of the duke. And Bonaparte is represented as astonished at, and complaining of the unfriendly language of Russia and other foreign Courts.

28th.—M. Laforêt's notification of Bonaparte's new title is treated with ridicule, even by those who will not hesitate to acknowledge it. M. de Hardenberg, alluding to it yesterday in conversation, spoke in terms of contemptuous indignation of this latest act of Bonaparte's *folle ambition.* The news will doubtless be received in England with disgust and contempt.

June 1st—The king is absent, but it is understood that there will be no difficulty in continuing communications with France under the new form of government. It is expected by Bonaparte that embassies will be sent from the foreign Courts to congratulate him.

The only condition this government will require is,

that Bonaparte will not claim any precedence or pre-eminence in consequence of his assumption of the Imperial dignity.

3rd.—The new style and title is announced to the smaller states in a manner more or less dictatorial, according to their influence, or degree of dependency.

It is confidently asserted that Bonaparte really desires peace, at least for the present, and that he has made propositions to that effect to the British cabinet. The Emperor of Germany, it is reported, has already sent new credentials to his ambassador at Paris. This Court is about to follow his example.

Letters from Stockholm state that great surprise is excited by an order received from the King of of Sweden, to arm, and to assemble at Stralsund part of his flotilla. The Swedes have shown great discontent at the prolonged absence of their king from his dominions.

6th.—The Emperor of Russia lately desired his minister at Paris, M. Oubril, to represent to M. Talleyrand " that the recent infraction of the neutral rights of the Electorate of Baden, which had resulted in an act that had filled Europe with horror and consternation, was, in His Imperial Majesty's estimation, a proceeding irreconcilable with any principle of justice or generally received laws of nations ; and that should any such act of gratuitous violation of neutral territory be permitted, there would no longer exist any security for the safety and independence of other sovereign states. He, therefore, considered it to be his duty, in his quality of guarantee and mediator, to express to the States of the empire his views respecting that proceeding, and to order the Russian resident at Ratisbon to forward an official note to that effect to the Diet of the empire; as well as to represent to it, and to its chief, the necessity of protesting against the further violation of German territory by the French Government. His Imperial Majesty also thought it incumbent on him to make known directly to the French Government, through his minister, his sentiments on this subject; being persuaded that the First Consul would readily listen to the just demands of the Germanic body, and would feel the necessity for immediately employing the most efficacious means for tranquillizing the alarm he had caused to these governments, and for putting an end to that state of things in Europe which at present threatened the safety and independence, which belonged to them by incontestable right."

7th.—Bonaparte's anger was great when this was made known to him, and under the influence of it he sent off immediately, to General Hédonville, instructions of a very violent and decisive nature. But after some hours of reflection, the cooler counsels of Talleyrand prevailed on him to recall them. A second messenger was despatched, with orders to take a shorter route, and to use all speed and every possible means to overtake the first. The two couriers entered Berlin almost at the same time, and the first despatches were sent back to Paris.

12th.—The Doge of Venice has proposed to unite

that country to France. Bonaparte, we hear, was
expected there about this time to complete the
arrangement.

16*th.*—His assumption of the imperial title is protested against by Louis XVIII., who has sent a letter
to that effect to this and to the other Courts of Europe.
No notice will be taken of his communication, here,
although the king, it is said, does not disapprove
of it.

24*th.*—General Hédonville arrived here to-day, in
sixteen days from St. Pètersburg. He will resume
his journey to-morrow, being anxious to reach Paris
for Bonaparte's coronation, which is announced for
the 14th of July.

Amongst the various projects we hear of for the
re-establishment of the Western empire, the most
recent one is, that Bonaparte intends to restore to
Germany the provinces lately ceded to France on
the left bank of the Rhine, and to hold them as a
distinct sovereignty, to which the electoral dignity is
to be annexed. He will then cause himself to be
elected King of the Romans, and, in time, succeed to
the Imperial crown of Germany.

This would seem to be a mere vain dream of
Bonaparte's insatiable ambition, never likely to be
realized. But we have only to recollect, in how
short time he has contrived to transform his in-
divisible republic into an empire, to regard it only
as a feasible scheme.

Russia desires to withhold, at least for a time, the
recognition of Bonaparte's new title, and urges the

King of Prussia to support the Russian note to the
Diet of Ratisbon, on the affair of Ettenheim.   But
Bonaparte has been already complimented from
hence,* and the "Berlin Gazette" announces that
M. Laforêt has had an audience of the king to deliver
his new credentials from "the Emperor Napoleon."
The vote of Prussia at the Diet will, however, be in
favour of the Russian Note; though Count Goertz,
the representative of this Court, is so fettered by
considerations of circumspection towards the French
Government, that its utterance will, no doubt, be
delayed until Bonaparte has devised some means of
evading the demand made upon him.

Letters—June 29th.—We are glad to hear that
Drake has safely reached the tight little island,
where, for the rest of his days, he will be allowed to
plant cabbages.   Perhaps the change of ministry
may not be favourable to his expectations in the
way of pension, but it will be felt, probably, that he
has gone through a great deal of worry and annoyance that he did not bring upon himself.   I
hope he told you his adventures.   He did not make
a handsome woman, and might have passed, had
there been occasion for it, through the whole of the
French army without any molestation, even without
male escort.   But don't breathe a word of this to
him; for what disguise he actually adopted, on his
journey to the coast, we ourselves scarcely know.

I hope the country is satisfied now Mr. Pitt is at
the helm.   The letters from England say that he is

* See Appendix No. 2.

considered to be as strong for every purpose of government as his best friends can desire. He never feared the run which was made against him, though his friends feared it for him, but now that the attempt has been unsuccessfully made, the universal feeling is that he has nothing further to apprehend. So far, that is pleasant intelligence. In *our* department, if things go on as they have begun, there is likely to be greater activity than there has been for years. Boney has given us ample employment, and the despatch of messengers from this and from St. Petersburg has been constant, though they have arrived from England only at long intervals. Now, we expect to be busier than ever, and we suppose the vacant secretaryship will soon be filled up. One messenger has lately been stopped on his way to Vienna, with Paget's riband, by the inundations. *On dit*, that the box containing it was lost, and that the bearer of it was himself in some danger.

July 2nd.—We have heard from Washington, from Mr. Merry, who was appointed to that mission after my brother was relieved from the idea that it was destined for him. Mr. M. is in every respect thoroughly disgusted with his situation. His account of the *capital*, of the manners of the people, their system of equality, &c., is enough to sicken the most enthusiastic admirer of the republic. When, after a long wretched voyage, they arrived in Washington, they found no house provided for them, and none to be had. After a month's misery and

extravagance at an hotel, he succeeded in procuring
two houses, with bare walls, and without water or
bells, which at an enormous expense were thrown
into one, and made habitable. Over a space of wild
country, about six miles square, are dispersed about
seven hundred houses; the communication between
most of them being in the winter season totally
impracticable, and at all times dangerous. Only in
one direction is there even a road made. As to pave-
ment, they will perhaps, he says, begin to think of that
in the next century. There is the greatest difficulty
in procuring the merest necessaries, the only market
being a few carts with provisions, which come, very
irregularly, from the country. The Spanish Chargé
d'Affaires, who gave a dinner to Mr. Merry and his
wife on their arrival, told him afterwards, that to
collect the materials for it his servants had travelled,
on their different errands, fifty-two miles. In
short, he considers his mission wretched and ruinous.
The president, to whom he went in full dress to
deliver his credentials—as had been the etiquette
in the former president's time — received him in
a manner as ridiculous as it was insulting; and,
altogether, what they have to undergo, in their
intercourse with the inhabitants, seems almost incredible. In addition to the brutality of their
manners, they make a point, he says, on every
occasion, of displaying the most inimical sentiments
towards Great Britain. This account makes us,
more than ever, thankful that my brother was not
honoured by being appointed to that mission, which

Lord Hawkesbury told him, at the time there was a question of it, ministers looked upon as one of the most important.

4th.—By-the-by, I must not omit to tell you that I have been vaccinated. I hope you are become a convert to that operation, which saves so many lives, and will, in time, make the small-pox as fabulous as the leprosy, or any other disorder no longer known. It seems to be more in favour here than in England. Certainly it is the most signal blessing which has for many years been bestowed upon humanity, and may perhaps be put in the scale against many of the evils we suffer.

Diaries—July 6th.—M. Lombard is obliged to leave Berlin, from extreme ill health, for the baths of Silesia; indeed, almost as a last resource, for he is hardly expected to recover. The king is at a country house near Potzdam, and Baron Hardenberg is gone to meet M. de Haugwitz, who is on his return. It is rumoured, that he fears the influence M. de Hardenberg is reported to have gained with the king. He has, indeed, been spoken of as likely to succeed M. de Haugwitz; but it is a report deserving perhaps little credit, for although the king has lost, it is well known, all confidence in the latter, yet his cabinet secretaries, with whom His Majesty is well satisfied, could hardly find a minister better calculated to suit their views. He dislikes business, and the general want of energy in his character leaves them full liberty to follow their own system in most branches of the administration.

10*th.*—Bonaparte, not venturing to put Moreau to death, has granted him the permission he sought to retire to the United States. The " Moniteurs " containing the bulletin issued on the occasion, have just arrived.*

14*th.*—The Emperor of Russia has expressed much surprise at the hot haste with which this Court has acknowledged the new empire.

It is rather surprising under present circumstances, that the autographic correspondence which has been kept up between the emperor and the king ever since their interview at Memel, and which has at times excited a high degree of curiosity, should still continue, as it seems in no degree to work any change in the sentiments of either correspondent. It was once expected, as the correspondence originated in personal friendship, that it would lead to important results, or a modification, at least, in the apathetic system to which this Court is still wedded.

. To what these communications especially relate, is not known, but it is hinted that they consist of a series of mere speculative political essays, to which no sort of application is intended to be given. Whether this be the case or not, the emperor must, ere this, have discovered that the soundest arguments have as little power to impart spirit and firmness to the feeble mind of the king, as they would have to stop Bonaparte in the impetuous career of his ambition.

17*th.*—Count Haugwitz has been too hasty, it appears, in returning to Berlin. His health will not

* See Appendix No. 3.

admit of his continuing to reside here, and His Majesty has, most reluctantly, he says, permitted him again to retire to his country house.

M. Beym has preferred M. de Hardenberg, to Schulenberg, as the Count's successor. He will, as a foreigner—Hanoverian—meet with many obstacles, but will doubtless do his best to overcome them, and to introduce, as far as the system of this Court will admit of it, a degree of consistency and dignity into its proceedings. But he will be obliged to follow, to a great extent, in the footsteps of his predecessor, and by every possible means to avert whatever might expose this country to the chance of a quarrel with France. To do the good, or to prevent the evil, which his own convictions would lead him to attempt, is thought to require a stronger mind and more determined resolution than M. de Hardenberg is supposed to possess.

29th.—Louis XVIII. has left Warsaw for Grodno, in order to hold a meeting with the princes of his family. The Prince of Condé and Duke of Orleans are coming from England to attend it. The French king wrote to the King of Prussia to inform him of his intention. The latter gave a friendly reply, and said he might make sure of a hearty welcome whenever he should think proper to return to the Prussian dominions.

Whatever may be done at this meeting, the effect of it on Bonaparte, when he hears of it—for both he and Talleyrand are now absent from Paris, delaying, it is supposed purposely, the communication of the

negotiation with which M. Oubril is charged by the
emperor—will be to dispose him to anticipate any
possible aggression of Russia; to extort the supplies
which the Hanse Towns are to contribute, and to
render the communication of England with the
Continent more precarious than it is at present.

30*th*.—Prince Henry is gone to Pyrmont, to have
an interview with his future father-in-law, Prince
Frederick of Denmark.

31*st*.—Shortly before Louis XVIII. left Warsaw,
a person named Coulon, who had served in a royalist
corps during the last war, and who now keeps a
billiard table in that city, gave information of an offer
having been made to him of a considerable sum of
money, if he would undertake to throw some
carrots, which should be scooped out and filled
with arsenic, into the soup preparing for the king's
table.

When the king was informed of this, he wrote to
M. de Hagan, president of the regency of Warsaw,
requesting to see him. That magistrate paid no
attention to the invitation, and a person of the king's
suite was sent to relate the particulars to him, but
both he and the courts of justice declined to interfere in the matter. Upon this M. d'Avarny was
charged to take Coulon's deposition in writing,
which the French king forwarded in a letter to
the King of Prussia, and, at the same time, to
the Emperor of Russia. His Prussian Majesty
expressed the utmost indignation and regret, and
gave orders that a strict judicial examination

should be made of the persons concerned in this affair.

M. de Hagan has been reprimanded for his negligence and inattention, and for the want of respect shown to the French king. His conduct is, indeed, considered unaccountable; for whatever may be the real state of the case, there was no apparent reason, for the police refusing to take cognizance of it. There are, however, grounds for believing that Coulon is himself the author of the story, and that he has invented it with the hope of obtaining a reward for his pretended discovery. But, as the laws of this country punish severely the act of preparing poisonous ingredients, otherwise than in the pursuance of some lawful avocation, an investigation was certainly called for.

The reason assigned for the conduct of the government of Warsaw, is, that a certain boyer, an unaccredited agent of Bonaparte, residing in that city, is one of the individuals named in Coulon's deposition. There is a spirit of recrimination shown in the language held on this affair by the agents of the Prussian Government. They accuse the attendants of Louis XVIII. with having too readily given credit to an idle story, fabricated, evidently, for the purpose of imposing upon them and the public. They have even gone so far as to say, that it is altogether a device of the French king himself, imagined solely for the purpose of holding out to the world a reason for throwing odium on Prussia, and for leaving her dominions.

August 10*th.*—Louis XVIII. has written, to some persons in Berlin, that he had been escorted' with every mark of respect through the Prussian territory, and had been in like manner received at Grodno, where he was immediately waited upon by the governors of the town and province. A house was prepared for his reception, and a captain's guard, with colours, ordered to be in attendance. This last honour he had declined, but, on the guard being withdrawn, two sentinels were left on duty. The other French princes had not arrived.

It has been discovered that Coulon and his wife had themselves purchased the arsenic which they pretended had been given to them for the purpose of poisoning the French king. This strengthens the supposition that the whole story is an imposture. But Coulon persists in his declaration of the proposal having been made to him by two Italians, who, however, are not forthcoming.

Letters—August 11*th.*—The King of Sweden has been lately hovering round these parts, but has never actually lighted upon us, which I am sorry for, as he is to my mind more interesting, and better worth seeing than the generality of sovereigns. He seems to have a good deal of his ancestor's—Charles XII. —blood in him; and if he is in some things rather *odd*, as people assert here, with an expressive nod of the head and tap on the forehead, it is very often on the right side. It must be confessed, that he gave the rest of the potentates of Europe a pretty smart reproof, by his conduct in regard to the Etten-

heim business; for he was the only one that did
anything to *prevent* the fatal catastrophe, though there
have been found, "at back hunt," some to resent it.
Though his efforts on the prince's behalf were of no
avail at the Corsican *Court*, and he has it not in his
power to punish the tyrant, yet he lets slip no occasion
of showing, most publicly, his detestation of the deed
and its perpetrator. The other day at Töplitz, a watering place near Dresden, the king was walking in the
rooms, with a little dog under his arm that belonged
to the unfortunate Duc d'Enghien, and which he
takes everywhere with him, talking with the prince's
late chamberlain, while he passed by Madame Laforêt,
the wife of the French minister at this Court, and
absolutely refused to be introduced to her; mortifying
her still more by the marked attentions he paid to
Mr. Wynn, who had come from Dresden, at His
Majesty's desire, to pay his respects to him. He was
very courteous towards all other strangers, distin-
guishing particularly the French emigrants, of whom
there are a great number at that place. He expressed
without the slightest reserve his partiality to the
cause of Great Britain. Mr. Wynn had a most
agreeable visit, and was much pleased with the king,
whom he accompanied on his excursions, and dined
with every day.

13*th*.—You have heard of the Coulon plot, which
in England, I believe, has been set down to Bonaparte's account. The man Coulon had once been
employed in the French king's kitchen, and therefore
continued to have access to it. It seemed strange to

everybody that he should be allowed to have a hand in the preparation of Louis' *pot au feu*, and to add to it his *carrottes farcis d'arsenic*; which, according to his own statement, he was about to do, when, suddenly conscience-smitten, and horrified at the atrocity of the deed he was in the act of committing, he hastened to make a full confession. This morning the letters from Warsaw tell us that the story of the plot from beginning to end, is pure invention, as Coulon and his wife have both acknowledged. Here the matter ends, though many persons still believe that the story originated with Louis XVIII. himself; while his friends assert that Coulon has been bribed, or threatened by the king's enemies, into confessing the plot, which Providence did not permit him to execute for them, to be the coinage of his own brain.

14*th*.—Young Pole, who goes to Constantinople with Mr. Arbuthnot, has just arrived, and announces his chief and another ambassador, Lord G. L. Gower. They will make a short stay in Berlin this week, on their way to their respective posts, if the French send no Coulincourts in pursuit of them.

I am grown too discreet, you say, and tell you no political news. I will tell you, then, that a report has reached Berlin that Oubril has left Paris. It is not confirmed by any official accounts, or even private ones upon which an absolute reliance can be placed. It is, however, an event daily looked forward to, and one might be the more inclined to give credit to it, when we remember that we had the

news of Lord Whitworth having done the same
thing several days before the official accounts were
received. If it be so, we shall have hot work of it.
And so far is sure, that Oubril had given it to be
understood to all Russian subjects in Paris, that they
should be ready to be off at a moment's warning, as
there was no saying what turn the negotiation
might take; but if the emperor stands stout up to his
pippins, war can hardly be avoided. If this piece of
news is not the talk of all the Bath tea-tables when
this letter reaches you, I beg, my dear mother, that
mum may be the word until it becomes so. Perhaps
I shall have less time than ever to write to you,
though fag has pretty generally been the rule with
us from early morning till night. But our new
chief is rather more alert than his predecessor; he
has turned over a new leaf at the office, and keeps
us all close to the collar, at home and abroad.
There is no chance of my brother seeing England
this year; though, in these uncertain times, we can
hardly tell what may happen from one day to
another, and it might chance that we should *both* pay
you a visit, even sooner than you wish. For, supposing the pending negotiation between the Emperor
of Russia and *his brother* Boney to end in war, who
can tell what part His Prussian Majesty would take.

Diaries—Aug. 19*th.*—The Duke of Brunswick has
claimed the interference of this court with the French
Government, in reference to the seizure, by the
French commander, at Celle, of the goods sent from
Hamburg, and other large towns of Germany, for

the fair at Brunswick. The goods of one merchant, who made the immediate and proper application of six hundred louis d'ors, were released. The value of what is retained is reckoned at half a million of dollars.

The conduct of the commander will doubtless be disowned at Paris; but he and his subordinates will be left in possession of the sums they have extorted from the merchants.

Bremen was blockaded at the same time, and has had to pay fifty thousand marks for the removal of the blockade and the renewal of postal communication with the south of Germany. The post from Hamburg to Brunswick had also been stopped.

23rd.—The Emperor of Germany, it appears, made it a condition of recognizing Bonaparte's imperial title, that he should be acknowledged Emperor of Austria. I have seen in a Vienna paper the patent published by the Emperor of the Romans on assuming the imperial title of his hereditary dominions. The title of Hereditary Emperor of Austria, is to follow immediately that of, Elected Emperor of the Romans. The motive for this change is, stated to be, the keeping up of a perfect equality in the relations of the House of Austria with France. The latter expression appeared, at first, to give some umbrage here, but it will be considered, I believe, that, as France does not claim precedence of other royal Courts, a perfect equality with that power implies nothing more than the equality of rank which Prussia has claimed with

France, and which has been admitted. The new
dignity of Austria, with this reserve only, will be
acquiesced in.

31*st*.—The King of Sweden intends to set out
from Leipsic in a few days, on his way to Stralsund,
where it is now said His Majesty will pass the
winter. But he observes the greatest secrecy respecting his journey, and has applied to this Court,
through his Chargé d'Affaires, for a general order for
his free passage to be sent to the Custom Houses on
the Prussian frontier, not choosing to state the exact
route he means to take. His object is also, supposed
to be, to avoid any compliments or marks of distinction that would probably, as on former occasions,
be shown to him by the king.

His return to his own dominions, though said to
be owing to the urgent persuasions of the Emperor
of Russia, is known to be chiefly occasioned by his
want of money, which is so great that he has lately
been sometimes at a loss for the means of defraying
his ordinary travelling expenses.

Sept. 2*nd*.—His Swedish Majesty has taken exception to the notification of the Emperor of
Germany, that he intends to assume a new title, as
being by no means sufficient to satisfy the forms of
the constitution. "The Diet," he says, "should
assemble and deliberate on the subject, and that, as
guarantee of the constitution, he felt himself called
upon thus frankly to declare his sentiments, notwithstanding his reluctance to express any opposition
to His Imperial Majesty's views."

4th.—This Court takes much credit to itself for its early and unconditional accession to the wishes of the French Government; considering its conduct and policy thus placed in a more favourable light than that of Vienna, whose recognition of Bonaparte's title has been made the price paid for the acknowledgment of that which the head of the House of Austria—following Bonaparte's example—has chosen to assume.

7th.—A fresh conscription of five hundred thousand men has been ordered by. Bonaparte to be immediately embodied. This menace has roused here very general apprehension for the continuance of tranquillity, though by some persons it is considered to be mere bravado, a defiance thrown out to Russia in consequence of the sailing of her squadron. Yet the king, it seems, is not so much alarmed at the hostile attitude of those nations as might be expected; he considers war, without the participation of Austria and Prussia, scarcely possible.

M. Oubril has left Paris, having received an unsatisfactory reply to the emperor's demands, which are believed to have been the evacuation of Hanover and Naples, and a suitable provision for the King of Sardinia. He is now at Mayence, the French Government not allowing him to proceed further until it is known that the French Chargé d'Affaires at St. Petersburg has crossed the Russian frontier.

Bonaparte and Talleyrand are at Aix-la-Chapelle, to which former seat of Charlemagne's empire the Austrian minister and the representatives of the smaller states are to repair to present their credential letters.

Some of the German princes are much alarmed for the integrity of the empire, owing to the facility with which the new title assumed by the Roman emperor has been acknowledged by Prussia; as it would seem to announce a perfect agreement between this Court and that of Vienna.

It is said here, that the latter Court has a very mean opinion of the talent for business of its representative, Count Metternich, and that upon any emergency it would send Count Mehrfelt on a special mission. It has, however, been observed that the Austrian count, who is a man of very pleasant, conciliatory manners, has been at considerable pains to cultivate an intimacy with M. Laforêt, though his present opinions are known to be entirely opposed to those of the French minister, and his habits of life very different from his. This circumstance has, therefore, excited considerable attention in several quarters. Perceiving, probably, that his conduct had led to some abatement of the friendly advances he had met with *chez nous*, Count Metternich has lately appeared desirous to do away with the unfavourable impression, which the *empressement* of his manner towards the members of the French mission had created, by showing himself more solicitous to keep up the cordial footing on which he was received by my brother. He is supposed to have been acting under orders from his Court. He is leaving now for Sans Souci, to deliver the emperor's letter to the

king, announcing his assumption of the title of
Hereditary Emperor of Austria. His Prussian
Majesty came from Paretz, for the double purpose of
receiving this letter and giving audience to a M.
d'Arbery—a young man whose family has considerable property in Flanders—who is a *ci-devant*
count; whose father is a lieutenant-general in the
Austrian service, his mother an attendant of Madame
Bonaparte, and he himself holding the office of
auditor of the Council of State. M. d'Arbery's
arrival in Berlin, and M. Oubril's departure from
Paris, were announced here on the same day, and
created an impression similar to that caused by the
publication of His Majesty's message to parliament,
and the simultaneous appearance of General Duroc
at Berlin, eighteen months back. The General came
to announce Bonaparte's intention to occupy Hanover
in case of war; M. d'Arbery is supposed to be
charged to give notice to the king of the early
invasion of Swedish Pomerania, and consequently of
the Duchies of Mecklenburg, through which it would
be necessary to pass to reach the Swedish territory.
He is the bearer also of a complimentary letter from
Bonaparte, thanking the king for the early acknowledgment of his new title, and assuring him that he
should "take pleasure, on all occasions, in con-
tributing to the lustre of the Prussian monarchy and
the splendour of His Majesty's reign."

M. d'Arbery, as auditor of the Council of State,
holds nearly the same intermediate situation between
Bonaparte and his ministers as that occupied by

M. Lombard in this country. From this circumstance having, with much affectation, been made generally known by the French legation, it is evident that M. d'Arbery's mission is meant to be a sort of a *pendant* to that of M. Lombard to Brussels, last year; the success of which corresponded with the great dissatisfaction Bonaparte was known to have felt at the low rank of the person sent to him, which he thought by no means equal to the distinguished one held by his envoy, General Duroc, both in his army and in his household.

With regard to Bonaparte's intended operations, it can only be inferred, from what we already know of the King of Prussia's "system for securing to his people the blessings of peace," that His Majesty will grumble a little and submit. His minister has, however, announced to the French party that "*il y à un point où la patience se lasse*," and that, to that point they are fast driving the king; that fresh attacks on the Hanse Towns, and an invasion of the Duchies of Mecklenburg cannot be seen with indifference, and that this Court, although it is not upon good terms with the King of Sweden, cannot permit a body of French troops to establish themselves in Pomerania. Whether the king will confirm this declaration, and, if so, whether the declaration may not turn out to be mere empty words, remains to be seen. For my part, I wish the Kings of Prussia and Sweden could change places. The latter would perhaps employ to some purpose the army of this country—amounting to near two hundred and fifty thousand men—more perfect, it is allowed on all hands, in every detail of its organization than at any former period, and sufficiently imbued with the spirit of patriotism effectually to resist the troops of the new empire.

The finances of the country are also known to be in a more flourishing state than they have been since 1790, when the late king made the first inroads on the treasure left by Frederick the Second. But the *vis inertiæ* of the king paralyzes the whole force of the Prussian monarchy, and renders it as completely null, for all purposes of beneficial influence, as are the smallest of the states of Germany, or of the Italian republic.

Letters—September 9th.—Our society, owing to the unfavourable weather, is returning by slow degrees to Berlin; the watering-places grow dull, the camp at Prague yet detains some of our set, but it will break up at the end of the month, and the Court will come earlier than usual from Potzdam, as the queen lies in the latter end of November. Prince Henry's journey to Pyrmont has resulted in his betrothal to a princess of Denmark—the daughter of Prince Frederick—but as she is only fifteen years old, the marriage ceremony is postponed for a twelvemonth.

10th.—As you have now got Drake safe amongst you, and have heard from himself the story of his adventures, I send you a description of a French caricature of his *flight*, which has given occasion for many a hearty laugh at his expense, both here and at Munich. Our hero is represented in woman's dress, *flying* away from the latter place, very heavily

weighted with immense folio books; his pockets full
of small bottles, with labels hanging out, marked
"sympathetic ink." His family motto, "*Aquila non
capit muscas*," in very large letters, surmounts the
whole, and beneath it is written, "*Non, en verité,
M. Drake n'est point un gobe-mouche.*" It was published in Paris, and has had so great a sale that I
cannot get a copy for you, as I intended. I regret
this, for the likeness is good and the expression very
ludicrous. *En revanche*, however, we have another
representing the *purple-decked* emperor seated on his
throne, and the woman, who lately stole the Russian
princess's diadem of diamonds, imploring for mercy
at his feet, and exclaiming, "*Est ce donc un si grand
crime de voler un diadême?*" Perhaps you have not
noticed the article in the "Courier de Londres," on
the appointment of M. de Portalis, secretary of this
legation, to Ratisbon. And, indeed, to fully appreciate the force of the concluding sentence, "*On
peut dire que c'est un singe qui represente un tigre*,
you must have known something of his character;
and have seen how far he is from being an Adonis
to understand how aptly the above expression applies
also to his *apish* style of beauty. I tell you these
things, because news of the kind you best like is
scarce. Our city has been for some time "a mighty
void," enlivened only by the temporary sojourn of
our ambassadors and their suites. Your recent
papers are also dull, especially after those containing
the bustling accounts of the Middlesex election. We
rejoice, and suppose every good Englishman does the

same, as much at the victory of M., as at the defeat of the baronet; for it would have been a disgrace to the county to have returned for its representative the man who was publicly pronounced unworthy to accompany the address. We are only sorry it was so hard run; but we know for certain that the opposite party held proof positive against two hundred of Burdett's votes. The effect produced here by the account of the shameful riots that took place on that occasion, is quite laughable to witness. In this country, where everything goes *vi et armis*, such scenes are incomprehensible, and nothing will convince some of our friends that our system of elections is not the worst of institutions, and that both candidates and electors are not great rogues.

18*th.*—To make up for our disappointment in not getting even a fortnight's holidays—for official business increases—we went over to Potzdam for the manœuvres. It was remarked that not a single English traveller was present; and it is, indeed, much better that they should be well employed at home. There are very few on the Continent, and those who now come through Berlin are fugitives from France, who have found means—by bribery or by the connivance from other motives of their gaolers—to escape from the imprisonment to which Bonaparte condemned them.

22*nd.*—I have received an amusing letter of the 2nd inst. from my aunt, who is at Dover. She is an enthusiastic *Pittite*, and, from her own account, when she paid a visit to Walmer, her enthusiasm

almost led her into theft. She says, " The Government is very active in constructing an intrenched
camp near the top of Shakespere's cliff, and in opening and embanking an immense ditch at the bottom,
with various other devices to impede the progress of
the French ; though I believe they dare as soon eat
fire as attempt to set foot on the Kentish coast.
However, it may be right to provide for the fortune
of war, and Bonaparte may have the pleasure of
seeing from his own shores with what zeal and
activity Kentish men are preparing for his destruction.   People at Dover are in great and lively hopes
that Mr. Pitt has some grand scheme in embryo,
with regard to this port, which they imagine is to be
made a royal harbour.   I passed a most pleasant day
at Deal and Walmer, which are so improved and
beautified even within these few years, that I really
hardly knew where I was.   They are absolutely lined
with most capital barracks, and interlined with
soldiers.

" My great delight at Walmer consisted in a minute
investigation of the minutiæ contained in Walmer
castle and its environs, as the residence of our
Kentish idol, Mr. Pitt, whom the stupid Opposition
think proper to dub 'the colonel.'   He has made
the castle a most comfortable residence, and has really
taught Eden to bloom in a perfect wild.   I never saw
anything so neat as his grounds, so flourishing as his
shrubbery, and his peaches had, to *my* taste, a flavour
peculiarly delicious.   His house and furniture are
neatness and comfort personified ; without a single

superfluity. I could have stayed there till this time,
examining his library,. looking through his famous
telescopes, and sitting on every couch that looked as
if it had had the happiness of receiving his wearied
limbs. Although it was one of the hottest days we
have had, I longed to steal a pelisse of his, lined
throughout with ermine, that hung by his bedside;
and if it had not been so costly, or had been more
portable, I really think I should have been tempted
to purloin it as a sacred relic. Oh, my dear George,
be assured we cannot fail of doing well now *he* is at
the helm; and though Bonaparte were to thunder in
our ears even ten thousand times more than he does—
and he now very often deafens us—I could never feel
the shadow of fear. I always venerated the wonderful talents of Mr. Pitt; but now—being as it were in
his very seat of empire—admiration is almost converted into idolatry. But I remember you did not
draw your first breath in Kent—so, perhaps, you are
not so enthusiastic a Pittite as I am. I wish your
brother could stir up your King of Prussia to second
Mr. Pitt's efforts. The reign of Bonaparte would
then soon come to an end."

Diaries—Sept. 23*rd.*—Some days ago a Frenchman,
who announced himself as Colonel Delgette, of one
of the foreign regiments in the service of Great
Britain, called on my brother at an unusually early
hour, and, pleading business of much urgency, and the
impossibility of his making any stay in Berlin, was
admitted. After producing letters of service, showing that he had been appointed by Bonaparte, *chef*

de bataillon, as well as other papers testifying to
his resignation of that post, and mentioning, besides
the high character he could receive from many persons of distinction in this city, he came at last to the
object of his visit—the offer of his valuable services
in France to the British Government. They were
immediately declined. He then urged the great
advantages which England would secure by the
acceptance of his offer—from the unusual sources of
information which he represented were open to him—
though he declined to furnish any written statement
respecting his views and means of action. Two days
after he made an application for another interview,
of which no notice was taken.. The next thing
heard of him, was that he had dined at the French
minister's more than once, and had, by some means,
contrived to get an introduction into Berlin society.
He had represented himself to M. Laforêt as an
officer in the army in Hanover, absent without leave,
and able to give information respecting the aims and
designs of Great Britain, that it was most important
for the French Government to be in possession of.
He proved to be a mere adventurer, and, notwithstanding his great effrontery, was obliged immediately to decamp, in order to escape the consequences of the indignation that was excited by the
discovery of his real character.

The public of Berlin take an exceeding interest
in everything relating to France, and are often quick
in seizing the ridiculous side of a subject. Lately,
especial amusement has been afforded by the appear-

ance amongst them of a Parisian *beau*—reared amidst
the horrors of the revolution, but remodelled after
the fashion of the new imperial Court—in the person
of M. d'Arbery, who has made himself a very conspicuous object in Berlin. He has just returned to
Mayence with the king's answer to Bonaparte's letter.
It is understood that the new emperor's compliments
have been but ill received. They were thought ill-
timed, and somewhat equivocal from the character
of the person selected for this special mission. M.
d'Arbery has been treated by the Court, and the
society of Berlin, with a coolness exceeded only by
the disgust which his manners and appearance excited.
Since his departure, it is made public that, besides
compliments and thanks for prompt and disinterested
acquiescence in Bonaparte's views, his new Imperial
Majesty had commanded his envoy to say, that should
the king desire to follow the example of the Emperor
of Germany, and assume the imperial dignity, it would
give him pleasure to be the first to recognize it, and
to use his influence with other powers in order to
obtain their concurrence.

M. d'Arbery, it appears, in the course of the
audience granted him, urged on the king the consideration of his imperial master's overtures. To
this extraordinary proposal the king replied, " that
as he did not conceive any additional honour would
accrue to himself, or any increase of happiness to his
subjects, by his adoption of any other title than that
he already possessed, he preferred to retain that,
being the one he had inherited from his ancestors."

M. d'Arbery, however, was honoured with a present of the king's picture, set in diamonds.

23rd.—It seems that a suspension of diplomatic relations between Russia and France is to be the only consequence of their *present* disputes. Russia, it is now understood, will resort to war only in case of some *new* provocation. This is an additional reason for the security felt by this Court respecting the differences that exist between France and Russia.

Oubril is still at Mayence.

25th.—Louis XVIII. is expected to return immediately to Warsaw. A letter addressed to him by the King of Sweden was sent to Berlin by express, and, contrary to the form hitherto observed, was addressed " A Monsieur mon frère, le Roi de France." The king recalled his minister, M. d'Engeström, on account of his sympathy with the views of this Court. No other minister has been appointed, and the present Chargé d'Affaires, M. Brinckman, has not been informed by His Swedish Majesty of the recall of his minister from Paris, which is thought extraordinary, at the least.

The coolness that now exists between Russia and Sweden is a remnant of the animosity which the discussion respecting the frontier in Finland gave rise to. The proceedings of the king were generally thought to be rash and ill-advised, and Count Woronzow conceived so much personal enmity towards him that, but for the emperor's forbearance, and his consideration of the closeness of their family connection, the opportunity would have been seized of taking possession of Finland. The king's long absence from his dominions, and his residence at Munich and Carlsruhe, have been unfavourably looked upon at St. Petersburg. But the anxious wish of the king to take a conspicuous part against France has not met with the consideration to which he thinks it entitled—his overtures on the subject having been answered only by a recommendation from the emperor to return to Stockholm.

The sentiments entertained towards the King of Sweden at Berlin, are even less friendly; on account of the part he has acted at Ratisbon, his undisguised opinions of Prussian politics, and those he has expressed, with as little reserve, respecting the King of Prussia himself.

One of the strange circumstances of the King of Sweden's situation is, that most of his ministers at foreign courts are advocates of the cause which their sovereign appears to hold in so much abhorrence. He yesterday left Magdeburg for Stralsund, and his minister, Baron Armfelt, is expected here to compliment the King of Prussia, in return for a similar mission when His Swedish Majesty passed through the Prussian dominions.

27th.—The French Chargé d'Affaires at St. Petersburg is not allowed to proceed further than Riga, on his return to France, until it is known that M. Oubril has left Mayence.

Oct. 2nd.—Baron Armfelt arrived a few days since with a letter from the King of Sweden. He passed on direct to Potzdam, to deliver it in person

to the King of Prussia, without any communication
with the Prussian minister. The Baron dined at
Court, and immediately after left Potzdam for Berlin.
He made no request to be presented to the queen,
and left no card with any person of her Court. Such
entire disregard of the usual form and etiquette has
created great dissatisfaction, and is calculated—as one
object of Baron Armfelt's mission was to ask Prussian
protection for Swedish Pomerania—to indispose the
king to commit himself to any promise of support to
the King of Sweden's plans. It is feared also that
the hasty departure of the Swedish envoy may excite
the attention of Bonaparte, especially as the king
has again expressed very decided opinions with
regard to him, and openly censured the conduct
of the French Government.

8th.—A Russian vessel is detained at Cuxhaven by
the French commanding officer. And it is reported
that the French army is about to take possession of
the Hanse Towns, owing to the impossibility of
drawing any further supplies from Hanover.

Orders have been given by this government to
stop the exportation of rye, the crops having failed
to a great extent this year, and the bread for general
consumption being made of that grain in this country.
Spirits are also not to be distilled from either rye
or potatoes. Wheat and oats have been productive,
but have risen in price, owing to the deficiency in
the rye crops.

15th.—The King of Sweden has been prevailed on
to suspend his armaments in Pomerania by the assur-

ances he had received of Prussian protection.   His
Majesty intended to return to Stockholm, as soon as
he knew of the effect on Bonaparte of a note he had
written to the French Chargé d'Affaires in Sweden.

The French minister here has been known to say,
that it is the rule with his Court to pay no attention
whatever to the conduct of the King of Sweden.

17*th.* — An intimation has been sent to Louis
XVIII. to suspend, for the present, his intention of
returning to Warsaw.   It is said to be conveyed to
him in terms amounting almost to a general prohibition to his again taking up his residence in the
Prussian dominions.

There exists much dissatisfaction with the present
proceedings of the Bourbon family.   It is felt that
the meeting of the French princes in Sweden has
so much the appearance, under the circumstances of
the moment, of active hostility to Bonaparte, that
this country cannot consistently afford any further
countenance to the members of that family.   It is,
however, whispered, that M. Laforêt, on leaving
Mayence, was desired by Bonaparte to solicit this
prohibition from the king, and that the granting of
Bonaparte's request was facilitated by the fact of
Louis having shortly before written to the King of
Prussia, to inform him that the Emperor of Russia
had offered him an asylum in his dominions.

M. Oubril's being at Frankfort, gives rise to a supposition that Bonaparte has attempted to renew the
negotiation.

23*rd.* — The King of Sweden's letter to the French

Chargé d'Affaires at Stockholm was not made known
to Bonaparte, it seems, until he had left Mayence
and had arrived at Treves. He was most violently
irritated on reading it,—sent off an *estafette* instantly, to make it known at Berlin, and wrote with
his own hand, " J'ai reçu l'infâme note du Roi de
Suède. Je le méprise, et je l'exposerai au mépris de
sa nation. C'est au dessous de moi de lui faire la
guerre. Mais je rappellerai mes agens commerciaux."

The King and Queen of Sweden, by the last
letters, were about to embark for Ystadt; and it had
been thought advisable to give publicity at Stralsund
to the hopes entertained of immediate assistance from
Russia. The proceedings of the king are narrowly
watched by this Government. The King of Prussia
has written to His Swedish Majesty.

25th.—There were gay doings at Mayence during
Bonaparte's stay there, to which Madame B. and her
ladies added the grace of their presence. Besides
" the emperor's " reviews, there were " the empress's "
receptions; balls, theatricals, and other festivities
every evening. M. Laforêt finds Berlin insufferably
dull since his return from his sojourn with the
brilliant Imperial Court.

26th.—The king has promoted Colonel Knobelsdorff
to the rank of major-general, on sending him to
Paris to compliment Bonaparte for the mission of
M. d'Arbery—a new proof of the influence of his
cabinet advisers, with whom the measure originates,
though it entirely coincides with the views of the
king, who, resolved to maintain peace at any price,

finds nothing more natural than to have recourse to any and every means for securing it.

Several Prussian officers and other persons are going to Paris to see the ceremony of the coronation. The Elector of Baden, it is thought, will also visit Bonaparte on that occasion.

27th.—We have been under much apprehension lately for the safety of our beautiful queen, who was for some time thought to be in a very critical, if not dangerous, state. Last week she was removed from Paretz to Potzdam, and is now so far recovered that it is expected she may come to Berlin in the early part of next month. Notwithstanding her great experience in such matters, she has erred in her calculations, I understand, to the extent of two months, in the time announced for her eighth confinement.

We have not one English visitor at this Court at the present time, a circumstance which has not occurred for years, I am told. *En revanche,* we have an unusual number of Russians, and among them some extremely clever, as well as very pleasant, people.

29th.—The approaching coronation had begun to be the one theme of conversation in Berlin ; and the great event, itself, we had supposed, would wholly occupy, at least for a time, the mind and thoughts of the mighty emperor and his Court. But at noon to-day, an *estafette* was received by M. Alopeus from the Russian Chargé d'Affaires at Hamburg, informing him that Sir George Rumbold had been seized, and carried off by a detachment of French troops, and his papers taken possession of.

Shortly after, came another *estafette* from M. de Grote, the Prussian minister, giving the details of this extraordinary outrage. In the night of the 24th, a body of near three hundred soldiers surrounded Sir George Rumbold's house at Altona. The commandant with about thirty of his men forced an entrance, and ordered Sir George to leave his bed and dress. Two officers took possession of his papers, which they placed in a carriage, and afterwards compelled him to enter it, when they drove off, accompanied by a strong escort, towards Hamburg ; whence Sir George was to be sent a prisoner to Paris. M. de Grote had demanded of the French minister at Hamburg an explanation of this flagrant breach of the law of nations, and he had expressed great concern at what had happened, but declared that he had received the first intimation of it from the syndic, Döorman, who had been to him, on the part of the senate. He had, already sent his secretary to Hamburg to inquire of General Frère on what grounds, and by what authority, he had acted, and he promised to let M. de Grote know the result of his inquiries.

30th.—This violation of the neutrality and independence of the German States, this fresh outrage of Bonaparte and the aggravated insult offered to the King of Prussia, are felt very deeply. They excite the highest indignation in all classes of people in this city, and have created no small bustle with us.

From my brother's situation, the first step in Sir G. Rumbold's behalf had necessarily to be taken by him, and for that purpose he went over to Potzdam, where he found the utmost agitation prevailing, to request the King of Prussia to send a messenger to Paris to demand Sir George's immediate release.

Nov. 1st and 2nd.—The king appeared to be extremely pained at the shameful occurrence, and to feel that it was incumbent upon him, as director of the circle of Lower Saxony, to interfere in the matter.

A messenger has therefore been despatched to Paris with an autograph letter from His Majesty to Bonaparte—in order, as it is therein stated, that " *les entraves diplomatiques* " may not occasion any delay—demanding the release of Sir George Rumbold, as the only reparation that can be accepted for this breach of the system agreed upon between the two powers ; and stating, further, that in case of refusal other means would be resorted to.

3rd.—Ten days, at least, must elapse before we can know how this demand will be received, and, of course, a longer period before we know how it will be enforced ; but it is made peremptorily, and we are in the midst of two hundred and fifty thousand armed men ; which in these times is no bad thing. It is reported that the military measures to be adopted, in the event of Bonaparte's refusal, are decided upon. The more *éclat* given to the demand the better.

The French minister at Hamburg has informed M. de Grote that the arrest of Sir George Rumbold took place by the order of Fouché, addressed to

R 2

Marshal Bernadotte. And that Fouché had received his instructions from Bonaparte himself, who had been led to believe that Sir George was engaged in the same machinations as those Mr. Drake and Mr. Spencer Smith were accused of.

4th.—General Knobelsdorff, who had been prevented from setting out on his mission at the time of his appointment, by an accident he met with when mounting a restive horse, had just left when the intelligence from Hamburg arrived. A messenger was sent after him to desire him not to proceed on his journey until he received further orders. If he should be found at Frankfort, he is to remain there under pretence of illness; if he has entered France he is to proceed on to Paris, but not to appear in public, and to say that his credentials will be sent after him by a courier.

The Duke of Brunswick is expected at Potzdam, to consult with the king on the course it may become necessary to pursue, should Bonaparte not give way.

5th.—It is a very striking instance of the subserviency of the German press that no newspaper at Hamburg, or elsewhere, mentioned even the bare fact of the seizure of Sir George Rumbold, or the steps taken by the magistracy of that town to reclaim their independence. Even in Berlin, an article on the subject, which was prepared and sent to one of the papers, was refused by the censor. Indeed, the newspapers of this country are not at liberty to relate even the ordinary events of the day, in a manner at all favourable to British interests—much less may they insert any comments, or use any arguments tending to show the justice of our cause. The "Leyden Gazette" has been suspended for venturing to express opinions displeasing to the French.

Her Imperial highness, the Hereditary Princess of Weimar, arrived to-day at Custrin, but has declined the invitation to visit Potzdam. Her refusal appearing to give umbrage to this court, the Duke of Weimar hopes, with the assistance of M. Alopeus, who set out last night to meet her, to prevail on her imperial highness to change her mind and to come this way.

6th.—Some days ago, letters from London informed us, that four of our frigates had fallen in with four Spanish ships of equal force, off Cadiz, and had brought home three of them—the fourth blew up. Our frigates were acting under orders to detain vessels laden with treasure, as those vessels were, but the Spaniards would not be detained ; so there they are, as our letter says. The business, it was thought, might yet be amicably arranged, and the treasure, *perhaps*, restored. Since then, the French have been very busy in spreading the report, and endeavouring to impress the minds of all classes with the idea, that this engagement between the British and Spanish frigates, and the capture of the latter, form a sort of a set-off against their own violation of the law, in the seizure of the person and papers of Sir George Rumbold. But intelligence has just arrived which proves the fallacy of their report, by showing that the Spanish ministry had previously been made aware of the eventual order that had been issued to the cruisers.

10*th*.—The Paris letters state, that the recent attempt on the flotilla at Boulogne has produced a more important effect on the French soldiers and sailors than the execution actually done by the fire-ships ; for it has shown them to what extreme danger an armament would be exposed at sea, or when arrived on the coast of England, if, in the present instance, the enemy owe their escape from the experiment that was made for their destruction, rather to good fortune than to any means of defence they could employ, though favoured with every protection their own harbours and batteries could afford them.

13*th*.—Expectation is anxiously on the *qui vive* for Bonaparte's answer to the demands of this Court; the more so, as the king has committed himself so far, and has given so much publicity to the step he has taken, that a refusal must be considered the signal for war.

Meanwhile, His Majesty is in a state of anxious hope and fear, and remains at Potzdam almost inaccessible, except to his cabinet secretaries, who, with General Köchritz—unfortunately just returned from Silesia—will doubtless do their best to damp the ardour with which the king, at first, entered into the general view taken of this outrage, and to represent to him the probable miseries he has brought on the country, and the calamities that may result from the step he has ventured to take.

17*th*.—We learn that, on the 2nd, the news of Sir

George Rumbold's seizure reached Paris by an express to the deputy of Hamburg, who was ordered to claim his release, and that Talleyrand professed ignorance of the whole matter. The intelligence had created a great sensation in Paris.

The " Moniteur " of the 5th also came by the last post from Paris. It contains a circular despatch—a copy of which, it is pretended, has been forwarded to this and other Governments—to the effect that the French Government can no longer recognize the inviolability of any British agent on the Continent. This despatch is entirely a fabrication, and an after-thought of Talleyrand to serve as an introduction to the violence committed upon Sir G. Rumbold.

There is also an alteration in Fouché's published letter to Bernadotte. The phrase introduced, " s'il est en votre pouvoir," is considered as providing a saving clause by which the French Government may withhold its approval of the means employed to accomplish their ends, and yet profit, temporarily, by their crime.

The manner in which Bonaparte announces this atrocious act to the world looks like a sort of de-fiance thrown down, by anticipation, to those Governments who might think of interfering on the occasion.

There is scarcely an individual who denies that the honour and dignity of the Prussian monarchy are involved in the issue of the present question; yet such is the King of Prussia's known predilection for peace that advantage is taken of it, by a party in

the interests of France, to inculcate amongst the
public all the arguments that can be brought against
the policy of engaging in a quarrel with France.
And it is to be feared, that the king will be only too
glad to avail himself of any opening that may be
afforded him, to escape from the dilemma into which,
it is suggested to him, he has been brought by the
precipitancy of Baron Hardenberg.

The messenger sent after General Knobelsdorff
did not overtake him on the journey. He had
travelled by a different *route*, on learning that Bonaparte's coronation was again postponed, and the
messenger reached Paris two days before him.

Whilst we are all on the tiptoe of expectation for
the great emperor's reply to the king, a letter from
the Prince of Mecklenburg Schwerin informs M.
Alopeus of another flagrant outrage—an attack on
the king's messenger, Wagstaffe. He was the
bearer of despatches relating, we presume, to Sir
George Rumbold's business, to the British ministers
at Berlin, St. Petersburg, and Vienna. On his way
from Husum, just after he had entered the wood of
Victlübbe, he was stopped by five men, masked, and
fantastically dressed as brigands, armed with guns,
and with pistols and poignards at their waistbelts.
They ordered the postilion to dismount, and three of
them bound him to a tree, threatening him with
death if he raised any cry for help, or made any
attempt to escape. The two others had, in the
meantime, seized the courier, and, with their pistols
pointed towards him, demanded his money, which he

gave them, begging them to spare his life. He was answered by one of them, in German, though they spoke French among themselves, that his life was safe, it was not that they wanted. Having bound the courier's hands and feet, they took the carriage a little further into the wood ; one of the men, who appeared to be their chief, impatiently repeating, " Mais les papiers, les papiers." These he took entire possession of, private as well as public ones, stowed them away in the courier's bag, and rode off. The others ransacked his valise, and being pleased with its contents, bound it upon one of the horses, together with various small packages that had been forwarded to the different ministers—amongst other things, a box of baby linen for my sister's infant. The brigands then decamped with their booty, having, with many threats, previously charged both courier and postilion to remain quiet until they had disappeared. The postilion having succeeded in releasing himself, unbound the poor courier. They then made the best of their way to the neighbouring village of Draguhn, the inhabitants of which had seen five or six of these sham brigands pass through in the morning; their costume exciting as much curiosity as terror. On reaching Schwerin the duke was made acquainted with the outrage, and he immediately sent off an *estafette* to the Russian minister with the above particulars.

20*th* to 21*st*.—A courier has arrived from Paris with Bonaparte's letter to the King of Prussia. It informs him that Sir George Rumbold is released and gone to England by way of Cherbourg. The joy with which this news is received affords the best proof of the anxious state of public feeling previous to its arrival; for few were sanguine enough to believe that Bonaparte would give way, or that a plausible means could be found for averting what ought inevitably to have been the consequences of his obstinacy. The transaction is now considered *closed*, and great credit is taken by the Government for the firmness and energy they have displayed. People are, generally, disposed to lose sight of the insult offered to the German empire; of the infringement of its neutrality and independence, and are willing to regard the release of Sir George Rumbold as a sufficient satisfaction for what has happened, and a final settlement of all differences with the French Government. And yet that spirit of aggression, which the late appearance of the French troops at Altona, and the robbery of our messengers denote, is still at its height, and it seems extraordinary, under such circumstances, that persons can be found to flatter themselves that Prussia may preserve an independent existence, without any exertion of her own, beyond the moment that Bonaparte has fixed for her entire subjugation.

24th.—An acknowledgment of the *act of complaisance*, as it is termed, shown by Bonaparte to this Court, has been sent from Potzdam to Paris. At the same time, we learn that Sir G. Rumbold's papers are detained, and we see his release announced in the French papers, in terms intended to seduce

the world to believe that Sir George was taken
as a spy at the French outposts ; plausibility being
given to this insinuation by the condition attached
to his release, of his not residing within fifty leagues
of any French army.

28th.—The King of Sweden is said to be greatly
piqued at the expressions employed by the King of
Prussia in his letter of the 10th of October.   His
Swedish Majesty acts, no doubt, on a well founded
principle; but, as there exists at this Court so much
prejudice against him, it is to be lamented that he
assumes towards it the language of reprisal.   He has
again excited the displeasure of the king by demanding to know, with reference to the late transaction
at Hamburg, what steps would be adopted in pursuance of the king's declaration to him "that he
would defend the peace of the north of Germany
against *whoever* might attempt to disturb it."   He
has been given to understand that his interference
is uncalled for.

30th.—Bonaparte has been asked to evacuate
Hanover, and to allow a Prussian force to occupy it
until peace shall be signed between France and
England; Prussia then to decide to which of the
belligerent powers the electorate shall belong.

Dec. 1st.—The Emperor of Russia is not so well
satisfied as the King of Prussia with the termination
of the Rumbold affair.   But to move the king to any
further exertion in the matter, is not considered
possible.   He is too happy to have escaped from
the embarrassment in which he feared his temerity

would eventually involve him to regard the manner, however ungracious, in which his request to Bonaparte has been complied with.   There are Prussians who consider their country humiliated by it, and who feel keenly that the baneful influence exercised by Bonaparte throughout Germany, and the injury suffered, by Prussia in particular, by the blockade of the Elbe and Weser, are the consequences of his not having been stopped *in limine.*

I heard, yesterday, a person of some distinction at this Court say, with much earnestness, that the substantial interests of the crown and people are sacrificed to the king's love of peace, and his selfish dread of any disturbance of the enjoyment he finds in the pleasures of a calm and tranquil life.

5th.—The "Moniteur" of the 26th announces that the French Government intend to communicate to foreign Courts the nature of the papers seized in Sir G. Rumbold's house.   This is a fresh annoyance to the king, as it was understood they were to be suppressed altogether, and further interference respecting them made unnecessary.   This violation of his word has caused a new burst of resentment against Bonaparte, though considerably stifled, in some quarters, by the dread of being involved in a new quarrel with him.   The Emperor of Russia has again declared that the release of Sir George is a totally inadequate satisfaction for the violation of German territory; but the king, putting aside that view of the question, has positively declared that "he will not go to war for a box of papers."

The said papers, however, are not likely to be sufficiently edifying to be honoured by publication in the
" Moniteur."

Letters—Dec. 7th.—Although we have actually
been employed, almost without intermission, for the
last thirty-six hours, in despatching a messenger, I
send you a line by him to certify that we are not
yet carried off. Your October letters are probably
gone to amuse Napoleon Bonaparte by his fireside
at St. Cloud; for Wagstaffe brought nothing but the
clothes he wore, and hardly expected to escape with
a whole skin.

My brother certainly did not write the note you
saw in the papers under date of the 5th of November;
what he did write you will probably have seen ere
this. It should, at least, have some merit in Sir G.
Rumbold's eyes, as it contributed, no doubt, to
shorten his abode in the Temple. What her ladyship will think of it is another ·question; probably
that she might have had timely notice of the
baronet's arrival at Richmond at one o'clock in the
morning. She is a dashing mother of forty, with
two very handsome girls, of whom she often passes
for the eldest sister. I daresay she would prefer a
Richmond or a London life to the humdrum round
of the Hamburg factory. Perhaps, as you say,
you may have the satisfaction of seeing the " freed
captive" in the Pump-room, as it is reported he is
going down to Bath to visit Lord Harrowby. We are
anxious for the next post, to learn what has been the
effect of Lord Harrowby's fall, and whether the Bath

waters have proved beneficial. His health appears
to be so bad that I should not be surprised if he did
not hold office long, although he has not hitherto
been deficient, in activity, at least.

11*th*.—We are in expectation of accounts from
Paris of the coronation, which was to take place on
the 2nd. It affords a subject of conversation to all,
to some of mirth, to others of sorrow. My idea is
that such a state of things cannot last. I feel persuaded that Bonaparte will end as he deserves, and
that every step he takes is one towards " the height
from which he is to be hurled by the hand of
Omnipotence," as Burke said, on a very different
occasion ; and the faster he goes the better. At all
events, his emperorship has certainly had to retreat
a step, and that, in time, without which you know
nothing can be done, may lead to what my sister
would elegantly call a genuflection, but which I
prefer to write, coming down on his marrow bones ;
At all events, we excommunicated, " profaneurs de la
morale et de la réligion politique," have adopted the
spiritual motto of *Dum spiro spero.*

I have had another letter from my Aunt Henry,
chanting the praises of Mr. Pitt. It made us laugh,
and reminded us of the advertisements that set forth
the excellence of Packwood's incomparable razor
strops.

12*th*.—To return to Boney, we have learnt,
amongst various particulars respecting the arrangements for his coronation, that he has altered the
etiquette hitherto observed by the kings of France

in their interviews with the Pope. Instead of kissing his hand, he advanced with extended arms to embrace him. His Holiness did not meet the great Liliputian in a similar manner, but let fall his arms by his side, and said, "Je me jette dans vos bras;" after which, he gave him his apostolic benediction.

Paris letters mention that Bonaparte has it in contemplation, during the Pope's stay in that capital, to unite the Protestant and Catholic persuasions under one common system. The same letters also state that the King of Spain is about to abdicate, and that the queen and the Prince of Peace are to be at the head of a regency, to the exclusion of the Prince of Asturias. Bonaparte's acquiescence is alone wanting for the execution of this plan, but he has hitherto withheld it; having devised some other method of disposing of the Spanish peninsula. Popular commotions were expected to take place at Madrid and other towns.

We have here, on their way to England, two families who were arrested at Paris on the breaking out of the war, but obtained leave, lately, to come to Germany—Mr. and Mrs. Peploe, the latter a niece of Lord Malmesbury, and Mr. and Mrs. Greathead. Mr. G. is an author, and *was* a famous democrat, but has undergone a cure by the treatment he met with in France. I believe he has written something for Mrs. Siddons, who lived in his family as an attendant on his wife

Diaries—Dec. 15th to 17th.—Particulars of the cere-

mony of the coronation of the new emperor and
empress are given in glowing language in the
French papers. The weather, we hear, was not
favourable for the Imperial pageant, which is described as one of extraordinary splendour. The
enthusiasm of the people, when the herald proclaimed that the "glorious and august Napoleon"
was crowned and enthroned, is said to have been
frantically expressed ; and Bonaparte was, of course,
pénétré d'émotion when he announced that he
ascended the throne by the unanimous wish of the
senate, the people, and the army. The whole thing
seems to have been a success, and Paris resounded
with the cry of "Vive l'Empereur, vive l'Impéra-
trice !" The French mission was illuminated again,
on the arrival of the news, as brilliantly as it had
been on the 2nd, and an entertainment was given in
honour of the auspicious event.

20*th*.—An affray has taken place at Embden
between a few drunken sailors, a part of the crew of
H.M.S. *Scorpion*, and some people of the town, and
complaints of the violent conduct of the former have
been forwarded to Berlin. The matter was about
to be satisfactorily arranged, when the Prussian
minister was informed that Captain Carteret, of the
same ship, had violated the neutrality of the Prussian
territory by boarding an American ship in the Ems.
The fact was admitted, but Captain Carteret explained that he had acted on the suspicion of there
being English sailors on board the American vessel,
and that an infraction of the neutrality of the river

was not intended—an explanation which has not given full satisfaction. Six men of the crew of the *Scorpion* afterwards deserted to the French, taking the ship's cutter with them to Delfzyl.

23rd.—The business with Spain seems to be on the point of terminating in hostilities. Mr. Frere was nearly out of the Spanish territory on the 25th ult., and was daily expected in England. The correspondence between Russia and England, the same letter says, is less likely to end in smoke than seemed probable a short time ago.

27th.—Subsidy to a large amount has been offered to the King of Prussia to engage him to unite with England in opposing the further encroachments of Bonaparte; and every argument has been used to show him his danger, and to excite him to take measures to avert it while yet there may be time, and before his country becomes a prey to Bonaparte's insatiable ambition. But the king declares that he has adopted a system of perfect neutrality, as most consonant to his wishes, and best calculated to secure the interests of his monarchy; and he hopes it may be in his power to maintain this system—Bonaparte having given him the most solemn assurances that he will not interrupt the tranquillity of this part of Germany.

Every one thinks it extraordinary that the king can so deceive himself; that he can place the smallest reliance on Bonaparte's assurances, in the face of the aggressive conduct he steadily pursues, and the intolerable principles set forth by M. Talleyrand.

But, when the king's character, and the influences
to which he is open are taken into account, the
hopelessness of prevailing on this Court to adopt
a line of conduct becoming its dignity and power,
will then be patent to all.

28*th*.—The Grand Seigneur, who refuses to acknowledge Bonaparte's new title, has requested the good
offices of Prussia to make known to the French
Government that he declines to do so, not from
hostility to France, but from circumstances out of his
power to control.

The King of Sweden, whose language and bearing toward this Court prevent the return to the
friendly understanding so desirable between the two
sovereigns, has just added to the irritation his measures create by signing a Convention with England.
It is notified to him that should the suspicion
entertained on that head prove to be well-founded,
the neutrality of his dominions will be no longer
acknowledged.

The mediation of Prussia, which Bonaparte was so
anxious to secure for the settlement of his differences
with Russia, seems to be unavailing—the pretensions
of the opposing parties being so irreconcilable.
The proposal of Prussia to hold Hanover during
the continuance of hostilities between France and
England—which she desired to make a *sine qua
non* with France for employing her good offices in
an accommodation with Russia—is rejected by Bonaparte and opposed by the emperor. It has also
been allowed to appear, that an impression exists at

the Court of St. Petersburg that Prussia is more anxious to obtain possession of Hanover than to insist on the evacuation of the north of Germany by the French.

30*th.*—From recent statistical reports, it appears that the Prussian army has been increased by 26,000 men since 1791. It now amounts to 248,205, besides supernumeraries in almost every regiment. Many details have also been attended to, and so much amended during the present reign that, in the opinion of all military men, the arrangement for the troops are now much more effective than heretofore, and the Prussian army, as a whole, never in finer condition than at this moment.

About 30,000 stand of arms have lately been manufactured, of which the muskets are shorter, and the bayonets longer than those before employed; but they will not be brought into use until the full number required for the army, or at least a large proportion of it, is ready.

Whether these advantages over former times are not more than counter-balanced by the weak, wavering policy of the present government, and the timidity and indecision prevailing in that quarter whence the general spirit that should animate the troops should receive its first impulse, remains to be seen. That these influences have had some effect on the higher ranks of the army is plainly perceptible; but amongst the officers, as a body, a feeling of emulation and spirit of discipline still exist; sufficiently active, it is asserted, to enable a commander, with capacity to turn them to account, to lead the Prussian army to exploits worthy of the most brilliant epochs of the monarchy.

The same returns state that the population of the Prussian dominions is now rated at nine millions of souls—an increase of a third since 1791. But this proceeds only from the increase of territory, without calculating the progressive increase of numbers observable in those parts of Germany that have not been engaged in war.

The late partition of the German empire has had an injurious effect on the recruiting of foreigners for the Prussian service, as there was formerly one recruiting officer, at least, in every imperial city, and the chief reliance is now upon deserters from other services. Even this resource has been, of late, diminished by an order—given partly from complaisance to the French Government, and partly from other motives—to admit no French deserters into the ranks. On the other hand, from the great increase of territory His Prussian Majesty has acquired, a much larger proportion of the native population can now be obtained for the military service.

The increase of revenue has not been so large, in proportion to the territory acquired, as might be expected, but it is estimated at four millions of dollars; making the whole revenue of the crown to amount to about twenty-nine millions. This is the weak part of the Prussian monarchy; and it is felt, that—while every source of revenue is now strained to the utmost—to supply, on an emergency, the

means of carrying out any extraordinary operations
would require the genius of a Frederick.

1805.

Letters—Jan. 5th.—What with the ice, that now
blocks the harbours and rivers, and the French police
ever on the alert to intercept the despatches and
letters that do by some means get landed, a double
barrier is raised at this season between us and England, and our communications are, of course, more
irregular and uncertain than ever. Several mails are
now due, and we are anxious, on many accounts, for
their arrival. The last letters left Lord Harrowby
in very bad health; so much so as to preclude the
probability of his continuance in office, even should
his fall not be attended with fatal consequences.

The political barometer is in a very fluctuating
state; but that by no means affects our enjoyment
of the festivities of the season. We have the usual
friendly and family gatherings, where cart-loads of
gimcracks and toys, that were displayed in the
booths of the Berlin fair, are again displayed to more
advantage on lighted tables in the houses. The
usual family hops, interrupted at midnight by hugging and kissing and laughing, only to be resumed
with more vigour, and kept up till near daylight.
But these, for the most part, are but bread and
butter affairs. We are waiting for our queen's
perfect recovery from her recent confinement to
begin, in serious earnestness, the gay doings of the

carnival, which has generally to be put forward or backward to accommodate Her Majesty—without whose bright presence, the carnival would be considered no carnival at all. This reminds me of Stevens, who, notwithstanding some rather precise notions respecting the frivolity of these amusements, enjoyed them, I believe, more than he thought right to acknowledge. I had a letter from him by our last arrivals. He has got back to Oxford; writes out of spirits, and alludes regretfully to his Berlin life. Diplomacy, however, no longer vexes him with hankering thoughts. *Il a pris son parti*—has taken priest's orders, and thus, as he says, " is now wedded to the church for life." I think he has done wisely, and I trust the union may prove a happy and prosperous one. He has some expectation of travelling, as tutor, with Lord Kinnoul.

Diaries—Jan. 7th.—The members of the French mission are taking considerable pains to accredit a report, circulated by their own agents, that a reconciliation is about to take place with Russia. Yet every succeeding day tends to show that no result can be expected from the mediation of this Court between Russia and France. The other night, however, M. Laforêt openly complimented the Russian minister on the subject, and he, as publicly, declined to accept the compliment.

As to Hanover, it is said that France would, perhaps, not object to give it over in trust to the King of Prussia, provided he would come under a positive engagement that it should be used as an object of compensation in any future negotiation for peace, and would prevent the transit of British merchandize, and the enrolment of recruits in the electorate, for the British service.

12th.—The Paris bulletin, speaks of a warm attack having been made by Bonaparte, at a recent levée, upon the Austrian ambassador, whom he questioned with much asperity respecting the recent movements in the Tyrol.

It is again given out that the project of invading England is abandoned.

16th.—The King of Sweden has been warned, that this Government will think it right to put a stop to any offensive operations he may commence in Pomerania. The king left Stralsund on the 7th to remove the queen, who is near her confinement; for, according to the constitution of Sweden, a prince born out of the kingdom is not capable of succeeding to the crown.

General Armfelt is now in Berlin, but leaves to-morrow for Stralsund.

22nd.—The Elector Arch-Chancellor and the Elector of Hesse Cassel have been endeavouring to negotiate at Paris an union of German princes, and have obtained Bonaparte's promise of protection to such an association. But, that the second prince of the empire should debase himself so far, as to solicit the interference of a foreign power in its concerns, has caused general and extreme indignation.

The Court of Vienna has taken offence at these proceedings of the German princes; also at those

of the French Government, both with reference to
this affair and to Italy. Bonaparte's violent behaviour to Count Cobenzl has likewise given great
dissatisfaction, and something very like the lauguage
of resentment has been expressed on the subject.

25th.—We hear that the treaty between Russia
and Sweden is signed, as well as that of subsidy
between England and Sweden. Baron Armfelt, who
prolongs his stay until the 27th, talks with the utmost
confidence of the extensive form of the campaign he
has traced out, and expects to surmount, with great
facility every obstacle that may oppose his intended undertaking. The General has a happy confidence in his
own talents, and in the bravery and spirit of the troops
to be employed. He expects, by the month of March,
to have formed magazines in Sweden, to have arranged for the transport of the Russian army, &c.,
yet His Swedish Majesty had the utmost difficulty
to procure the sum necessary to defray the expenses
of his journey from Stralsund to Stockholm. However, the General certainly looked to the supplies
he was to receive from England.

29th—It has been announced to this Court, in the
usual manner, by the Spanish Chargé d'Affaires, that
war has been declared by His Catholic Majesty against
Great Britain.

Letters—Jan. 30th.—Our carnival and all its gaieties
are postponed. The queen is again in perfect health,
and was ready to grace the ball-room with her presence, and take her share of the dancing. Two days
ago the Duke of Brunswick, who had been invited

for the festivities of the carnival, arrived in Berlin ; but on that very day the queen-mother was seized with a paralytic fit. Her physician gives but little hope of her recovery, and probably she will not live many days. It is, indeed, to be wished that she may not, as, with half her body paralyzed, she can only be a burden to herself and others. The king is deeply afflicted, for he is most affectionately attached to his mother, and the queen and all the royal family participate in this feeling, and share fully in his grief.

I too, unhappily, have much cause for grief in the unexpected death of Henry Löwenstern. You know my attachment to the Löwenstern family, and the friendship that exists between me and Otto, the eldest son. About ten days ago Henry and I went out together to skate, and he being a novice came down upon his knees several times on the ice, but was apparently as well as usual when he returned home. The next day I was surprised to hear that he was in a high fever. This increased during the day and following night, until it became wild delirium and fury. Two attendants could scarcely hold him, and restrain his violence. Nor was it, indeed, calmed down until the near approach of death. A blow on the head was supposed to have produced this fatal result; and, though I could not call to mind that in falling on the ice he had struck his head, I was wretched under the idea that he had received his death blow in that way, and that I, indirectly, was the cause of it by inducing him to attempt to skate. Otto had left

Berlin the day before this happened, M. Alopeus having sent him to St. Petersburg with despatches, and M. Löwenstern was also absent in Livonia. I therefore passed two nights with Henry, while the Countess Hagan strove to comfort the afflicted mother and sisters, who were overwhelmed with grief and despair, and whom it was necessary to exclude from the room where the poor youth lay; for their presence only increased his ravings. When this scene of sorrow was ended, and the cause of poor Henry's death ascertained, I was relieved from much of my distress of mind, by the statement of his servant that he had returned from walking covered with snow, on the day preceding the skating, and had told him he had had a terrible fall *Unter den Linden.*

The surgeon who attended him, accompanied by a confidential servant, has taken the body to Livonia, where M. Löwenstern waits to see it deposited in the family vault. Before their departure, the room in which poor Henry lay in his coffin, was hung with black, and lighted up—after the custom of their country—and an impressive sermon was preached by a Lutheran minister. The Countess Hagan and myself, with some other friends, assisted at this ceremony. Henry was a fine youth of sixteen. His death has affected us all very deeply.

Feb. 2nd.—It was reported last night that the queen dowager was better; that her illness had taken a favourable turn. It is now hoped that she is at least in no immediate danger, and her physician thinks she may eventually recover, should she survive

the ninth day from her attack. We are to launch,
they say, into the dissipations of the carnival next
week. It is a little *mal à propos*, this delay in the
rising of the curtain ; for many foreigners have come
to Berlin to take part in the diversions. If they
really do commence, after this second postponement,
no doubt everything will be done to make amends to
the queen for lost time.

There has lately been so much high play at the
supper parties—where Macédoine has been introduced, and has quite eclipsed Loo—that His Majesty
has expressed a wish that it should be discontinued.
This has been complied with ; but as Macédoine
occupied twenty to thirty people at once, the effect
this sudden change has produced at these *réunions* is
rather a dull one. I was the other night at the
first supper where Macédoine was not played. The
Macedonians were like a defeated army. Individually
they knew not what to do, and had no general
point de ralliement. Two or three different parties of
men sat down together to try a sober game. The
desperate gamesters, however, disdained a rubber,
and sat yawning on the sofas, making feeble attempts
at conversation, in which the Germans do not greatly
shine. It was dreary work ; and even when supper
was announced, welcome sound though it was, yet I
think the repast was not enjoyed so much as when
the excitement of Macédoine had raised the spirits,
whetted the appetite, and given more glibness to the
tongue. If His Majesty has set his face against Macédoine, then, as a *pis aller,* Loo must regain its vogue.

3rd.—Ten mails arrived yesterday, yet they brought us no very interesting public intelligence, except that of "the reconciliation," and the nomination of Lord Mulgrave; though this is scarcely news, for the retirement of Lord Harrowby was long foreseen. Who would succeed him was, however, not so certain.

4th.—The reports of the queen dowager's health are less favourable.

Diaries—Feb. 7th.—People are now looking towards Vienna with some anxiety. The last advices state that M. de Rochefoucault had been some days in that city, but refused to present his letters of credence until the Austrian troops, lately placed on the frontier of Italy, had returned to their quarters. He had been informed, that measures regarding the internal arrangements of the empire could not be discussed with any foreign power.

There is certainly a desire to oppose some united resistance to the ambitious views of Bonaparte by those powers who are not actually at war with him. But doubt and hesitation are created owing to his pursuance of his well known system of urging his pacific intentions at St. Petersburg, at the same time that the members of the French mission proclaim loudly that he is negotiating for peace with Great Britain.

10th.—After having been very confidently informed that the invasion of England had been abandoned, we now learn that Admiral Verhuel is on his way to Holland, if not already arrived there, to

superintend the armaments in the Texel ; Bonaparte having ordered a renewal of the preparations
for the invasion. The opinion gains ground that
at length something is really to be undertaken, and
the sailing of the Toulon and Rochefort squadrons
is thought to confirm it.

The admiral has asserted that he can answer for
the safe arrival of a fleet on the English coast; and
this opinion, which he has used every endeavour to
impress on Bonaparte, is said to be general throughout the Dutch navy.

14th.— General Wintzingerode, aide-de-camp to
the Emperor of Russia, arrived last night with a
letter from the emperor to the king. It was known
some days since that orders had been given for the
Russian troops, in Livonia and Esthonia, to hold
themselves in readiness to march.

The emperor is said to be determined to oppose
the occupation of Swedish Pomerania by Prussian
troops. Prussia has, therefore, by her own fault got
into a dilemma from which it is difficult to say how
she will extricate herself. And the embarrassment
is likely to be increased, when France shall adopt the
language, which the evident and well understood
mission of General Wintzingerode to engage this
country to join the allies, will of course give rise to.

16th.—We have the "Moniteurs" by a courier
from Paris, who brings the news of the rejection by
England of Bonaparte's overtures, as well as an
account of the return to port of the Toulon squadron.
Two frigates and a ship of the line are reported to

have separated from it in a gale, in which the whole
squadron sustained much damage. It is, however,
surmised that the sight of the British squadron,
rather than the gale, was the cause of the enemy's
return; for letters from the south state that one
of Lord Nelson's frigates having reconnoitred the
French fleet in the outward road of Toulon, his
lordship had, by this means, early intelligence of the
French admiral's intention of putting to sea.

The language of the French Government is bitter
and irritating in tone, and the publication of the
correspondence with Great Britain is doubtless intended to create an impression unfavourable to her
in the public mind; while in the report of the Tribunate there occurs the expression—evidently used
ad captandum—that both Austria and Prussia are
the allies of France.

It is said that Bonaparte, in his letters to the
King of Prussia, has usually signed himself, " Good
brother, friend, and *ally*." The King confines himself
to the usual form, " Good brother and friend."

It has lately been observed that the queen has on
various occasions shown a disposition to obtain some
influence in public affairs, and that advantage has
been taken of this circumstance to secure that influence in favour of M. de Haugwitz. It appears,
therefore, that he has not lost sight of the possibility
of his return to power; and his friends think the
present crisis offers a favourable opportunity for
disposing the mind of the king to recall the Count
once more to his councils. With this object in view,

M. de Haugwitz now supports M. Lombard; and the prevalence of the cabinet secretary's opinions, which coincide so well with the line of conduct the king is inclined to pursue—and which would lead him to be a passive spectator of a war that would be carried on at no great distance from the gates of Berlin, or of being exposed to the hostility of a Russian army on the eastern frontier of Prussia—has excited some murmurs against the queen, from the supposition that she has been prevailed upon to countenance the views of the French party.

22nd.—A Court-ball that was to be given to-morrow evening is countermanded, the queen-mother having had a relapse. She is now in great suffering and danger.

Letters—March 8th.—As usual, we are anxiously looking . towards England for news, and waiting somewhat impatiently for the several mails now due; for my brother has not yet received any reply to, or acknowledgment of the despatches sent from hence in the first days of December. Yet the wind has been for some time westerly, and there are packets, we know, at Heligoland; but the quantity of floating ice on the coast of Sleswig prevents the boats from getting near the shore. In the meantime, we receive partial advices through Holland—the king's speech came that way—but many interesting particulars remain unknown to us. The chief advantage in this sort of conveyance, is, that we are sure to hear the worst side of every subject, and the good may come after—for such is the slavery in which the continental

press is held by Bonaparte, that hardly any newspaper dares to circulate intelligence favourable to
England, without having received our papers, from
which they sometimes venture to make an extract.

10*th.*—This has been an unusually dull winter,
and the death of the queen-mother on the 25th
ult.—one month from the time of the first attack—
has finally put aside all the dissipations we were
waiting only a favourable turn in her illness to
plunge into. Her Majesty was in her fifty-fifth
year, and was a daughter of Louis IX., Landgrave
of Hesse Darmstadt. The affliction of the king and
royal family is very generally shared by the public,
and her death will be felt as a misfortune by many
persons; for the late queen was extremely bene-
volent. She sought out misfortune, and relieved it
unsolicited, and her private acts of generosity were
numerous. Her funeral took place on the 4th. The
king, and the princes of the family, accompanied
the body to the vault, where the remains of Frederick
William II. are deposited.

13*th.*—The ceremony of the " Court of Condolence,"
which took place last Sunday, was, for such an
occasion, the most farcical spectacle I ever witnessed.
All those who assisted at the condolence assembled,
about half-past five, in a room of the palace—
the ladies in black stuff dresses, and entirely enveloped in veils, of black gauze, of from twelve to
fifteen yards in length, which fell in a deep double
fold over the face. As we had some time to wait,
the chatting and laughing went on gleefully ; and

the ladies, who had all thrown their veils back,
were amusing themselves with sprightly comments
on the droll effect of their dress. The military part
of the company—whose red coats, worn over black
waistcoats and inexpressibles, had certainly a very
odd appearance—came in for their share of tittering
raillery. But presently all this hilarity was silenced;
every face assumed a gloomy expression, and the
veils were drawn hastily down. The large centre
doors of the apartment had been suddenly thrown
open. Beyond them was a hall, hung with black,
and daylight was excluded; the darkness being made
still more visible by the feeble light of two candles,
burning at the further end of the hall, and by whose
pale glimmer you made out that a figure, enveloped
after the same mummy-like fashion as the other ladies,
was sitting there in an arm-chair, with several others
standing around her. It was Her Majesty and the
princesses. The princes of the family were ranged,
standing, down the sides of the hall. The ladies
entered first, single file, walked slowly up the hall,
made a profound curtsey to the queen, and passed
on to another room; the gentlemen followed. Not
a word was spoken, not a sound was heard, but the
dull "echoes of our feet," until we reached the outer
room, which was well lighted up, and where the
giggling and chattering had recommenced with
greater activity than before. The preparation for,
and conclusion of, this scene formed so striking a
contrast to the procession of *mourners* slowly passing
through the dark hall of the shadow of death, as it

were, that it produced a singular effect on those who witnessed it for the first time. The king was not present—his grief was supposed to be too over-whelming. Of course we have all been as black as crows since the queen-mother's death, and shall continue so for some time to come. This is a gloomy sort of consolation to me for the loss, as I fear, of my uniform, for the second time. Cavendish had been good enough to order it himself, that it might be correct in all its details. But nothing has been heard of it since it was sent, some months ago, from the Office. The French must have surely taken a fancy to this particular style of uniform. It was intended to grace the festivities of the carnival; however, I have no present need of it, and there is just the ghost of a chance that it may turn up with the final breaking up of the frost.

There are now, we hear, two candidates for the secretaryship of this mission : Hill, who was with my brother in Paris, and a Mr. King. As I am not to have the appointment, I must be content with discharging its duties and wishing success to Hill. As for King, he has been staying for some time in Berlin, and an odd sort of fellow he is; with much, I should say, of his mother's eccentricity of character. He is the son of the Countess of Kingston, who paid a visit to the French commandant at Hanover last year. When the expedition was on the point of sailing for Egypt, King was at college. Suddenly he took it into his head to set off for Portsmouth, without saying a word to anybody, and entered as a volunteer; wrote two lines to his mother, bidding her good-bye, and wishing her health and happiness should he see her no more, and so set sail.

16th.—We received seven mails on the 13th, and were much surprised at hearing, on the first opening of our communications with London, that the Hamburg baronet shortly intended to visit this capital. Owing to the detention of the mails, our time for wondering was short, for his arrival followed pretty quickly upon the notice of his plans. *On dit,* that he is obliged to run away from his creditors. However, he has completely *done himself up* by his *parole.* He comes to thank the king and my brother for getting him out of prison. The latter told him he was a lever that had broken in his hands, and says that, as far as he is concerned, it would not have signified much if Boney had kept him in *Le Temple,* together with what the king calls his box of papers, for anything there is likely to be found in it. Yet I must say, I feel for him; for I never saw any one so altered, and whatever his talents for diplomacy may be, we found Sir G. Rumbold a most pleasant gentlemanlike man, when we made a short stay at Hamburg on our way to Berlin. Now, it is hardly possible to live with him, his depression is so great; and the slights and reproaches he experienced in England so prey upon his spirits that, if in company any person happens to laugh, he immediately supposes it to be a sneer directed against him. During only the short time he has been here, this has frequently occurred; and all intercourse

T 2

with him is rendered, therefore, so painful, that I
shall be glad when he leaves for Dresden, which
I believe he intends doing as soon as he has had an
opportunity of personally thanking the king for his
release. Have you happened to meet his wife and
daughters? A Spaniard, who had resided some
time in England, was here last summer, and spoke of
the elder Miss Rumbold as the prettiest girl he had
seen there. I have since heard that she really is
uncommonly beautiful, but attends so little to the
hints and admonitions of the Bishop of Durham, that
the love of showing off an amazingly fine ankle has
prevented more than one offer from among the
crowd of her adorers. *Apropos* of pretty women,
Texier, the French play-reader, is now here with his
daughter. People are disposed to admire her beauty
far more than his performance, and not without reason.
The late dowager queen made a ridiculous fuss about
him, otherwise he would have completely failed
here. I never heard him in England; but he read a
play of his own at our house a short time ago, and
in a manner that pleased nobody. When he read
the part of a king, a sword and a crown were placed
by his side; for that of an old woman, a spinning-
wheel was drawn up before him. He has a son with
him, of about seventeen or eighteen, and being asked
the other day for what pursuit or profession he
destined him, he answered, " I have a great many
friends in England, and I hope in the course of a
few years to get him made a member of parliament."
His daughter, as I have already said, is particularly

handsome; but Texier is so impatient when she
is present that this should be generally and instantly
felt, that she has not been in company five minutes
before he begins expatiating to everybody near him
on her extreme beauty and great accomplishments, as
a proof of which I heard him tell the Duke of
Brunswick Oels that, in England, " Il y avait cinq
cents *lords* qui auraient été les uns plus heureux que
les autres de l'avoir." Our royal motto immediately
presented itself to my mind, as I trust it did to that
of the duke and others, if not, there must have been
difficulty in repressing the naughty ideas that suggested themselves on hearing M. Texier, with a
theatrical air, triumphantly proclaim his daughter's
conquests. The idle public of this city are just now
taken up with a man who reads lectures on skulls,
and shows by their conformation the different
propensities of their owners. As we have no time
to spare, we are not amongst this Dr.'s disciples.
His name is Gall. I have not yet heard that his
so-called discovery is to lead to any useful result.

Diaries—March 18*th.*—The King of Sweden has
himself, written to inform this Court, that in accordance
with the dignity that should characterize the acts of
an independent sovereign, he cannot allow his general
policy or his engagements with other countries, to
become a subject of discussion. And that should the
King of Prussia persist in his intention of invading
Pomerania, " He will, with the assistance of God and
his faithful subjects, defend himself to the utmost;
and will not be wanting in allies to support him."

23rd.—The proceedings of the French in Italy, and Bonaparte's journey to Milan, are exciting unusual interest. During his stay in that city, M. Humboldt, the Prussian minister at Rome, has received orders to reside there. We learn, from the "Moniteur," that Bonaparte has taken the resolution to declare himself King of Italy, this being, he announces, the only possible means of securing the independence of Italy and the countries belonging to it. He represents it also as a proof of his pacific disposition, and the most feasible expedient for the restoration of peace; intimating that, when Corfu is evacuated by the Russians, and Malta by the English, he will, in conformity with the public acts now made known, abdicate the throne of Italy in favour of some individual of his own selection.

As usual, this Court is highly indignant at the arrogance and overbearing ambition of the modern Charlemagne; but, as usual, it will conceal its sentiments, and adopt the extravagant reasons with which Bonaparte imposes on its weakness.

April 3rd.—The long talked of arrangement of the exchange of decorations is at last completed. For the seven "Golden Eagles"—as the insignia of the newly instituted Order of the *Legion d'Honneur* are called—seven black ones are returned. The former are destined for His Majesty; Prince Ferdinand, the king's great uncle—who accepts the decoration which was intended for his son; Prince Louis Ferdinand, who, however, expressed unwillingness to receive it; the Duke of Brunswick; Field-Marshal Möllendorff;

Baron Hardenberg, and Count Schulenberg. The
Black Eagles are for Bonaparte, his brother Joseph,
Murat, Beauharnois, Cambacèrés, Talleyrand, and
another member of his government, whose name has
not transpired.

A similar arrangement has been made with the Court
of Madrid in regard to the Order of the Golden Fleece.

Though it has been thought unadvisable to refuse
these orders, yet there is not one of the persons for
whom they are destined, except Prince Ferdinand,
who has been, throughout, a warm admirer of the
French Revolution, who is not ashamed of the new
decoration—some of them express themselves, undisguisedly, to this effect; and the feeling is not a little
strengthened by Prussia being placed, by this arrangement, on the same footing of dependence as Spain.

7th.—The French minister went yesterday to
Potzdam to deliver the insignia of the Legion of
Honour to the king, together with a letter from
Bonaparte. In the evening he had an audience
of Prince Ferdinand, for the same purpose. The
prince had invited to his house the whole of the
French mission, several foreign ministers, and many
of the residents of this city, to see him decorated
with the star and riband, which he immediately
put on. Visits were also made to the other persons
for whom the new honour was destined, and the
insignia were delivered to them with a letter from
M. Talleyrand. Field-Marshal Möllendorff had a
large party to dinner, to which M. Laforêt was not
invited. The insignia lay on a table for the

inspection of the guests. Only Prince Ferdinand
has, as yet, wor the order.

The Duke of Brunswick has sent to express his
great embarrassment on this subject, and his doubts
as to the acceptance of the decoration of the Legion
of Honour being compatible with his position as
a Knight of the Garter. Meanwhile, M. Laforêt
has delivered the insignia to his serene highness's
minister at Berlin, in the same manner as to the last
mentioned persons, with a letter from M. Talleyrand,
and not from Bonaparte.himself, as was expected,
considering the difference of his serene highness's
rank and situation.

8th.—The changes that have taken pláce in the
war department at Vienna, and the determination of
the emperor to postpone his journey to the Venetian
provinces, engross much . attention here. Both
Prince Schwartzenberg and General Loton are considered totally unequal to undertake the important
charges with which they are entrusted ; and it is
supposed that the influence of the empress has been
exerted, for the purpose of suppressing any disposition
that might appear in the Austrian Government to
oppose the progress of France.

9th.—The king has written to Bonaparte, in
answer to his notification of his having assumed the
title of King of Italy. His Majesty expresses an
earnest hope that the step he has taken may fully
answer the object that gave rise to it. That the erec-
tion of the Italian Republic into a kingdom may be
universally considered as a proof of Bonaparte's pacific

disposition, and the manner of doing it a proof of his moderation; and that the whole may lead to the desirable end of restoring peace to Europe.

As to the act itself, and the title adopted, His Prussian Majesty says that, the opinions of other powers, more immediately interested upon the occasion, must be referred to. Thus ends the letter, and it is addressed to the Emperor of the French, without the addition of King of Italy. This is doubtless the result of the language lately held to this Court by the Emperor of Russia; for, as Bonaparte made an act of the emperor one of the pretexts for that which he now announces to the world, the acknowledgment of his new title would be, in fact, to allow the justice of his complaint, and, in a certain degree, to take a part in his favour.

There has been, however, no refusal, but merely hesitation, to acknowledge this new dignity; and Bonaparte has not started that question, but now, as when he assumed the Imperial title, has taken it for granted that it would be immediately acknowledged by this and other Courts. The king's letter contains a great many compliments intended to palliate the effect of the concluding phrase.

14th.—The Duke of Brunswick has accepted the insignia of the Legion of Honour; and M. Laforêt is to receive from him, as well as from the king, a valuable present on the occasion. The duke, however, apologises to the King of England, and begs that it may be borne in mind that his country is surrounded by a French army, and that the honour is conferred

on him as a Prussian general, in which capacity he
made his acknowledgments to M. Talleyrand.

The king, who was consulted by his serene
highness, advised this course, and said the duke
could not act more conformably to his own interest
than by adhering to the system pursued by this
Court. The duke showed a desire to adopt a contrary
course; but was prevailed on to accede to the wishes
of His Majesty, on being assured that the acceptance
of the new honour was really as repugnant to his
feelings as to those of the duke ; but that, without
departing from the line of conduct he had laid down
for himself, he could not refuse it. He had, indeed,
gone so far as to set aside Bonaparte's proposal of
giving greater solemnity to the exchange of orders ;
he having desired that they should be delivered by
a chamberlain, sent expressly for that purpose by
each Government.

17*th.*—Bonaparte being in Italy, M. de Lucchesini
has followed him thither with the orders ; which are
left it seems entirely at his disposal, so that the
report that one was destined for Bernadotte is not
yet confirmed. Bernadotte has asked, and obtained
the permission of His Prussian Majesty, to be present
at the reviews to be held at Magdeburg towards the
end of next month.

20*th.*—M. Brinckman, the Swedish Chargé d'Affaires,
has received from the King of Sweden the insignia
of the Order of the Black Eagle, with directions to
return them to the Prussian minister, with the remark
that " Orders of knighthood were originally instituted

in honour of religion and chivalry ; and that, in his
quality of knight, the King of Sweden could not
consent to wear an order worn by Bonaparte *et ses
semblables.*"   It was intended to return them to
M. Tarrach, the Prussian minister at Stockholm, but
he declined to receive them, and M. Brinckman has
not yet been allowed an opportunity of fulfilling the
commission entrusted to him, as much displeasure is felt
at this act of the King of Sweden.   M. Tarrach will
be recalled, and a Chargé d'Affaires left in his place.

 25th.—The messenger who took the Prussian
Orders to Paris is returned, and brings the news of
the Toulon fleet having a second time put to sea and
again returned to port, and that there was reason to
believe it had been engaged and defeated by the
British squadron in that quarter.   A report has also
found its way here, the confirmation of which we are
anxiously awaiting, of the Brest fleet having been
defeated by Sir C. Cotton.

 Letters—April 27th.—Your last sunny spring letter
from Bath was quite cheering ; here, not a leaf is to be
seen.   After all the contumely heaped upon it, our
English climate is, perhaps, not the worst in the
world.   However, *en attendant* the spring of the
Brandenburg sands, and the waking up of Downing
Street from the trance it has lately fallen into, I
have enrolled myself amongst the disciples of Dr.
Gall, whom I believe I have already spoken of to
you.   There is a general rage for this man and his
system, and, in conformity to the fashion of the day,
I am attending a course of his lectures.   They

contain, as far as I have gone, much ingenious and
entertaining matter, together with a great many
mischievous notions. Dr. Gall is a physician of
Vienna. He fancies he has discovered an entirely
new system of the brain, by which he makes that important part of the human structure to consist, instead
of a marrowy substance, of a membraneous skin, which
can be opened and spread upon a table like a napkin.
He likewise divides the brain into various organs,
from which he pretends to account for different
qualities of the mind. Many of his notions have a
direct tendency to fatalism, as he says that a man
being born with the organs that dispose him to
theft, murder, suicide, &c., although his disposition
thereto may be modified by education, it cannot be
totally eradicated. This doctor has not yet published
anything upon his system; but if I can get a clear
statement of it in a concise form, I will certainly
send it to England, that the first part of it may
be received or refuted by the profession; for as
to the theory of the organs I think that, at best,
must remain an ingenious speculation.

29th.—I was amused by your fears of my being
concerned in a duel, noticed in some of the English
papers. You must never place any confidence in
what those papers report from this quarter. We
frequently see statements of occurrences here which
certainly never occurred. But the duel in question
did really take place; the principals were a M.
Krudener—connected with the Russian mission,
whose father, now dead, was the Russian minister at

this Court—and a Captain Mausinna, a son of the surgeon-general of the army. Society, as you may know, is in Berlin most rigidly divided into sets which, except in the case of a few young men, never associate with each other. Krudener, who belonged to the first circle, had chosen to join the subscription for the weekly balls of the second, which indeed includes persons of such position as the judges, privy councillors, the clergy, and officers of the garrison. At one of these balls the quarrel happened. Both the young men had been drinking very freely, and as both were anxious for the good graces of the same fair lady, they exchanged some very uncomplimentary words which ended in blows. Krudener being the weaker man came off rather badly, but the next day, after much consultation, for it is the first instance of a *noble* fighting with a *bourgeois*, he sent a challenge to Mausinna, with the declaration that one or the other must forfeit his life. The meeting took place at eight the next morning; shots were exchanged at the distance of eight paces, and Krudener wounded his adversary in the thigh. But, according to their previous arrangement, this was not sufficient satisfaction. They fired again, and Krudener's ball pierced his adversary's heart: he fell dead without uttering a word. This affair caused a great sensation in Berlin. As it was thus to be settled, I confess to being glad that Krudener is the survivor; though I doubt whether his existence is worth having. For, from what I know of his disposition, I believe he will suffer much from remorse when the excitement of

his present feelings has passed away.   His mother—
who about a year ago wrote a novel called " Valerie,"
which made a great noise—is *au désespoir*.   She is at
Riga; her son, with his second, Prince Lubomirski,
is at Dresden.   Krudener cannot return to his post
at Berlin, and the prince I imagine will prefer some
other Court.   *De mortuis nil nisi bonum*—yet it must
be confessed that Mausinna was a great scamp.   The
sympathy of the public, however, is with him and
his family, and has been very strongly expressed.

May 1st.—You have heard of the honours conferred
here by the Great Nap; and that the Golden Eagle
now flaunts his glittering plumage by the side of the
black one, at least on the breast of Prince Ferdinand,
the Great Frederick's brother!   He alone of the
decorés feels himself honoured.   What would have been
the feelings of that brother could he have stepped
from his tomb, and have beheld the *empressement*
with which the prince and princess received the
mighty man's minister, when he arrived to decorate
his royal highness, in the presence of a large company; having just returned from the performance
of a similar ceremony at Potzdam!   The king will
probably never wear his Order, unless his ill-fate
should force him to an interview with the Corsican
emperor.   The Duke of Brunswick is still greatly
embarrassed how to reconcile honour with dishonour,
the Garter with the Eagle.

7th.—We have Sir William Coll and his sister
with us, quite young people, who have been travelling for the last two years.   They left England just

before the breaking out of the war, and were among those English who owe their liberty only to the good nature of the commandant at Geneva, who had promised to give them timely notice of any unfavourable turn of affairs. The arrest of the English was, however, ordered without any previous warning. The commandant went to them with the order in his pocket; told them he should delay the execution of it for a few hours, and begged them to set off immediately. They did so, and Sir William and his sister, after another very narrow escape at Lausanne, reached Neufchatel, whence, after letting his beard grow, and both disguising themselves as peasants, they contrived to get away, and travelled on foot to Munich. They have been at Vienna for the last fifteen months, and are now on their way home. They amuse us greatly with stories of their adventures. You may remember their father, an old blind baronet, who lived at Lee. Our Hamburg baronet is still here, as miserable as ever himself, and making everybody miserable he comes in contact with. He thinks himself hardly dealt by, and perhaps he is ; but everybody answers, "his parole!" "his parole!" Drake, he says, had he been carried off as he was, and lodged in a Paris gaol, might have been induced to give his parole, too ; and he hears that Drake is one of those who cast blame on him. Neither one nor the other can again be employed, but Drake, having been made a catspaw of, will no doubt find consolation in the receipt of a good pension.

Kotzebüe, after whom you inquire with so much

interest, left this some months ago to pass the winter, I believe, in Italy. Upon his first coming here people were much disposed in his favour, but his unconscionable vanity and affectation of extreme sensibility sickened many persons; and he sank very low in every one's estimation after the publication of his memoirs, because of his pitiful and ignoble insinuations against those to whom he owed a deep debt of gratitude. For myself, I own that I was much surprised, notwithstanding all I had heard and seen of him, when, after reading his description of his feelings in the wood near Stockenanschoff, and the stream of tenderness that gushed forth when he thought of " his Emily," the mere repetition of whose " sweet name " calmed his sufferings both of mind and body, &c., I learnt that he had just married his third, if not fourth wife.

It was reported, about three months ago, that Kotzebüe had been arrested by the French on his road from Rome to Naples. A month or so afterwards there appeared in the " Hamburg Gazette " a letter from him, contradicting the report, and expressing his astonishment at the impertinence of the newspaper people in propagating it. He assured his *friends* that, so far from having met with any hindrance or molestation on his journey, he had experienced, wherever he met with a Frenchman, not only the urbanity for which that nation is celebrated, but the most distinguished and flattering marks of consideration and respect. This curious production ends thus : " Would to God my good countrymen would leave me quiet !"

and then, *pour surcroît d'insolence,* he signs himself
" Kotzebüe, Chancellor of His Imperial Majesty the
Emperor of Russia ;" which will certainly do him
no good at St. Petersburg.

9th.—We expect to have another brush with
Bonaparte if Mr. Taylor returns to Cassel.   M.
Bignon, the French Chargé d'Affaires at that Court,
has informed the elector that if Mr. Taylor is
admitted to his table at the same time as himself, he
will immediately quit Cassel. His electoral highness
is said to have replied, " Qu'il en était le maître." He
is, however, rather perplexed as to the course he
shall take, and has sought the advice of the king, as
well as desired to have the charges which the French
Government bring against Mr. Taylor stated in
writing.

Diaries—May 14*th.*—The Swedish Chargé d'Affaires
has fulfilled the king's orders, and delivered also a
letter he was charged with from His Majesty. No
notice whatever will be taken of it, and the Swedish
Order of the Seraphim will not be sent back ; but
directions have been forwarded to M. de Tarrach to
ask for his passports, and to leave Sweden immediately, with the whole of his mission.

M. Brinckman has been informed that he is at
liberty to remain in Berlin, but as a private person
only. It was at first intended not to proceed to that
extremity, but to treat the conduct of the King of
Sweden with indifference. M. Lombard and the
French party, however, persuaded the king to resent
the affront, and availed themselves especially of the

King of Sweden's expression "et ses semblables,"
which they represented as pointing directly to His
Prussian Majesty. At the intercession of the Russian
minister, permission was given to M. Brinckman
to remain in Berlin, but no other concession was
made.

16th.—Their Majesties are going to Fûrth on the
23rd, for the inspection of the troops cantoned in the
margraviates. They will afterwards pass some time
at a new bathing place, not far from Bareuth, called
Alexander's Bad.

Several French officers, besides Marshal Bernadotte,
are to be present at the reviews at Körbelitz. The
latter is to receive the military honours of a Prussian
field-marshal, and Lieutenant-Colonel Kreusemarck
is appointed to attend him and his suite during his
stay with the Prussian troops.

19th.—M. Laforêt observed yesterday, in conversation, that Bonaparte's assumption of the consular
dignity was followed by the restoration of the
blessings of peace, and he now hoped that his
accession to the crown of Italy would prove of
similar benefit to humanity. Bonaparte's reasons for
assuming the regal title are just announced to the
world by M. Talleyrand, in terms to which "qui
s'excuse s'accuse" may fairly be applied.*

The manner in which the Austrian Government,
without absolutely acknowledging Bonaparte's title
of King of Italy, makes it clear that they have very
little disposition to resist his claim to it, is con-

* See Appendix, No. 4.

sidered as a betrayal of their weakness in no small degree.

23rd.—Public attention is now almost exclusively directed to the expected arrival of M. de Novossiltzow, for whom Bonaparte has sent passports for his journey to Italy, for the purpose of entering upon a negotiation for a pacific adjustment of the differences existing between Russia and France. It is feared, however, that Bonaparte's inordinate ambition will prevent the possibility of coming to any reasonable terms with him. The French party, meanwhile, endeavour to divert the public mind towards that view of the matter which, as they represent, shows with what facility an accommodation could be effected, if the complicated interests that England is forced to attend to did not present a material obstacle to a peace. Yet they have made known, that Bonaparte has declared, that any menaces from the Russian envoy will prove fatal to the success of his mission.

25th.—My brother, having received leave to absent himself from Berlin for some weeks, presented me to-day, to Baron Hardenberg, as the person who had filled the office of secretary of legation for the last fifteen months, and who would make any application to him that the course of affairs might render necessary ; who would report to the British Government any circumstances that might occur during his absence with which it would be desirable they should be acquainted, and would take charge, generally, of the business of the mission.

Letters—May 26th.—I received yesterday a letter

from a friend in England. He says, "This is with us a season of *conjecture*, with respect to the fleets; of *apprehension* for the islands, and of *cavilling* at home on subjects that ought not to have been introduced at a critical time like this. Thoughtful people tremble for the state of the nation. The king, whatever you may hear of his perfect recovery, be assured, is far from being *compos mentis*. His disposition is so very volatile, and so difficult to do business with, that ministers know not how to act. He thinks of nothing but pleasure and expense, in unbounded degrees; the presents he makes—something quite new with him—cost enormous sums. His dislike to the queen increases daily, and he is now devoted to *two young favourites*. What a deplorable state of things for a nation circumstanced as we are! Yet we, whose duty it is to be, as those who seeing, see not, console ourselves with the thought that an old dotard, if he càn work no good, may do less evil than a drunken profligate.

"Do you know that our friend Nott is named *sub*-preceptor to that poor child the Princess of Wales? You have had, no doubt, a full and particular account of the Installation, reported as the most magnificent spectacle ever seen in England. I can add, and the most *ennuyant*. Sir Isaac Heard will pocket some thousands by it, which may console him for the unlucky accident he met with. It is a sort of windfall to him; for he told me he never expected or supposed there would be an Installation in this reign. I could tell you some anecdotes that would make you laugh, about that event, and matters more domestic of our virtuous court. But I forbear, for they should perhaps be considered subjects rather of grief than of mirth. I know, too, that your letters are often waylaid by the enemy. This goes by a pretty safe conveyance, or I should not have ventured to give you even this little peep under the curtain.

" The great emperor, they tell us, knows as well as ourselves, what great George and his hopeful heir would be worth to us in the hour of danger. But he knows also what sort of spirit pervades the people, and how, if it comes to the point, the whole nation will rise and do its own work, and brush him off our shores very thoroughly.

" The spirit of the King of Sweden's declaration to his cousin and brother of Prussia is generally admired. Had he but the needful resources, or neighbours with something like the same chivalrous boldness and valour, for which we give him credit, he would soon carve his way, I fancy, through Prussia to France, and beard the lion in his own lair. Adieu, my dear George. Don't let us two old Westminsters drop our correspondence. You have heard from Mrs. J. of the changes at that seat of learning, I know. How is it your brother does not apply for the vacant Berlin secretaryship for you ? I, who, being in the office, ought not to let you into its secrets, believe that Lord M. would give it you. You are thoroughly up to its duties ;. and they tell me you are now full six feet in height, fond of the ladies, and a devilishly good-looking fellow." B.

Diaries—June 3rd.—The Swedish Chargé d'Affaires is ordered to ask for his passports and to leave Berlin immediately.

4th and 5th.—Countess Voss has written, from Magdeburg, that Bernadotte had excused himself from attending the reviews on account of indisposition. But Berthier was there ; of whom she says, " Il est très poli, mais du reste, pas grande chose." M. de Lucchesini had arrived at Fürth, from Milan, in five days. He brought the news that the Doge of Genoa awaited only the arrival of Bonaparte to complete the arrangement for the union of that country with France. The event is officially announced by the French, this morning, as having actually taken place, with the further information, that Bonaparte had acceded to it solely at the entreaties of the Genoese, and to give them an additional proof of his pacific dispositions and his desire to ensure the independence and welfare of that part of Italy.

My brother, who is at Dresden, writes that he had, on the 3rd, a private audience of the elector, and that at an evening Whitsuntide drawing-room—the only one held there during summer—he and his wife were presented to the whole of the electoral family. The Court resides at Pilnitz, a very pretty chateau, and famous for the interview that took place there in 1791 between the Emperor Leopold and the late King of Prussia on the subject of the affairs of France. The agreement formed between them was afterwards converted by the French revolutionists, and by our opposition, into a treaty for the partition of France ;

and was made the *cheval de bataille* both in France
and in our Parliament, in order to prove the iniquity of
the last war, and of the views of the coalesced powers.

The Emperor of Germany arrived at Prague on the
30th.   The Chancellor of Bohemia, only, accompanied
him.   Immediately on his arrival he convoked a
meeting of the chief magistrates and *capitaines de
cercles*.   His journey was suddenly undertaken, but
its object is supposed to be, to find if possible, a
remedy for the sufferings of his Bohemian subjects,
arising from the scarcity and consequent high price
of all the necessaries of life.   The condition of the
inhabitants is represented as most wretched.   Specu-
lators are however inclined to think that an interview
with the King of Prussia may be intended, as, after
the Fürth reviews, he will be near Bareuth, not far
from the frontiers of Bohemia.   The march of the
Austrian troops towards Italy, consisting of ten
regiments of infantry, four of cavalry, and three parks
of artillery, has, it is feared, been countermanded.
The *semestriers* who were ordered to join their regiments are also dismissed.

The King of Sweden has invited the British,
Russian, and Austrian ministers at Stockholm to accompany him to the camp at Scania.   M. Brinckman
has not yet applied for his passports; he postpones his
departure as long as possible, thinking it not impro-
bable that the king may be prevailed upon to make
up matters with the King of Prussia, and that he,
perhaps, may be employed in the work of concilia-
tion.   There are many good reasons for supposing the

contrary, but so strange a thing would not be without a precedent.

6th.—A person, who professes to have overheard the matter discussed between Count Metternich and M. Laforêt, at the house of the latter, assured me this morning that Austria has acknowledged Bonaparte's title of King of Italy, and that the King of Prussia on being informed of it, immediately, *in a great huff*, sent off fresh letters of credence to M. de Lucchesini ; observing that, if a power so much more nearly interested in the question than Prussia, as Austria was, had recognized Bonaparte's proceedings, there could no longer be any reason for Prussia withholding her recognition of the title he had assumed

Letters—June 10*th.*—Bonaparte has dismissed the Archbishop of Turin from his office, because he declined to accept the *cordon* of the Legion of Honour, and refused to *incense* him at the door of the cathedral. The Piedmontese nobility appear to have set an example to their more powerful, but less magnanimous, neighbours. Women, as well as men, have refused the most distinguished places in the new-fangled Court. Nothing can equal the discontent prevalent in Italy. People of all ranks make no scruple of publicly avowing their sentiments, and the usurper's disappointment and vexation are equally undisguised.

12th.—The Russian negotiators have received, by the last " Moniteur," a gentle hint of what they have to expect. The paragraph referred to says " toute la paix d'Amiens—rien que la paix d'Amiens—la France n'en signera jamais d'autre."

13th.—Berlin is becoming a perfect desert, every-body is hurrying away to breathe the fine air of Dresden, which place has now more visitors than it can comfortably hold. But most of them are birds of passage on their way to the watering places in Bohemia. Two of the French generals, who were at the late reviews near Magdeburg have arrived in this city. The junior officer—Frère, of Hamburg notoriety—came without asking leave; and, indeed, without knowing that his superior officer was here. Allow, then, that he must have been taken rather aback when he met, as he was going to pay a visit to the French minister, Sir G. Rumbold at the door, and General Révaud on the staircase. The conduct of the latter while at the reviews was such as to annoy even his own officers. To some inquiries that were made after the health of Bernadotte, who had excused himself from attending on account of illness, Révaud answered with a shrug of the shoulders — His Prussian Majesty being present—"Il se porte aussi bien que moi." At a *fête* given at Brunswick, in honour of the French officers, the duke, it appears, wore his French eagle, which Révaud remarking, immediately expressed to his serene highness his satisfaction at finding that the report he had heard of his refusal to wear that decoration was incorrect. The duke was not well pleased at this freedom, nor with the familiarity with which the General constantly addressed him as " Monsieur le Duc," never " votre Altesse," or " Monseigneur."

14th.—An amusing circumstance occurred with

reference to Révaud's *avant-courier*, who contrived to
pick a quarrel with his postilion just as he reached
his journey's end. Wishing to convince the man of
his fault, by a forcible argument, addressed to his back
rather than to his understanding, he began belabour-
ing him unmercifully with the *flat* of his sabre. His
Majesty happened at that moment to be at a window,
and saw all that was going forward. Observing to
his aide-de-camp that, the gentleman, he supposed,
had forgotten he was no longer in Hanover, he gave
orders that he should be put under arrest, and, that
he might have leisure to refresh his memory, continue
in that comfortable situation during his master's stay
at the reviews.

The three French generals who assisted at these
reviews were Berthier, Kellerman, and Révaud.
Berthier was accompanied by his wife. They dined
each day with the Queen, and supped with General
Knobelsdorff. The Duke of Brunswick gave them a
very grand entertainment at his capital, and ordered
that the plays most agreeable to them should be
performed at the theatre.

All the Prussian officers, even the King and Duke
of Brunswick, were encamped during the reviews,
except Prince Louis, who preferred the conveniences
and delights of love in a cottage, as he had taken his
chère amie with him.

16*th.*—Sir George Rumbold has been very ill with
the ague and fever which affects so many people in
Berlin. I have constant attacks, more or less severe,
and do not expect to be entirely free from them while

I remain here. Sir George is going to Dresden for a change. The Metternich family set off for the same place this morning, also M. Brinckman, to whom the King of Sweden has sent peremptory orders to leave Berlin without loss of time. The Prussian minister is already returned from Stockholm.

Diaries—June 17*th.*—A French messenger has arrived from Italy, but has been twelve days on the road, having come round by Paris. M. Laforêt announces that he has brought no news, beyond that it was the intention of Bonaparte to return to Paris by the 12th of next month. But there are various *on dits*, of a not very conciliatory tone, on the subject of M. de Novossiltzow's mission, from which it is inferred that Bonaparte is inclined to treat the Russian negotiator in a manner very different from what his former professions led us to expect.* The French minister is at great pains to make it generally known that he has no instructions as to the place or time of the proposed negotiation; but he states, vaguely, that by the time M. de Novossiltzow arrives at Mayence Bonaparte's movements will be more certain, and that the former will then be informed when and where he can be received.

18*th.*—The king is at Alexander's Bad; to which place the Electors of Bavaria and Hesse are also gone to consult with His Majesty on the present position of affairs, in regard to their electorates. It has been rumoured, and has caused general alarm, that the king intended to make a tour in Switzerland

* See Appendix, No. 5.

before his return to Berlin. It is feared that he would, in that case be drawn into a meeting with Bonaparte, from which only unfavourable results are augured.

24th.—An *avant-courier* arrived on the 22nd, and announced that M. de Novossiltzow might be expected in Berlin that night. Instantly, I despatched a courier to Dresden to give my brother the first intelligence of it. The people of Berlin are so anxiously interested in this negotiation for peace between Russia and France, that numbers were waiting merely to get a glimpse of the Russian negotiator, as he entered the city. They were however doomed to disappointment; for M. de Novossiltzow did not reach Berlin until late last night, having been twelve days on his journey.

The *quidnuncs* were all on the alert this morning, when a further subject for speculation was afforded them by the arrival of my brother, about eleven o'clock, in an open carriage and four. He had travelled all night, with the hope of arriving as soon as M. de Novossiltzow, and is now gone to visit him.

26th.—Bonaparte announces that he will not receive M. de Novossiltzow at Milan, but in Paris. The latter will wait for an interview with the King of Prussia. This, it is hoped, will put an end to any project that may have been formed for a tour in Switzerland.

27th.—We had M. de Novossiltzow and ten others to dinner last evening, and paid him the compliment of a *diner Russe* cooked by a Russian *chef*. M. de N. himself, is however, *Le Russe le moins Russe* I

have seen for a long time. Polite and *prévenant*,
yet with a frank and open manner that at once
inspires confidence. He has the appearance of being
very young, though he is near upon forty; *il louche*,
and has not, exactly, an air *distingué*, yet his manner
of presenting himself, and his evident *bonne foi*, at
once prepossess you in his favour. I have noticed
him thus particularly, because so much is expected
from his talents as a negotiator, in this business
between Russia and France.

29th.—The incorporation of Genoa has made so
great a sensation at St. Petersburg, and also at Vienna,
that there are hopes that the latter Court may be
induced by it to take some vigorous and decisive
steps in conjunction with Russia. It is even proposed,
in consequence, to break off the negotiation with
France; though M. de Novossiltzow will proceed on
his journey to the place Bonaparte may appoint, in
order to give Austria time to receive the succours
that may be sent to her. The actual recognition of the
title of King of Italy by Austria, which the French
mission reported had taken place, is now said to have
been a fabrication.

30th.—The king has notified his intention of returning to Berlin to receive M. de Novossiltzow.

July 3rd. —Disturbances have taken place in some
of the provincial towns, owing to the distress which
the high price of corn and other necessaries of life
has caused among the poorer classes. But it is not so
severely felt in the Prussian dominions as in Saxony
and Bohemia. The turbulent spirit which, from the

same cause, has occasionally shown itself amongst the
populace of Berlin has been allayed by the measures
taken to diminish the consumption of grain, by prohibiting its distillation, and to secure a supply for
the markets by stopping the exportation of bread,
even to the neighbouring villages. At Halle these
measures were not seconded by others that were
necessary to enforce obedience to them. In consequence the people of that town, after many riotous
acts, went to the length of destroying several houses,
and putting to death several supposed monopolists.
For the popular vengeance—as too often happens—
fell chiefly upon innocent victims. But the worst
feature of these disgraceful proceedings is, that they
occurred in the presence of a whole regiment of
infantry, in garrison at Halle. After causing full
inquiry to be made into this circumstance, the king
has cashiered the field officer of the day, and two
other officers of the regiment.

5*th*.—Count Schmettan, a Prussian general, and
a very clever fellow, has availed himself dexterously
enough of the circumstance of the King of Sweden
having returned the Black Eagle to the King of
Prussia. The Count had the Swedish Order of the
Sword, but no Prussian decoration. He, therefore,
wrote to the king, suggesting the propriety of returning the *insignia* to His Swedish Majesty, and begging
to receive the king's orders to that effect. The king
replied, that it was not necessary to return the
Swedish Order, but as it might not be agreeble to him,
under existing circumstances, to wear it, he sent him

the Red Eagle to supply its place. It is said that the Count looked higher, he expected to bring down the Black Eagle, and was somewhat disappointed when he found his colour red.

Mr. Pierrepont, our minister at Stockholm, and his Russian colleague have been amusing themselves greatly at the Swedish camp, and have been royally entertained there. Everything was at His Majesty's expense ; houses, horses, carriages, &c. &c. The camp consisted of about nine thousand very fine-looking fellows, in every respect very well equipped. The king laid aside all etiquette, and was extremely affable and attentive to his guests.

7th.—The affair of Genoa creates, apparently, no uneasy feeling at this Court, notwithstanding the agitation it has caused at St. Petersburg and Vienna. It is not enough for the King of Prussia to see the knife at his throat, the blow must be given before he will believe that danger threatens him.

10th.—The King of Prussia arrived yesterday at Charlottenburg and gave audience to M. de Novossiltzow. The result is that he does not proceed on his journey to Paris, but returns Bonaparte's passports to the Prussian minister, and in a day or two will set out for St. Petersburg. The Russian troops are already marching towards the frontier in different directions.

The king, it is generally believed, will not be moved by any arguments to depart from what he calls his system, which is, in fact, no system at all ; being founded on nullity, and a determination to be entirely governed, and not at all guided, by events

as they arise, and to resign himself submissively to
whatever may appear, at the moment of unavoidable
choice, to offer the least immediate danger. In short,
nothing but actual force will stir the King of Prussia
from the ground he has taken as the basis of his
political conduct.

12*th*.—Mr. Taylor having returned to Cassel, the
French minister, M. Bignon, took the liberty of
addressing himself to the elector on the subject, and
in language so intemperate and threatening, that
his serene highness has submitted the matter to
the king. He has expressed his intention to continue to receive Mr. Taylor, yet asks for advice in
the embarrassing position he is placed in. The
king has approved of the elector's resolution, and
advised him to persevere in it.

14*th*.—As the Prussian Government has been the
medium through which the mission of M. de Novossiltzow has been conducted thus far, it will also be
charged to convey to Bonaparte the motives that
render it impossible for Russia to proceed in the
negotiation, at a moment when he is arbitrarily
taking possession of every point that was to have
become a subject of discussion.

19*th*.—Very early this morning M. de Novossiltzow
left Berlin for St. Petersburg, and will travel with
great speed. He has made here the most favourable
impression. His personal qualities, and his conciliatory manners, would have been likely to gain
the esteem and good will even of our enemy. He
left a note, addressed to the Prussian minister, to be

communicated to M. Laforêt. The latter has refused
to receive it, alleging that it is conceived in terms
offensive to the dignity of the emperor, his master.
As M. de Novossiltzow desired that all publicity
should be given to it, it was forwarded to Hamburg,
and has appeared in the newspapers of that town.
Curiosity is now piqued to see what effect it will
have upon Bonaparte.*

It is generally admitted that the British Government could not have given a better proof of its
sincere wish to put an end to the war, or the
Emperor of Russia of his readiness to second that
wish, than by the manner in which this step towards
a negotiation has been taken. The most inveterate
antagonists of Great Britain must allow that an
attempt has been made to meet the overtures of
France upon fair and dignified grounds, and that it
has been done in the most unexceptionable manner.
The choice of the negotiator is thought to be an
unequivocal proof of the sincerity with which it was
sought to restore to Europe independence and peace.
The King of Prussia is fully convinced of it. He
has felt irritated at the conduct of the French
Government, and displeased with M. Laforêt for
returning the Russian note. He himself gave orders
that the French minister should be made acquainted
with his sentiments. And, speaking of Bonaparte's
ambition, he said, "Qu'il ne croye pas que je le
suiverai dans toutes les sottises qu'il jugera à propos
de faire."

* See Appendix, No. 6.

The Hamburg papers have published the note of M. de Hardenberg to M. Laforêt on returning the passports of M. Novossiltzow.*

Letters—July 23rd.—The Russian business having been brought to an unexpected close, my brother thinks it right to await at Berlin the intelligence he is expecting, both from England and Russia, rather than to avail himself further of his leave of absence. My term of office, then, is ended. Though short, it has been satisfactory. My correspondence, both public and private, has been pronounced by my chief, " very commendable." But a damper, or rather an extinguisher, to my hopes has arrived by this mail. My brother's urgent solicitations to Lord Mulgrave are answered by the announcement of Mr. Bartle Frere's appointment as secretary of legation. My aguish attack was on me, and what I could not, momentarily, at least, help feeling, I think made it sharper than usual. However, it is past now, and I am going for a few days to Dresden. I have worked almost day and night during my brother's absence, and the change, he thinks, will do me good. Frere was at Felstead with Francis—his junior and his *fag*. He is, I believe, a pleasant, gentlemanlike young man, and will, no doubt, be an agreeable addition to our circle. King, who wanted the secretaryship of this mission, and remained in Berlin ready to pop into it when his friends, as he expected, had secured the post for him, was appointed to Dresden, under Wynn, our youthful minister at that

* See Appendix, No. 7.

Court. King, however, on receiving notice of it was highly indignant; and, although he has never filled any appointment whatever, actually wrote to Lord Mulgrave, saying he had better keep so good a thing for some one of his particular friends. He is certainly very amusing, but terribly harum-scarum, even for an Irishman. He is now off to Greece, and of course will not turn his thoughts again to a diplomatic career.

Lord Mulgrave has made himself very unpopular with the juniors. He has given orders that no clerk shall "on any account ever leave the Office" without asking permission. Some of the young men, I have been told, being too proud to ask leave to go to dinner, prefer to go without, and remain in the office till all the doors are closed, and they are almost turned out.

Dresden, 31*st*.—I left Berlin with my friend Löwenstern on the 24th. While changing horses at Potzdam, we were much amused by the facetiousness and thoughtless loquacity of a French courier, who drew up at the post-house nearly at the same time as ourselves. Little suspecting that he was communicating his information to a Russian, and an Englishman, he told us he had been sent off at an hour's notice, and was the bearer of only one small letter. But he did not end his story there; and when he proceeded to give us the particulars of what was passing in Paris, of the anxiety felt by all classes for the safety of their boasted Armada, and of the journey of his "imperial master" to the coast to

superintend, not to accompany, the flotilla about to
attempt the long threatened invasion, we could
hardly contain ourselves for laughter; and had not
our order from M. d'Engelbach to the postmaster
made him more alert than usual, we should certainly
have been betrayed by our hilarity. As soon as we
arrived at Dessau we sent off the particulars he had
favoured us with to Berlin.

We looked at Wörlitz *en passant*, then continued
our journey in a heavy rain and dark night. We
were praising the goodness of the roads, and congratulating ourselves on our prosperous journey, when,
suddenly I was raised high above my fellow traveller,
who was as suddenly seated on a level with the
road. We fancied that the carriage had fallen into
a deep hole, but soon discovered that one of the
wheels had come off. Nothing was broken, and, as
luck would have it, in spite of the rain and the darkness, we succeeded in finding the nut of the wheel,
which had come unscrewed, and was the sole cause
of our change of position. Notwithstanding this
contre-temps we got to Leipsic early in the morning,
having accomplished the last post, which is four
German miles—and the roads the worst on the
whole journey—in five hours. Leipsic is a very
dull town except during the fair. We assisted at a
Lutheran baptism, at the church of St. Nicholas,
the handsomest modern church I ever saw. We left
Leipsic at four, and arrived within half an English
mile of Würze by six. Here we had the mortification of being detained thirteen hours by the over-

flowing of the Mülde, owing to the late excessive rains. A miserable ale-house, every corner of which was already taken up by persons in the same predicament as ourselves, was the only accommodation the place afforded. We had nothing for it then, but to make up ourselves for the night in the carriage that stood in the inn yard; not a little worried, however, by a quarrel with our postilion, who, upon our arrival, said he would give his horses a feed, and take us round by Crimma. Accordingly we enjoyed a quiet dish of tea, and made acquaintance with a Saxon lieutenant going to join his regiment at Toyau, expecting in an hour or two to proceed on our journey. But our friend the postilion, in the interval, had had such frequent recourse to the brandy bottle that, from a very good humoured, gay postilion, he had become the surliest bear I ever had to do with. Neither the threats and authority of the Office, nor our own more persuasive language could make the brute stir, so we were obliged to give it up, and be content to turn into the carriage, and await the morning. Our Saxon friend was furious, wrote to the postmaster at Würze, and entreated us to lay our complaint at the office at Dresden. We, however, on our arrival in this city, felt so indifferent in the cause of public justice, that it was only from a sense of what we owed to the advocate who had so enthu-siastically espoused our cause, that we took any further step in the matter. The Dresden office has referred us to Leipsic, which ends the affair, and fortunately so for the drunken postilion.

On our arrival, we made the usual round of visits
and presentations. At noon we accompanied Wynn
to the princes' and princesses' apartments, and were
very graciously received. Thence we went to the
elector, who talked a good deal with everybody. I
expected to be passed by, and was therefore the more
surprised when I found him very chatty with me
also, telling me, amongst other things, how pleased
he was to have made my brother's acquaintance.
But not thus condescending was his consort. She received us, as is usual, in the dining-room, the dishes
being already on the table; the grateful savour of
which had, I suppose, so sharpened her appetite, that
she would hardly allow Wynn time to pronounce our
names, and she held no conversation with anybody.

Saturday we had a supper at Wynn's; the guests
were mostly Russians, including the Princess Hohen-
zollern and her set. The Princess Troubetzkoi, who
was there, is, I think, at least by candle-light, almost
the prettiest woman I have seen on the Continent.
The Czartoriskis play the *campagnards*, and will not
join in the *raking* of the town, which I am sorry for.
At Wynn's there was, at first, but one card-table,
and that for men; but just as supper was about to be
announced, the Duchess Acurenza took it into her
head to wish to play, and a Boston was accordingly
arranged for her *Grace*.

What remains of my leave of absence I shall spend
chiefly with my friend Löwenstern's charming family
at Breisnitz, whence we shall make excursions in
La Suisse Saxonne.

Diaries—August 9*th.*—Returned to Berlin this afternoon. Heard at Dresden, what I find confirmed here, that Bonaparte has said he was neither surprised nor dissatisfied at M. de Novossiltzow's return to Russia as his mission was so unlikely to lead to any successful result. From a paragraph in the " Moniteur," intended to express his sentiments, it appears that Bonaparte is desirous of negotiating directly with England.

10*th.*—Count Bernstorff, brother of the Danish minister, has been sent to Berlin for the purpose of removing some obstacles that have arisen to the completion of the negotiation for a marriage between Prince Henry and the Danish princess. They relate to a correspondence which has been carried on between the princess and a young officer in the Danish army. The prince considers that some explanation should be forthcoming on the subject.

The vexations to which the Elector of Hesse is exposed, by the conduct of M. Bignon, and the orders of the French Government, with respect to Mr. Taylor, may lead, it is feared, to serious consequences. The king has sent a remonstrance, and has said that if any well-grounded complaint can be brought against Mr. Taylor, it would be judged of according to the established rules of the laws of nations.

The Elector and Prince Witgenstein were at Pyrmont, where Mr. Taylor also had been to pay his respects to the elector. His serene highness displayed great anxiety, and entreated Mr. Taylor to leave Pyrmont. This, at first, he declined to do, but has

since determined to return to Cassel; to remain there
for some days; to despatch a messenger to England,
and afterwards to go for some weeks to Dryburg.

The insolence of the orders sent by the French
Government, and the impetuosity of M. Bignon in
attempting to execute them, have excited both
alarm and indignation. For it is felt that it is but
a mere pretext for the subjugation of the Elector of
Hesse, and other princes, and is to end, if not checked,
in usurping the same authority in the Prussian
dominions.

11th.—A Frenchman, who described himself as *un
littérateur*, lately applied in Vienna for a passport, to
go to Hungary; but, being recognized as an officer
who had served in the last war as aide-de-camp to
General Massena, the passport was refused. Bonaparte
made this a subject of complaint, as being inconsistent
with the relations of peace and unity existing between
the two countries. The cause of the refusal was
explained, and it was added that such complaints
came with an ill grace from France, where several
Austrian officers had been arrested by the police, and
had obtained their release with the greatest difficulty
through the intervention of the Austrian embassy.
An explanation of the armaments going on in Austria
was then demanded. The answer was, they were
occasioned by those of France, where nearly three
times the number of troops were assembled beyond
those under arms in Austria.

12th.—Prince William of Brunswick having lately
had occasion to reprimand one of the young subaltern

officers of his regiment, he replied in so insolent a manner that the prince, in a moment of great irritation, struck him. The officer immediately drew his sword, attacked the prince, and wounded him. He then rushed away, to surrender, as he said, but, instead of doing so, went to his rooms, and shot himself through the head. For some reason this unfortunate affair is hushed up; and though it is well known to be a fact by every officer of this garrison, the truth of it has been denied in a way that indicates that no public notice will be taken of it. The reprimand, it has transpired, was as intemperate as the retort.

16*th*.—It has always been thought likely that General Rüchel, colonel of the regiment of Guards, and governor of Potzdam, would be named to one of the first commands, in the event of the Prussian army taking the field. He has just been appointed to succeed General Kreusemarck, who retires from the service with the rank of field-marshal, as governor of Königsberg. His nomination to this post is considered to be, in some measure, connected with the present state of affairs. But while it is asserted, on the one hand, that the king is determined to maintain the tranquillity of the north of Germany, on the other, it is denied that any armaments are in contemplation. Such, however, is the state of readiness in which the Prussian troops are maintained, that some time might elapse before any steps so openly significant would be taken, as the recall of furlough men, the dislocation of regiments, or the purchase of artillery horses.

The military magazines which, according to the constitution of this army, should always be full, in order to supply any unexpected demands, have not been completed since the peace of Basle ; owing to the high price of corn.

In the course of this year, from the failure of the last crops and the consequent want and misery of the poor, which exceed everything we know of in England in our years of scarcity, it became necessary to open these magazines, for the assistance of the provinces, when it was found that they contained very little more than was required for that purpose.

We received yesterday the account of Sir R. Calder's success which, as a commencement, we may be satisfied with, but which, if followed by no other more decisive operations against the enemy, would leave a feeling of regret that they should escape so well. However, we should still have supported the honour and superiority of our flag. The joy here is almost as general as in England, though there are some persons who do not think it prudent to proclaim it so loudly.

19th.—We are waiting anxiously for the confirmation of a report, just received, of Lord Nelson and Admiral Cornwallis having fallen in with the combined squadron, and taken sixteen sail of the line.

22nd.—The " Frankfort Gazette " contains a most insolent and scurrilous article on the subject of M. de. Novossiltzow's mission. The French resident at Frankfort would not allow the editor of that paper to publish the Russian note. A remonstrance was therefore sent to the latter for giving insertion to the above-named article, when permission was granted for the appearance of the note; with comments immediately following it, furnished to the editor by the resident.

28th.—The Russian army entered Gallicia, at Brody, on the 22nd inst. The vigour and resolution of the Emperor Alexander, and the prospect of the speedy beginning of a continental war, have caused great excitement in Berlin amongst all classes of people. Nevertheless, the course to be taken by this country will probably remain uncertain until no choice is left to it.

The Elector of Würtemburg has applied to be included in the line of neutrality, which he hopes the King of Prussia will draw for himself and his confederates. The reason for this application is, that Bonaparte had made a requisition at Darmstadt for the largest possible number of troops, with the necessary cannon and ammunition, to be got ready for service without delay, and held at the disposal of France. Although he would consider such a proposal as altogether inadmissible, yet, in case it should be made, the elector urges on the king an armed neutrality as desirable, and the more so as information had come to him from Strasburg, that quarters and magazines were preparing there for thirty thousand men.

30th and 31st.—Mr. Taylor's business has caused my being despatched on special service to Hanau— a small present compensation for a recent disappoint-

ment, which I feel much more than I care to let my
brother know. I got as far as Weimar this morning
at half-past seven. The duke, for whom I had
some information of importance, was already out
hunting. I transacted my business, therefore, with
Baron Eglestein, and left my excuses to his highness
for proceeding, as I was obliged, on my journey. A
fracture in the carriage compels me to spend a longer
time here—Eisenach—than pleases me, while it is
botched up by a smith.

The question of Mr. Taylor's recall or dismissal
remains undecided. He is in a most unpleasant
position. The elector, to a certain extent, is still
determined to resist the demand of France, and the
King of Prussia continues to approve of his determination, and to promise his protection. Mr. Taylor's
correspondence, published in the " Moniteur," proves
only, that his conduct has been unexceptionable, and
that of the French insolent and most unwarrantable ;
thus, the charges brought against him are utterly
refuted by what the French have themselves made
public. Yet they persist in their demand, and
Prince Witgenstein—the Prussian minister at Cassel
—has allowed himself, in opposition to the views
of his own Court, to encourage the elector in that
deference and submission to France which his highness's own ministers recommend. The key to this
enigma is that the prince, in the various pecuniary
and commercial speculations in which the elector is
engaged—and by which he turns to a very profitable
account the immense capital he possesses — is, in

fact, little more than his serene highness's broker. Loans, at very high interest, upon property, either real or personal; purchases of corn in large quantities, to be retailed when advantageous opportunities offer, are amongst the principal sources of this part of the elector's revenue. Prince Witgenstein receives a large percentage for his agency, and the elector employs him in preference to the Frankfort Jews ; whilst other parties concerned, consider that their engagements with the elector have an additional surety by being contracted through the medium of a Prussian minister. In the midst of all this traffic, it is not surprising that there should appear in the conduct of the elector so little of dignity or consistency, or on the part of Prince Witgenstein so strong a repugnance to see his electoral highness purchase either, at the risk of disturbing so lucrative a business. The King of Prussia, although he has repeatedly assured the elector that he will not suffer him to be molested in consequence of his continuing to receive Mr. Taylor at his Court, yet says that he cannot, with that object in view, send troops into Hesse beforehand, nor can he prevent the elector from yielding, if he thinks proper, to the views of his own ministers, or to defer to the private opinions of Prince Witgenstein. As the elector himself will not adopt, it is clear, any more decisive line of conduct towards Mr. Taylor until forced to it, my business is, to persuade that gentleman to leave Hanau, and put the elector to the test, by returning to Cassel, and, remaining quietly at his post; allowing nothing, short of His Majesty's commands, to remove him.

Hanau, September 3rd.—I reached this at five yesterday evening ; gave Mr. Taylor an account of all that was going on at Berlin, and explained to him our reason for desiring his return to Cassel. He read all the papers I brought him, and, after discussing the subject, he determined on returning to his post. We set off together this evening, and expect to be at Cassel early to-morrow.

7th.—Mr. Taylor has resumed his residence at Cassel without let or hindrance. He is to remain long enough to incite the French, if they are determined to oppose his stay at this Court, to some fresh act of violence. Bernadotte's army is encamped round Cassel, and a very fine sight it is; for the town and environs are exceedingly pretty, and the French encampment certainly lends the charm of animation to a very picturesque spot. The elector had sent a message to Bernadotte demanding an explanation of the formation of an army round Cassel. The General answered that it was not intended to molest his electoral highness, or to invade his territory, but merely to form a camp of observation in that quarter.

The elector is also assembling a camp of sixteen thousand men, with which he intends to defend the entrance to his country, and, in case of necessity, to fall back to Eichsfeld, where he would be joined, he expected, by a sufficient number of Prussian troops to resist the progress of the French. But General Berna-

dotte's army is supposed to be destined to join that
under General Marmont, and to act against Austria
in the empire.

The general opinion at Cassel is, that a direct attempt to force Prussia into a war with France would
be unsuccessful, and it is equally probable that the
king would not, for the sake of preventing any
military operations from Stralsund, risk the consequences of a war with Russia.

Berlin, Sept. 12*th.*—I returned from my mission to
Cassel to-day, and find great excitement prevailing.
War is the general topic. How Prussia is to stand
aloof nobody knows, except, perhaps, the king.
General Duroc is here, and the little man is no
doubt doing his best to turn the mouths of the
Prussian cannon against us. He pays great court to
the queen ; and there is a story afloat that, having
greatly admired a scarf which Her Majesty herself
had embroidered, she requested his acceptance of it
for Madame Duroc, who is the daughter of M.
Hervas, formerly the Spanish Chargé d'Affaires at
this Court. The General arrived here on the 1st
inst., having left Boulogne on the 25th ult. Part of
the army of Boulogne had begun its march towards
the Rhine on the same day, and Bonaparte himself
had left, with the same destination.

13*th.*—Similar demands to those made at Darmstadt have been extended to the Electorates of
Bavaria, Würtemberg, and Baden. The French
ministers at those Courts were authorized to state
that Bonaparte having determined that they should

not remain neutral in the impending war, it rested
with the electors to decide whether they would
declare for or against him. At Stutgard, M. Didelôt,
the French minister, added, from himself, that he
would not require an immediate answer, but in the
course of a few days would do himself the honour
of waiting on his electoral highness to receive his
decision.

The elector naturally feels a great repugnance to
declaring himself against the emperor, at the same
time he cannot but be aware that his country is at
the mercy of whichever power should first occupy it.
He seems to rely but little on the intervention of the
King of Prussia, though he has again very urgently
solicited it.

It is the general opinion that it is become impossible for this country to remain neutral; and though
it cannot be precisely known to what aims General
Duroc's exertions may be now directed, yet a variety
of circumstances favour the suspicion that he is the
bearer of a message, perhaps less offensive in form,
but not very different in effect, from that which the
princes of southern Germany have received.

Count Haugwitz has been sent for from Silesia,
and M. Lombard has returned from Leghorn, where
he has been for the benefit of his health.

Great complaints are made of the conduct and
threatening language of the Russian officers, of the
armaments, and of the proceedings generally on the
side of Swedish Pomerania.

Orders have been given to put eighty thousand

men on the war establishment, besides the whole of the artillery in garrison at Berlin. Some other regiments will be added, making altogether a force of ninety thousand men.

The accounts received of the movements of the French troops, and the assembling of Bernadotte's corps round the city of Hanover, give rise to the suspicion that Prussia intends to take military possession of the electorate. M. de Hardenberg asserts that the French have made no such proposition, but that if made it would be acceded to; it being for the advantage of the country as well as for England, to whom it would be restored at a general peace.

The alarm is great lest the Russians should attempt to force a passage through the Prussian territory. Advantage will perhaps be taken of it to remove the obstacles which this country has threatened to oppose to the operations of the allies on the side of Swedish Pomerania.

General Marfelt arrived yesterday from Vienna, for the purpose of urging the King of Prussia to join his forces to those of the allies.

15th.—An express from Munich this morning informs us that the Austrians had crossed the frontier on the 9th, and that Count Walmoden, who commanded the advanced party of Uhlans, went forward to parley with the commanding officer of the Bavarian troops, who destroyed the bridge on the Inn and retired. The Elector of Bavaria arrived at Anspach on the 11th, on his way to Würzburg.

16th.—The Elector of Darmstadt has represented to
this Court the distress of his position, in consequence
of his being required to hold, at Bonaparte's disposal,
three thousand infantry, some artillery, and one
thousand horses. But as the king can afford neither
help nor protection to the princes of South Germany,
the elector is advised to place his valuables in a
place of safety, and is offered a residence in Franconia,
for himself and the electress.

17th.—The officers of the garrisons of Berlin and
Potzdam have not only been ordered not to ask for
leave of absence, but to get their camp equipage ready
for service without delay. It is also certain that
battalion guns have been sent off for the use of the
three regiments of infantry nearest the Mecklenburg
frontier, together with a detachment of foot artillery,
six guns, and two howitzers, and another detachment
of horse artillery, eight guns, and thirty-two powder-
wagons. It has been remarked that the ·cart-
ridges preparing in this arsenal are for grape and
grenades; none for cannon of large calibre. All
this seems to point to the operations on the side of
Stralsund, which are no longer a secret, as the
Russian Admiralty has engaged transports throughout the Baltic for that port.

19th and 20th.—The Courts of Copenhagen, Dresden, and Cassel, have been urged to accede to the
neutrality of Prussia, and to set on foot a respectable
force for the support of that system. But Denmark
will be cautious of acting contrary to the interests of
Russia; Saxony will follow her usual policy, and

seek to gain time; while the question is already decided for the Elector of Hesse—as we learn by express that Marshal Bernadotte marched through Cassel, on the morning of the 17th, with seventeen thousand men. He previously sent a message to the elector to say that, as. the peace of Germany was still inviolate, he requested a passage for his troops through the Hessian territory *to return to France.*

The request was granted. The elector put the garrison of Cassel under arms, and the rest of his troops were drawn up at a short distance from the town. The French army, with Bernadotte at their head, then marched by the elector, rendering him all military honours. It must have been a very imposing spectacle, and I almost regret not to have seen it. The elector was not, as has been reported in Berlin, desired by the king to consent to this measure—he has now, however, given in his adhesion to the neutral system of Prussia, with what probability of abiding by it remains to be seen.

Permission is asked for the march of the Russian army through a part of the Prussian territory; and every argument is urged to move the king to make common cause with the powers allied against Bonaparte. But the pernicious counsels of his confidential advisers confirm him in the obstinate tenacity with which, when pressed to adopt a more energetic and dignified attitude, he pleads, and clings to his system of neutrality. The king has said, also, that if the Russians do cross the frontiers of his dominions he will consider it the signal for war. He has ordered

the whole of his army to be put on the war establishment, and has determined on immediately seeking an
interview with the emperor at Brzesco : and on this
will depend the final decision of the king. But that
he will decide for taking active measures against the
common enemy, few, if any, are so sanguine as to
expect.

Count Haugwitz sets out to-night for Vienna with
the hope, it is said, that he may be able to prevent
the commencement of hostilities; but it is whispered
about that he is despatched on a fruitless errand, in
order that M. de Hardenberg may be freed, for a
time, from a troublesome colleague.

22nd.—The French have left between four and
five thousand men in Hanover, and reinforcements
are shortly expected. They took with them two
thousand five hundred horses, and about one hundred
and fifty thousand dollars in cash and bills of exchange. The States were ordered to provide for the
march of the troops through Hesse, where everything
was to be paid for. It is believed they are gone
to Frankfort.

23rd.—Further advices state that they appear to
have determined to evacuate the electorate of
Hanover altogether. General Ebelé, who commanded
the artillery, and two thousand men who were left
in the city, set out, five days ago, after having
demanded from the States fifty thousand dollars for
the gunpowder he left, and five hundred louis
d'ors for his own purse. Large quantities of gunpowder have likewise been given to different con-

tractors in exchange for the horses with which they. have agreed to furnish the French army.

24th.—General Marfelt set out this morning on his return to Vienna. He has been treated with the greatest distinction by the king, who has always shown a particular esteem for him. He was presented with His Majesty's picture, set in diamonds of more than usual value. The General, however, had no better success in obtaining a favourable decision from the king than those who before him trod the same ground. Perhaps he made some impression upon him ; for General Marfelt possesses, in an eminent degree, the talent of developing, and placing in various and striking points of view, the arguments he employs; and being thoroughly master of his subject, he put it before the king in so clear a light, and with that mild earnestness of manner that characterizes him, that His Majesty had not a word to say for himself. He, indeed, improved upon everything General Marfelt said against Bonaparte, in favour of our opposition to him, of the necessity of union, &c., but always ended with, " I cannot decide upon war."

Two days after this audience, an answer came from Vienna to the proposal brought to Berlin by Duroc. It states, with respect to the independence of Switzerland, Holland, and the German empire—which Bonaparte had offered to guarantee—that it is not supposed that any additional security can be derived from new engagements, if those already contracted by France should be insufficient. That the actual

status quo in Italy which Bonaparte wished to see
maintained—reserving to himself his late usurpations
—was so far from being admissible, that it was the
very object of the armaments now going on in
Austria; and, finally, that His Imperial Majesty was
so closely connected with the Emperor of Russia, that
he could listen to no terms that would not give equal
satisfaction to that sovereign. The same messenger
brought the intelligence that the Elector of Bavaria,
after a short negotiation with Prince Schwartzenberg,
had agreed to put his troops under the command of
the Austrian general, who by this time had taken up
his intended position on the Lech. Doubts are,
however, entertained of the elector's sincerity, which
casts a damper on news that would otherwise be most
welcome.

25*th.*—A courier has brought a second letter from
the Emperor of Russia, again urging the king to
make common cause with the allied powers, and
again requesting a passage through his territory for
the Russian army. As an inducement to join the
allies, Russia holds out to the king the probability
of recovering for Prussia her late possessions on the
left bank of the Rhine. But this bait is by no
means an enticing one to His Prussian Majesty. He
sees in it only a prospect of being brought into
contact with France, and of being exposed to endless
disputes with Bonaparte. However, this budget of
proposals, entreaties, and requests, was unfolded
before him two days ago, and has caused him, no
doubt, many an uncomfortable moment. It is

believed that *he*, in his present anxious state of indecision, would be easily overcome, if his advisers were
not divided; and though the honestest half may be
on our side, yet I am afraid it is the weakest. But
decide he must, and that very shortly, between a
war with Russia or a war with France. M. Alopeus
is ordered to allow three days for deliberation, and
then to deliver the same Declaration—*mutatis mu-
tandis*—that Romonowski presented at Vienna.

The head-quarters of the Russian army were advanced on the 15th from Brzesco to the Pelica, and
the troops will probably begin their march across south
Prussia and north Silesia into Lusatia and Saxony.
The Prussian armaments in those parts are certainly
not sufficient to oppose their entry. The first operations would be to disarm the regiments one after the
other, and take possession of the whole country east
of Warsaw. Let us hope, however, that things may
take a more favourable turn.

The attention of this Government seems to be
chiefly directed towards Stralsund.

26th.—A report is afloat to-day—and full credence
is everywhere given to it—that the Russian general,
Buxhövden, arrived privately at Potzdam, on Thursday, and after a long interview with the King of
Prussia, which had no more satisfactory result than
that of others which preceded it, returned immediately to his post at Grodno.

27th.—Meanwhile, General Duroc and the French
minister seem to be very calmly waiting the result
of the present state of agitation and uncertainty into

which the lamentable indecision of the king has
plunged, J may say, nearly the whole of Europe.
Their couriers and messengers are constantly passing
to and fro between this and Paris, and, doubtless,
they are fully informed of all that is going on.

It has transpired that Duroc has been commissioned to offer the king a hundred thousand men and
a considerable subsidy, in case he should decide
on acceding to Bonaparte's proposal of an alliance
with France—and thus become involved in a war
with the two imperial courts—besides a large increase of territory on the successful termination of
the war, including the whole or greater part of the
Electorate of Hanover.   He can, of course, afford to
be very liberal in his promises ; and the facility
with which he no doubt flatters himself of being
able to perform them at the expense of others, or of
leaving them unperformed, renders no excess in the
generosity of his offers incredible.

But the king rather desires to stand aloof, equally
from Bonaparte and the allies.   His idea is to preserve the " imposing attitude," which the Prussians,
generally, believe their country to have now
assumed.

28*th*.—It is announced that fifty-three thousand
horses are wanted for the service of the different
regiments.   The first *corps d'armée* to be assembled
is General Kalkreuth's.   His head-quarters are to
be fixed at Pasewalk, a few miles to the N.W. of
Stettin, and a short distance from the frontier of
Mecklenburg and Swedish Pomerania.   The Duke

of Brunswick will shortly take the command of the different armies.

It is generally credited that a secret treaty exists between Bonaparte and the princes of south Germany. The Elector of Bavaria, especially, is suspected of being in league with the enemy.

29th.—The march of the Russian army through the Prussian territory is suspended until after the interview which the emperor has proposed to the king. But it is under the supposition that this Court will ultimately accede to the views of Russia.* The Lombard interest is, however, just now completely in the ascendant; besides which, military men, generally, are much piqued at the pretensions of Russia, and a feeling of resentment against her has lately sprung up amongst them; so that a contest with that power would perhaps be popular, as far as such a term is applicable to a country and government like this.

We are particularly anxious for letters from England, where, as here, all eyes must be turned towards the King of Prussia. The enemy is profiting by the delay which his wavering policy has caused in the proceedings of the allies, and much damage to our cause may result from it.

Our chief seems anxious, at this critical moment in the fortunes of Europe, to distinguish himself by vexatious changes in the Office, which make him extremely unpopular, and petty arrangements respecting the private correspondence of the foreign

* See Appendix, No. 8.

ministers, which occasion inconvenience and annoyance to them, and probably will not be a saving of five shillings a year to the country.

The expense of living at Berlin having greatly increased of late, the Russian minister has in consequence received a large addition to his salary.

Oct. 1st.—The king has granted an increase of five dollars per month to the pay of the subaltern officers. A corps of observation is to be formed at Sieratz, between Breslau and Warsaw; but no regiments have yet left their usual quarters for that or any other destination that has been named.

It is now positively known that an engagement was long ago entered into between the Elector of Bavaria and the French Government for the junction of his army with that of Bernadotte. The latter is arrived at Würzburg; the Bavarians are stationed in and about Augsburg, in the Upper Palatinate, where there is easy access for one column at a time across the territory of Nürnberg, without touching that of His Prussian Majesty.

The elector received Bernadotte on his entrance into Würzburg, and a council was immediately held. The next day the citadel was occupied by a French garrison, and Bernadotte took the command of the Bavarian troops. M. de Gravoureuth, the elector's war minister, demanded a free passage through Anspach for the Bavarians retiring from Augsburg to Würzburg, and asserted that General Mack had declared his determination not to respect the Prussian territory. The president of the regency of

Anspach immediately wrote to the General for an explanation. And he in very unequivocal and energetic terms convicted the Bavarian minister of falsehood. The treachery of the elector excites great indignation at Berlin and other parts of Germany.

A strong corps of Austrians is marching towards Augsburg, and other troops, that were destined for the Grand Army, are advancing in the same direction. The Emperor of Germany is at Stoskarh. The order to halt, which it was reported had been given to a part of the Austrian army, was, it appears, to one column only that interfered with the line of march of the rest. Its march was resumed twelve hours afterwards.

There are probable, though not certain, accounts of a corps of Austrians having advanced from Feldkirch, and occupied Coire.

The arrival of a British force is anxiously looked for, and its occupation of Hanover and Holland much desired. In the latter country it is supposed that it would have no less success than in the electorate; for the Dutch are said to be impatiently waiting for deliverance from the yoke of the French, and to have drawn together a military force in the town of Amsterdam to defend it against them.

2nd.— Marshals Bernadotte and Marmont have effected the junction of their armies, and are proceeding towards Franconia. The Austrians are hastily throwing up works round Ulm, and the peasants of that part of the country had been em-

ployed for that purpose. The Elector of Würtemberg has complained of this, and of the requisitions,
extortions, and oppression of the Austrians in the
heart of his dominions ; as well as of their forcing on
the inhabitants, in payment of the commodities taken
from them, paper that had no currency in his country ;
and of their seizing his subjects and compelling them
to work at intrenchments, formed even out of the
electoral states.

The Austrian light troops had advanced, on the
25th ult., as far as Nagold, eight German miles from
Strasburg, and would be able to cut off a corps of
Bavarians assembled on the Danube, and prevent
them from joining the French.

The French army crossed the Rhine on the 29th
ult., in four columns.

5th.—Prince Dalgoruski, the Emperor of Russia's
aide-de-camp, arrived yesterday with a letter to the
king. His Imperial Majesty was at Brzesco, but
intended to leave on the 30th for Pulawy, a magnificent country-seat belonging to Prince Czartoriski,
which is destined to be for some time the head-
quarters of the 2nd Russian army. The troops
assembled at Brzesco consist of forty thousand men.
Several regiments are now on their way to Sieratz.

7th.—Several acts of violence have been committed by the French troops, since their arrival in
the neighbourhood of Würzburg, in the villages
within the territory of the margraviate of Anspach.
Remonstrances were sent to the French commander,
by whom suitable apologies were offered ; and

Bernadotte declared that the first of his soldiers who should be guilty of such irregularities should be shot.

Notwithstanding this, on the 3rd inst., two French officers rode into Uffenheim, and presented an order to the Prussian magistrates to furnish quarters for twenty thousand men. Immediately they sent off a messenger to Marshal Bernadotte, requiring an explanation of this extraordinary proceeding. Before the messenger returned, four regiments of cavalry, under General Kellerman, appeared before the village of Sickenhausen, where an officer with twenty-five hussars had been posted. He at once challenged the advanced guard of the French column ; informed them that the territory they were about to enter was a part of the Prussian dominions, and that he had orders to oppose the passage of any force that might attempt it. General Kellerman replied that he had received positive orders from Marshal Bernadotte to advance, and that with the force he had under him resistance to his march would be useless. The march was then sounded, and the French regiments passed by the Prussian detachment. The officer requested and received from General Kellerman a written attestation of his having done his duty in attempting to defend his post. The General added to it that, he himself acted under the express orders of Marshal Bernadotte, whom he supposed to have sufficient reasons for giving them.

In the evening of the same day Bernadotte took up his quarters at the town of Windestein. M. de

Schaukman, president of the regency, protested against this step. Bernadotte was profuse in expressions of respect for His Prussian Majesty, and of his extreme regret that his orders, given to him by Bonaparte himself, were so peremptory in their terms that he dared not disobey them.

The column of cavalry was to proceed by Anspach and Gunterhausen; the Gallo-Batavian army, under General Marmont, by Morgentheim; the Bavarians by Fürth, and the whole to rendezvous at Neuburg, on the Danube; whence, it is supposed, they intend to fall upon the rear of the Austrians, while Bonaparte himself will attack them in front.

When intelligence of these proceedings of the French was brought to the king he was very violently affected by it, and in the first ebullition of his anger gave orders for the immediate dismissal of the French minister and General Duroc. Upon reflection he countermanded them, but summoned a council to deliberate on the course he should take. Could he but be kept long enough in this frame of mind some good to the common cause might result from it. But if this new insult to the crown of Prussia should excite merely momentary resentment, instead of rousing him to feel the necessity of vindicating the honour and dignity of his crown and sovereignty, and of doing it effectually, Prussia will hereafter sink into the miserable predicament into which Spain and Naples are fallen. However, the event has raised *our* spirits, and we allow ourselves to hope that good may eventually come of it.

8th.—All that we now know of the Austrians is that the advanced guard, which was to oppose the before-named corps, had reached Augsburg, and had been reinforced by about six thousand men, chiefly cavalry from Bohemia. The last intelligence of the Russian army, under General Kutuzow, was dated the 27th ult., when it was crossing the road from Prague to Vienna, at Jagelsdorf, five German miles from that capital.

9th.—Whether the interview of the sovereigns of Russia and Prussia will take place at present seems doubtful. The king cannot now, it is thought, absent himself from his capital, and there is no certainty that the emperor will advance in this direction; though advantage having been taken of the late events in Anspach to obtain permission for the Russian army to cross the north part of Silesia, the interview may, without inconvenience, be postponed.

Field-Marshal Möllendorf, yesterday morning, made public at parade the unexampled violation of Prussian territory that had just taken place at Anspach by order of Bonaparte. The recital of the flagrant circumstances attending it seemed to infuse new spirit and animation into both officers and men, and they heard with eager satisfaction that they were soon likely to turn their arms against the invader of their country. This news was rapidly circulated amongst the people, and joy is undisguisedly shown at the prospect of Prussia uniting her efforts with those of the allied powers to crush the common enemy of the peace and independence of Europe. People exchange in the streets congratulations on the subject, and the genuineness of the sentiments generally expressed cannot be doubted, except in those persons avowedly devoted to the French interests.

M. de Schaukman sent immediately by express to Vienna an account of what had taken place at Anspach. It will therefore be known at that Court that some support may probably be looked for from this quarter. But news has just come in, of Bonaparte himself having got as far as Ludwigslust and taken the command of the Würtemburg troops, which has greatly lowered the hopes of those who looked to Prussia for energetic action on the side of the allies.

The Landgrave of Darmstadt on being summoned to send his contingent of troops to the columns of the French army, disbanded them, and retired with a small body of light horse to Giesen.

It is conjectured that Bonaparte must have taken the step of entering Prussian territory, and there concentrating his troops for the purpose of striking a decisive blow at Austria, from having been misinformed by his agents of the present state of the relations subsisting between Russia and Prussia. They may have been misled by the circumstance of the openly declared intention of the former to march her army through this country, and that of the latter to regard it as a signal for war—which would compel her to accept the alliance proposed by France.

10*th*.—General Kalkreuth sets off to-morrow to arrange with the emperor the march of the Russian army quartered near Pilawy, the king having consented to its passage through his dominions. It will be under the command of General Michelsen, and will take the route of Warsaw and Breslau.

The army of Stralsund is also declared to be at liberty to proceed in its operations unmolested by this country. It is, however, much to be regretted that General Tolstoi, who commands it, cannot leave Stralsund without further orders, as the Prussians will doubtless take military possession of Hanover, unless a Russian or British force should occupy it before them.

The interview, which it was proposed should take place at Cracow, between the two Emperors and the King of Prussia is now finally set aside, as the latter, under the present state of things, cannot leave Berlin.

11*th*.—In to-day's " Berlin Gazette," under date of Anspach, it is stated that the Bavarians, in their march through the margraviate, committed every kind of excess. They broke open the royal store-houses and supplied themselves from them with the necessaries the king's officers had refused to give them, and placed a garrison of three thousand men in Nürnberg. General Tauentzien, who commanded at Anspach, remonstrated strongly with Bernadotte, and insisted on seeing the orders he said he had received from Bonaparte. The French marshal complied with his demand, and also told General Tauentzien he might be quite easy on his own account, for Bonaparte had written him word that the whole measure had been previously concerted with the Court of Berlin.

General Tauentzien took the judicious step of sending an officer to General Mack to acquaint him with the march of the French columns and the circumstances under which it occurred. By this means the evident tendency of this falsehood will have failed in its effect.

These instances of French perfidy have made their due impression in this city.

Bonaparte was at Heilbron, by the latest accounts. The French army, in great force, marched through Stutgard and Ludwigsburg, in defiance of the elector's request that they should go round those towns.

15*th.*—Bonaparte has written to the king in a tone of insolent superiority exceeding anything he has yet ventured to adopt, even towards this country, and in terms altogether so disrespectful that His Majesty is greatly displeased. It has been made known to M. Laforêt, and General Duroc, that the king considers himself absolved from every promise he has made the French Government, in consequence of the late proceedings in Anspach; and that the Russian army would therefore cross his country, and part of his own army occupy the electorate of Hanover. The French negotiator suggested that some arrangement might probably be made for the delivery of Hanover to the king; and, extraordinary as the project seems, there is an idea entertained that the Prussians may occupy the country, and a French garrison remain in the fortress of Hameln.

16th.—The Prussian army will be assembled at four different stations. The largest corps, seventy thousand strong, in Franconia, under Prince Höhenlohe. The second, force unknown, at Hildesheim and Halberstadt, under the Duke of Brunswick The command of the third will be given to the Elector of Hesse, who will join his own troops to it. It will be stationed in Westphalia, in Münster, Minden, and Paderborn.

General Blücher, who commands in the last-named province, has been ordered to allow of no further transports of French troops or baggage.

He is an officer of much talent, spirit, and resolution, extremely well disposed towards us and our cause, and will probably have, under the Elector of Hesse, the command of the operations of the Westphalian corps.

The fourth army is to be the reserve; and of this the king will take the command. It will be composed of the household troops; the garrison of Potzdam; the regiment of gendarmes; the grenadiers of the Berlin regiments, and several other corps now on their march from Pomerania. The king has often said that, from motives of ambition, he would never draw the sword; but surely a war more just or necessary than that in which Prussia is about to engage could never have been undertaken.

The Russian army, under General Michelsen, will form the right wing of that commanded by Prince

Höhenlohe. The communication between the Russian and Prussian head-quarters will be frequent, and it is desired that the Austrian Government should send an officer to communicate as much of their plans as may be necessary for military concert between the two countries.

It is inquired, with great anxiety, what the views of Great Britain may be with regard to the force which was said to have been destined for an expedition to the Continent, but which the last letters from England reported as not likely to be employed this season.

Very early this morning intelligence was brought here from Würzburg and Ratisbon that a corps of Austrian grenadiers—differently estimated at from eight to eleven battalions—had been surrounded by the French at Wertingen, a town between the Lech and the Danube, and made prisoners with their colours, artillery, &c.

M. Otto is at Würzburg with the elector. Letters thence describe the rapid and irresistible progress of the French armies, which, it is added, are to replace the elector, without delay, in his residence at Munich. These accounts are, however, in the usual bombastic style of the French reports, and are a good deal confused, perhaps designedly so.

Whether the Austrian corps was taken by General Murat's column, which is said to have passed the Danube near Ulm, or by that under Davoust, cannot be discovered. Probably, the disaster has been exaggerated, though something of the sort must,

unfortunately, have occurred ; for subsequent letters
from Swabia speak of the passage of Austrian prisoners through that country. If French accounts
may be credited—amongst which is a letter from
Bonaparte to the Elector of Bavaria—their columns
are in possession of both sides of the Danube. The
Austrians made an unsuccessful attempt to destroy
the bridge of Donauwerth. Bernadotte passed the
river at Ingoldstadt, the Bavarians at Kelheim, and
both corps were marching to Landschut. Bonaparte
had ordered an attack on General Kienmeyer, who
had retired to Aicha.

The direct communication of the Austrian army
with Germany is interrupted, but if, as stated from
Ratisbon, their head-quarters were at Guntzburg,
much of the preceding tableau would be changed.

If the Austrian general can succeed in concentrating his different corps before they are attacked in
detail, Bonaparte may have cause to repent of the
precipitation with which he has advanced, without
magazines, and with comparatively little artillery.

Some apprehension is felt lest the Russians, under
General Kutusow, who were transported in wagons,
at the rate of six to eight German miles a day, and
consequently, without cavalry, should not have been
able to retire behind the Inn, where the main Austrian army was endeavouring to gain a position.

It is already, most unfortunately, very perceptible
that the French faction, which exercises its pernicious influence near the person of the king, has
succeeded in abating the resentment His Majesty so

keenly felt, and so warmly expressed, when he first
heard of the insult put upon him by Bonaparte,
But the want of energy that so lamentably marks
the character of the King of Prussia; his dread of
plunging into a greater embarrassment than that he
conceives submission to the encroachments and overbearing insolence of the French to be; his dread, in
a word, of encountering a power so formidable as
that of Bonaparte, has afforded advantages to those
about him who are daily pleading the cause of
France, in opposition to the opinions of his friends
and advisers. These, see with regret the humiliation
of their country, and urge for active measures that
she may retrieve her position; but their efforts are
ever counteracted by the insidious counsels of subordinate agents, and they have the utmost difficulty in
prevailing on the king to follow a line of conduct in
only the smallest degree consistent with his dignity
and honour.

17*th*.—An intercepted correspondence has made
known certain schemes of Bonaparte for the revo-
lutionizing of Poland. His emissaries, under various
disguises, are seeking to disseminate opinions, and to
awake dormant feelings unfavourable to the present
rulers of that country.

One of the letters made public, is from Bonaparte
to Lucien. In order to induce the latter to repudiate
his wife, who was the widow of a Paris stockbroker,
Bonaparte promises to provide for her when divorced
by giving her a principality in Germany. As Lucien
and his wife are just gone to America, he is sup-

posed to have turned an unwilling ear to some previous proposal of the same kind.

The king is at present greatly displeased with the conduct of Prince Henry, who has very unequivocally declared his dislike to the marriage that was arranged to take place next year between him and a princess of Denmark. She is supposed to be deeply attached to a lover far below royal rank. The explanation given of the young lady's correspondence with a subaltern officer has been more satisfactory to the king than to the prince. The marriage is now finally broken off, and much surprise is expressed that Count Bernstorff, after such a rejection, should prolong his stay in Berlin. He had recently returned from Travemünde, where he had been to consult the prince royal as to the part Denmark would take in the impending war. The prince has replied that Denmark will preserve a perfect neutrality. The delivery of this message may serve to retard the departure of Count Bernstorff, and to veil, in some degree, the unsuccessful result of the matrimonial mission.

An account is just come in of a second advanced corps being cut off near Ulm, which is thought to prove that General Mack is retiring with the main body of his army behind the Inn, and that he may be able to effect there a junction with the Russian army.

Another account is received. General Mack has concentrated his army on the left bank of the Iller, with the rear towards Strasburg. Bonaparte has

posted himself on the opposite bank. A general
engagement was expected on the 14th.

Bernadotte entered Munich on the 13th.

Reports are flowing in apace, vague and con-
tradictory.

18*th.*—An express is sent off to Husum to detain
the packet, and a Prussian order to the postmasters,
for horses to be in readiness all along the road. I
leave Berlin this evening for London, with the news
that the king has at last determined on various
military operations; the first of which is, to send an
army to take possession of Hanover, for the purpose
of restoring it to His Britannic Majesty. The king
is also ready to enter into a treaty of concert, and
to arrange for an eventual subsidy for himself and
the German princes, his confederates. If this is
not entirely satisfactory, it is more than we have
dared to hope for; and Bonaparte must now be
reduced if the Austrians do but make a tolerable
defence. If they are defeated, this country will be
the chief bulwark against the overthrow of the
whole Continent. So much is this felt to be the
case, that the partial losses which Austria has
suffered have produced here rather a good effect
than otherwise.

The Prussian army is in very fine order, and is
very well disposed. The Anspach affair has done
wonders in rousing the spirit of the troops. Yet
the ebbing and flowing in the disposition of the
Government, according to the circumstances of
greater or less encouragement in the course of

events, and the more or less success of the intrigues
of the French party, must still be taken into consideration.

Harwich, Oct. 23rd, 1805.

Letters.—You will have heard from General
Ramsey of the speed with which—bad roads and
dark nights considered—I reached Husum. A fine
breeze was blowing, and I went on board immediately. I am now just arrived, and find here two
messengers, with despatches for Mr. Pierrepont and
the commander of the Russian army, waiting for a
change in the wind that has brought me over so
swiftly. While the horses are being put to the
chaise, I write this line to send by one of the messengers, and then set off instantly for London.

London, Oct. 24th.—I arrived in town a little before
ten o'clock last night, and went directly to the Office.
Mr. Ward was out of town, and Mr. Hammond over
the way at Mr. Pitt's, where a council had been
sitting which Lord Mulgrave had just left. I therefore sent to Mr. H. to inform him of my arrival. He
immediately crossed over and took the despatches,
and shortly after a message came from Mr. Pitt,
desiring to see me. He received me in the civilest
manner; said your despatches were highly satisfactory, and seemed in great spirits from reading
the good news you had sent him. After congratulating me on being the bearer of it, and expressing his satisfaction at the expedition I had used
on my journey, he questioned me as to the general

spirit that reigned at Berlin, the march of the Russians from Stralsund, and what was known at the former place relative to the reported defeat of the Austrians.

On the first of these points I left him little to desire, assuring him that nothing could be better than the spirit that animatéd all ranks of people at the present moment, or more general than the deep sense entertained by them of the insult offered to Prussia by the recent proceedings of the French at Anspach.

On the second, I could only repeat the intelligence received at Berlin on the day I left it; adding what I had learnt on the road—that the advanced guard of the Russians was expected at Schwerin on the evening of the 18th or 19th.

With regard to the business of Wertingen, I told him that the only knowledge you had at Berlin on the subject was derived from French reports, on which, from the vagueness and uncertainty of their tone, little reliance could be placed. It was supposed, however, that the successes of the French at Wertingen and Ulm were greatly exaggerated, but that if the news of this check of the Austrians had had any particular effect at Berlin it was rather favourable to the common cause than otherwise, by showing the necessity for prompt and vigorous measures.

I had been with Mr. Pitt more than half an hour when he said he would not detain me any longer that night, as I should probably not be sorry to get a little rest, but that to-day, at one o'clock, Lord Mulgrave would be very glad to see me. Accordingly I went, but his lordship was engaged, and I saw only the two under secretaries, who were both remarkably civil.

25th.—I returned to the Office to-day by Lord Mulgrave's appointment, and had a long conversation with him. His reception of me was as gratifying as that I had met with from Mr. Pitt. He began by expressing his extreme satisfaction at the receipt of the welcome intelligence contained in your despatches, as well as at the clearness and fulness with which you had gone into details, leaving him, he said, little to inquire. There were, however, one or two expressions in them on which he wished for some information; and he then adverted, with evident anxiety, to that part of your conversation with Baron Hardenberg relative to the delivering over of Hanover to the king by Prussia. He observed that that might possibly bear two constructions, and wished to know if it was to be the result of any future arrangement at the close of the war, or whether the King of Prussia would be ready to carry out his intention as soon as a proper force should be sent to take possession of the electorate; hinting to me that *that* was the destination of the expedition now nearly ready to sail. I answered, that I was not able to give him a positive assurance to that effect, but I certainly understood that such was the intention of the Prussian Government. Another point on which, he said, he did not feel himself

perfectly at ease, was the idea which Prussia held
out of adopting an armed mediation; and he desired
to know whether I considered it merely a pretext
made use of for gaining time and concentrating her
forces, or that such a line of conduct would eventually be pursued. I thought myself justified in
stating that nothing further could be intended by it,
and that from the general spirit of indignation which
pervaded the whole kingdom, I considered war, on the
part of Prussia, as almost inevitable.

His lordship mentioned, in terms of great approbation, the conduct of Baron Hardenberg. It was
his conviction, he said, that had it depended on his
Excellency, things would long ago have taken a
very different turn. He then expressed some anxiety
as to the stability of that minister's present position,
and asked me on what several hints in your late
correspondence were founded, from which he had
been led to infer that a change of administration was
probable. I ventured to assure him that, however
trying and critical M. de Hardenberg's situation
may, at times, have been, he now stood upon very
firm ground. That it could not be denied that there
was a moment last year—alluding to the business of
Sir George Rumbold—when the popular clamour
ran high against him, and when it was feared that
his advice to the king would be overruled by the
.counsels and secret influence of the cabinet secretaries.
But that the momentary loss of credit he then
experienced had been amply made up to him by the
reputation which the success of his interference on

that occasion had gained him, and which had enabled him to combat successfully the subsequent efforts of his enemies to withdraw the king's confidence from him. And I assured his lordship that the hints he referred to must have proceeded rather from your know-ledge of the many difficulties the Prussian minister has to encounter than from any actual indications of an approaching change in the government. Lord Mulgrave then put many questions to me respecting the character of the King of Prussia himself, which I answered as faithfully as I could, referring him at the same time to a separate despatch I recollect on that subject of the 17th September, 1804. But I should observe, that he seemed to have mistaken the hitherto wavering and timid policy of that monarch for cowardice, and spoke of him as a man deficient in personal bravery.

He then mentioned your Russian colleague, of whose abilities he seemed to have but a very poor opinion. He attributed the want of confidence shown him by his Court to his attachment to French prin-ciples. The younger Alopeus he thought far superior to him, and said he was looked upon at St. Petersburg in a very different light from his brother. He was surprised, he said, that the cleverer one should be sent to Stockholm, when his abilities might be turned to so much more profitable account at Berlin.

I told him, in answer, that no one could be more thoroughly anti-Gallican than the elder M. Alopeus, and that, if we might judge from the general opinion entertained of him on the Continent, he was by no means deficient either in talent or experience.

His lordship was also very anxious to know the real dispositions of the Duke of Brunswick; and I soon found that both he and Mr. Pitt had paid more than ordinary attention to those parts of your correspondence which had any reference to his serene highness, and particularly to one passage where you speak of the fairness of his *language*. Here I could only repeat your own expressions, corroborating them, however, by calling to his lordship's recollection the exertions of his serene highness to induce the king to allow of the passage of the Russian troops through his dominions.

Speaking of the indignation excited at Berlin by the late violation of Prussian territory, Lord Mulgrave observed, how very ill-advised and injudicious a measure it was, on the part of the Russians, to think of forcing their passage—a measure which, however weak the conduct of Prussia had been, it could never be supposed would be practically submitted to by a power possessing such ample means of making herself respected.

With regard to Baron Jacobi, his lordship's conversation was a complete recapitulation of the contents of the despatch you read to me on the same subject, the day of my departure, with this addition, that, in a conference he had just had with him, Jacobi had declared he now saw the moment approaching when the dearest wishes of his heart were about to be accomplished.

·Lord Mulgrave ended this conversation by informing me of the intended special mission of Lord
Harrowby—which I had already heard of from
Mr. Hammond, on the night of my arrival—observing
that, if the allies would but act with union, and lay
aside all individual jealousies and mistrust, naming
particularly the ancient rivalry between the Houses
of Hapsburg and Brandenburg, it must be all over
with Bonaparte, who could never withstand the
united efforts of the three great continental Powers
joined to those of England. Lord Harrowby's mission, he said, anticipated, in a manner, the object of
my journey, and rendered my immediate return
needless. I might go down to Bath for two or
three days, provided I held myself in readiness to
come up at a moment's warning. And he suggested,
that that moment would be as soon as Lord H.'s
arrival on the Continent is known here. I go down
to-night, and shall return in a few days to press my
departure if I find it likely to be at all delayed.

And now, my dear brother, I conclude this long
letter by expressing my thanks to you for having
secured me so welcome and flattering a reception on
my first return from the Continent.

&c.,   &c.

GEORGE JACKSON.

Reilly's Hotel, Nov. 5th.—On my return to town,
my dear M., I found my table covered with cards,
invitations, and letters. Amongst the latter one
from Lady Hester Stanhope, expressing her regret

at having missed seeing me when I called upon her
before I left for Bath, and saying she should be in
town again this week, and hoped I would not fail to
call, as she should be happy to show every civility
in her power to the brother of her old friend. In
a word, nothing could be kinder or more polite.
Owing to the non-arrival of the mails, no determination is come to respecting my departure. I am therefore completely tied by the leg. As to news, there
is none, except what you see in the papers, which
is by no means considered in a doleful light by
Mr. Pitt, or indeed by any one who is not a decided
croaker, and will give himself time and trouble to
reflect. There is a report, but I think it unworthy
of credit, of the total defeat of a corps of French
near Güntzburg, under Marshal Ney, who was said
to have been killed in the action.

Francis has, no doubt, by this time heard of Lord
Harrowby's mission. I believe he will feel it very
much; and, indeed, after three years of incessant
exertion, when he hoped to reap the only reward he
cares for—the gratification of concluding what he
had begun—it is poor encouragement to have another
step in to snatch away the prize at the moment it
was within his reach. So much has been said to me
on the subject, that in writing to you this observation
escapes me, but I beg of you to say nothing about it
to anybody.

Nov. 6th.—When you learn, my dear M., that I
am off with the glorious news from Trafalgar, which
you will read in this night's extra " Gazette," you will

not expect from me more than a few lines, until I get to my journey's end. I enclose them with two gazettes, dripping wet from the press, which I shall send as a parcel by this night's mail from the Gloucester coffee-house. The event has proved how necessary it was to be constantly in waiting, for, with the very best intentions, they could not, had I been in the country, have sent for me in time ; and I should never have forgiven myself, if, from my own fault, I had missed so favourable a stroke. You had no idea that my maxim of " Push on, keep moving," would so well answer, and answer so soon.

Adieu, &c.,
G. J.

P. S.—I just now learn that a corps of Austrian cavalry, six thousand strong, commanded by the Archduke Ferdinand in person, fell in with and captured, near Nordlingen, a detachment of French troops, six hundred foot and eight hundred horse. This was an escort to fifty pieces of artillery and one hundred ammunition wagons, which also were taken. The Austrians had crossed the Danube, near Ulm, and were marching across the Upper Palatinate to join the combined armies on the Inn. But this is old news. I send you a packet just put into my hands. It is from Otto Löwenstern, and will give you all the reports of the war that have reached Berlin to the 30th ult., the last date we have from thence. Do not fail to return it by the first messenger. Once more adieu.

From M. Otto Löwenstern—translation.

Berlin, October $\frac{18}{30}$th.—I have done my best, dear
George, to keep you *au courant* of all that is going
on in your absence.   It is an anxious, busy time
with every body, and with our mission especially,
as our emperor is here. $\frac{11}{23}$rd. A few days after
you left, General Kalkreuth sent a messenger to
announce that His Imperial Majesty, having heard
of the obstacles that prevented the King of Prussia
from leaving his capital, would himself visit Berlin,
and might be expected on the $\frac{13}{25}$th. He particularly desired that all ceremonies might be omitted
on the occasion.   It was ordered, therefore, that the
guns of the garrison should not be fired, but that the
king's equipages should be sent for the emperor's
use to a certain distance from the city, and several
Generals and Staff officers to meet him.   Preparations
were ordered to be. made to receive him, both at
Berlin and Potzdam, and the emperor was himself to
decide at which palace he would take up his residence.   Three days, it was said, would be the extent
of his visit.   But Prince Dolgoruski, the emperor's
aide-de-camp, was expected that evening, and from
him a more particular statement of His Imperial
Majesty's wishes and intentions was looked for.

The public records were referred to for precedents
of the etiquette observed on any similar occasion.
But as no Russian emperor had visited Berlin since
the time of Peter I.—who came in the suite of his
own ambassador—little or nothing was found in the

usages of that day applicable to those of the present. The records inform us, that the Czar Peter associated with much familiarity and condescension with the ministers of the elector; that he strongly recommended his electoral highness to take the title of king; that he was very profuse in his assurances of good will, and that His Imperial Majesty indulged freely in copious libations of wine.

General Kalkreuth also sent us intelligence that confirms the last reports from the Austrian army. From Anspach and Ratisbon, we hear that Bonaparte on the $\frac{2}{14}$th, actually attacked the Austrian forces on the Iller, and succeeded in forcing their positions. The precise situation of the respective armies is difficult to ascertain; so conflicting are the statements on that head.

The French and Bavarians assert that thirty thousand Austrians have laid down their arms; that fifty thousand have, in another place, been taken prisoners, and that some pieces of cannon have been captured. But we make large allowances for French brag in all these accounts. Bonaparte issued a proclamation at Ratisbon on the $\frac{1}{13}$th, in which he made known the great exploits he meant to perform, and the people of that part in their terror looked on them as *faits accomplis*, and immediately reported them as such.

A report that " scattered detachments of Austrians were retreating in disorder across the Upper Palatinate," was sent here by a subaltern officer of the regency of Anspach, but it was not accompanied by any connected account of what had taken place.

The intelligence that the French had passed through the centre of the Austrian line; that one part of Mack's army had retreated to the Vorarlberg and Tyrol, and that the other is crossing the Palatinate, with the object of effecting a junction with the army on the Inn, is considered trustworthy. Orders have been issued, at least so it is asserted, since these reports arrived, for the Prussian armies to move forward to the support of the imperial troops, as soon as they reach their different destinations, and the whole force is expected to be ready to march by the $\frac{10}{22}$nd proximo. If such a decision has been taken, we owe it no doubt, to the announcement of Alexander's visit.

I write *à differentes réprises*. Dolgoruski came in this afternoon $\frac{12}{24}$th. He says the emperor will stay here but a very short time, and that from Berlin he goes to meet the Emperor of Germany. However, accounts were brought in, in the course of the night, which may compel some change in his arrangements; for I am sorry to say that the defeat of the Austrians on the Iller, is confirmed by these accounts. They run thus :—" The engagement was begun by Bonaparte, on the $\frac{2}{14}$th. In the course of that day he made eight successive assaults on the Austrian line, and was each time repulsed. On the $\frac{3}{15}$th he returned to the charge, and was again repulsed, with immense slaughter, until about noon, when a considerable impression being made on the Austrian line, it gave way, and separated into two corps. The right wing has escaped, it is conjectured, in the direction of the Tyrol; but no certain accounts have been received from that quarter. A part of the left wing threw itself into Ulm, and if it has not already surrendered, as reported, must shortly be captured."

" A corps of twelve thousand men, with the Archduke Ferdinand at their head, forced their way through the French army. It was this corps which, in its retreat towards the Upper Palatinate, captured the park of artillery and its escort." An *estafette* from Bareuth, to-day, tells us that " the archduke and his troops had passed through that town on their way to Eger, whence they hoped to reach Prague, though a detachment of French, under Murat, was in close pursuit of them."

The usual exaggerated accounts from French and Bavarian sources are in circulation. They state the loss of the Austrians at twenty to thirty thousand men, and thirty general officers, amongst whom is General Mack.

Our imperial master arrived yesterday $\frac{13}{25}$th, at two o'clock. On the preceding day, the king's first aide-de-camp, General Köchritz, went out some miles on the road by which the emperor was to enter Berlin, to meet and to compliment him. Yesterday the king's brothers, the Princes Henry and William, rode a German mile out of Berlin to receive him. At the gates of the city the governor, and commandant, F. M. Möllendorff, and General Götze, were waiting to welcome him.

An immense assemblage of people filled the streets to see him pass, and gave him a noisy but no doubt as hearty a welcome as any he had received. Indeed, if the tumultuous joy that now reigns throughout Berlin may be said to mean anything, I should say that the whole city is delighted at His Imperial Majesty's visit.

All the troops that remain in garrison were drawn up in the neighbourhood of the palace, where the king and queen, the whole of the royal family, and the Court, were assembled to receive their illustrious guest.

The peculiar position in which the French mission is now placed prevented any invitations from being sent to the *corps diplomatique*.

Between three and four the Emperor and their Majesties left Berlin for Potzdam. Prince Dolgoruski, Counts Tolstoi and Liewen accompanied them; also General Woronzow, who came in in the morning from Warsaw.

Prince Czartoriski, who has two secretaries with him, followed in the evening. He sent word before he left, to the English and Austrian ministers, that the emperor would give audience to them during his stay. Saturday he passed with their Majesties at Potzdam. Yesterday, Sunday $\frac{16}{28}$th, after the garrison had marched in review before the emperor and the king, he and the whole of the Prussian Court returned to Berlin, when, under the title of Le Comte du Nord, His Imperial Majesty paid visits in person to the various branches of the royal family, F.M. Möllendorff, and Count Schulenberg.

He then assisted at a gala, and a dinner at the palace, served on the state service of gold, to which not only the royal family, but also the ministers of state and lieutenant-generals of the garrison were invited.

In the afternoon His Imperial Majesty gave private audiences to the ministers of Russia, England, Austria, Turkey, and Mecklenburg Schwerin; and in a room adjoining the audience-chamber he received the ministers of other friendly states.

In the evening he went with their Majesties to the theatre, where the people received him with such marked enthusiasm and joy as are very rarely evinced by the public of Berlin.

17th.—Our emperor has won the hearts of the Berlinois. All classes of people are chanting his praises. He has a manner that wins popularity; much affability, which, without losing dignity, does not oppress by apparent condescension.

Yesterday he went to the Arsenal, and, after the conference that was held in the morning, visited several of the public buildings and institutions of Berlin. The Duke of Brunswick, who assisted at this conference—about which you will learn all the particulars when you return—arrived here on Sunday night.

The emperor dined with Prince Ferdinand yesterday, and passed the evening with their Majesties.

The conference with the king and his ministers was resumed to-day. What impression has been

made on His Majesty I have not yet heard, and I
doubt if it is yet known to Alopeus. In the afternoon we had a parade of the *gendarmes*; and I hear
that, after dining at Charlottenberg, the Emperor will
accompany their Majesties to Potzdam, where there
is to be a grand manœuvre of the garrison to-
morrow.

The good people of Berlin were again gratified by
a sight of Alexander to-day. He rode through the
principal streets with a very brilliant *cortège*, both
Russian and Prussian; for according to the etiquette
of this Court several officers of high rank, both civil
and military, have been appointed by the king to be
in constant attendance on the imperial visitor.
Count Kalkreuth is one of them, and, as usual, finds
many things on which to exercise his amusingly
caustic wit. From what I have told you of our
emperor's doings you will think, perhaps, that the
real object of his visit to the king has been less
attended to than pleasure. But it is not so. He
gives to business several hours every day. Our
mission, and the members of his own suite, have had
no idle time on their hands, I assure you. All have
been constantly employed, and many couriers daily
arrive from, and depart for, St. Petersburg and the
different Russian armies.

In case you should not hear it from any other
quarter, I should tell you that a detachment of
Prussian troops—Kleist's regiment, a few squadrons
of dragoons, and a battalion of light infantry—under
General Bila took possession of the city of Hanover

on the $\frac{13}{25}$th.   The French garrison retired to Hameln on the preceding day, and the Prussians have occupied the defiles leading to that fortress.

The last piece of news 'I am able to give you by this mail is, that this morning, $\frac{13}{30}$th, a courier reached Berlin from Vienna, which he left on the 24th, and announced the immediate arrival of the Archduke Anthony, for whom he had ordered horses all along his journey.   Metternich instantly set off to Potzdam to inform His Majesty, who ordered that Sans Souci should be prepared for his reception.   The Count returned without delay, and only just in time to receive the Archduke, who went on to Potzdam without stopping in Berlin, except to change horses.

It is seven o'clock, and a messenger for England leaves in the course of an hour.   But I add to this budget, that I was just about to close, that one of our secretaries has told me that the archduke has made this rapid journey to Berlin for the purpose of entreating the king to afford the Austrians the immediate support of a Prussian army.   He is to urge him to give instant orders for its march through Bohemia to the defence of Vienna, which city now depends for its safety wholly upon the army on the Inn.

Under such pressing difficulties one can hardly believe that the King of Prussia will not yield to the Archduke's urgent request.

The army under Prince Höhenlohe is nearest to the scene of action; but it is calculated that it cannot arrive on the Elbe in the neighbourhood of

Dresden until the $\frac{2}{14}$th of November, though it might with excellent effect march through Thuringen and Franconia to the Danube, and thus check Bonaparte's progress, even should his troops have been pushed beyond the Inn. I hope to see you back before the next messenger leaves for London. Your brother, I know, looks forward anxiously for your return. To lose his right hand at this busy moment is no joke, *mon cher* George, &c., &c.

OTTO LÖWENSTERN.

Duroc, I hear, is about to leave Berlin.

Mr. F. Jackson to Mrs. Jackson.

Berlin, Nov. 3rd.—I am in eager expectation of George's return. I reckon upon his having sailed yesterday, and unless the wind which favoured his passage over should impede his return he must be here in a very few days. He has done very well, and has met with the reception which his assiduity and talent for business deserve. My object in despatching him at this important moment was to give him a good introduction to people in power. It has fully answered the purpose, and I now, for many reasons, want him back very much. For the rest, we are going on very well. The Emperor of Russia arrived on the 25th ult., and leaves on the 5th. I had a private audience of him on Sunday. Nothing can exceed his affability and condescension, but his good understanding and the joy that his presence has created here. He had determined yesterday to leave Potzdam to-day; but the business in hand did not allow of his doing so. He therefore will not set out until Tuesday, in compliance with a Russian custom of not beginning a journey on a Monday. During his stay here, he has principally applied himself to gaining over those individuals who stood in the way of his wishes, in regard to the object to which we owe his visit, or whose more active co-operation might hasten their accomplishment.

The Duke of Brunswick he particularly distinguished, and conferred on him the Order of St. Andrew, with a diamond star worth 3,000*l.* Baron Hardenberg also received that order, and Count Haugwitz will obtain some substantial proof of his good-will. He gave Beym one of the cabinet secretaries, a diamond ring, which is valued at upwards of 1000*l.* His attentions to their Majesties themselves, and to every person belonging to their Court, have been unremitting. He is a very fine, handsome young man, and the evident goodness and amiability of his character seem everywhere to have made their due impression. For my own part, I am very glad to have had the opportunity of paying my respects to him, &c.

F. J. J.

Mr. J. Jackson to Mr. G. Jackson.

Berlin, Nov. 9th.—I fully looked for your return yesterday, or for a letter to announce it. I have, instead, the intelligence that Lord Harrowby is coming

out.   I do not therefore expect you just yet, still I
would not have you delay your departure, if there
should seem to be nothing worth waiting for.

· It would be both useless and improper to enter
into particulars upon the subject of Lord Harrowby's
mission, but I may say that I feel deeply the mortification of being superseded, even by a person of Lord
Harrowby's presumed abilities, at a moment when I
had, as you know, after years of anxious labour, arrived
at a point which was the summit of my wishes.   I
must, however, rejoice at the present state of things,
although another is to reap the crop that I have sown.
I hope I shall continue to bear this disappointment as
I ought, having the testimony of my own conscience,
and, indeed, of the king's government, most fully
expressed, that I have not deserved it.

You will have seen by my letter to our mother
that, like the rest of the Berlin world, I was well
pleased with Alexander.   He told me, at the audience
I had on the 27th, that he was satisfied with the
progress he had made for the success of the object he
had in view, and that the king and his ministers
seemed to be well disposed to co-operate with the
allies in the present critical state of affairs.   He said
he was quite aware of the sort of influence exercised
here by persons in the Cabinet, and well acquainted
with the secret springs that too often impede the
motions of the ostensible Government.   What he
was himself doing arose, he said, from no interested
motive, beyond the gratification he should feel in
rescuing Europe from the disastrous situation into

which it had fallen from the wild ambition of an obscure individual. The unfortunate reverses of Austria render, as he observed, the alliance of this country more necessary than before. " And," he added, taking me by the hand, " I am resolved not to leave Berlin till the work I have undertaken, and which is satisfactorily begun, shall be successfully completed."

After a week's negotiation, conducted almost in despair of bringing Prussia to accede to the views of the allies, an agreement was come to, and Count Haugwitz is charged with the important commission of conveying to Bonaparte the substance of the Treaty of Potzdam, based on the armed mediation which this Government announced its intention of employing.

The Treaty of Potzdam was signed on the 3rd, and the ratifications exchanged.

The emperor left Potzdam early on the morning of the 5th. He took leave of their Majesties in the vault in which the remains of Frederick II. are deposited. Various plans were suggested for an interview of the two Emperors and the King of Prussia at Prague or Dresden ; but the events of the war must decide whether any one of them can be adopted. The emperor was to pass two days at Weimar, and to be at Dresden to-day ; thence to proceed to Bohemia to meet the Emperor of Germany, who, it is supposed, will come some part of the way for the interview. Count Haugwitz was to have set out for Paris on the evening of the 5th, but he is still here, owing solely to his habit of procrastination.

Duroc left on the 3rd. He went to Potzdam on the 2nd, to take leave of the king. He was not invited to dinner, but was presented with a snuff-box, with the king's picture set in diamonds. Duroc pretends that Bonaparte is without information of what is passing here. It is, however, difficult to understand that no notice should be taken of the declaration of this Court of the 14th of October.

I hear that the French General endeavoured to make an acceptable apology for the affair of Anspach, as General Murat has also done for an action which took place at Bareuth between his corps and the retreating Austrians. I cannot go more into details, you will learn them on your arrival. Lord H. is making a long journey of it. I have heard nothing of him.

&c., &c.,
F. J. J.

Letters—Berlin, Nov. 19*th.*—I promised, my dear mother, that you should hear from me as soon as I arrived. The newspapers—those ever watchful Arguses over the motions and actions of *great men*— will have cleared up your doubts as to the time of my actual departure from London. When I got my gazettes from Mr. Rolleston's office, where I left them all busily employed in making up packages for the Continent, it was past ten o'clock. I set off immediately, full gallop, into the city, which, as well as the West End, was, as it were, on fire.

What with the news itself, the pleasure my commission gave me, the noise and hurrahs of the crowd —
which was often so dense as to impede the progress
of my four steeds—I could get no sleep that night;
and by the time I was out of London the horses
were so tired—from my having had them before the
door ever since four o'clock, waiting solely for the
coming out of the gazettes—that I was much longer
getting to Romford than I otherwise should have been.

At all the places I stopped at on the road, the
utmost joy was expressed by every soul who heard
the glorious news I was the bearer of. A packet
was waiting my arrival at Harwich. I embarked
immediately, and, after a voyage as tedious as it was
boisterous, landed at Hamburg on Saturday the 16th.
I provided myself with a carriage—having left my
brother's, which I had expected to return in, at
Husum—and proceeded with all possible expedition
towards my destination. As the clock struck six
yesterday morning I entered the gates of Berlin, and
very soon after roused my brother and his household
from their beds. What was my mortification, then,
to find that a report, stating the sum and substance
of my gazettes, had got before me; having reached
Berlin late on the preceding evening. But though
vexed, I was not surprised; for in the two first
days of my voyage, and afterwards, when beating
about by contrary winds, I had the *pleasure* of seeing
the vessel which sailed from Yarmouth at the same
moment as myself, with a gazette I gave the commander, for our fleet off Texel, making the best of

her way to that station, *grace* to the very same storm
that retarded my progress.   What I then apprehended, precisely happened, and the report, *viâ*
Holland, reached this a few hours before my arrival.
However, they were not sorry to have it confirmed
in so satisfactory a manner; and that, and a most
kind and handsome letter from Mr. Pitt, which he
himself delivered into my hands, for my brother, at
the end of a very flattering conversation I had with
him just before setting off—and from which it would
seem that he feels for the awkwardness of his situation, and wishes to alleviate it—so raised Francis'
spirits that it would have done you good to have
seen him.   He at first proposed to celebrate the
victory by a grand ball, which has since been changed
for a great supper.

  23rd.—Everybody sought invitations to it, and
more than everybody that had them came.   I was,
for that evening, a hero, and it would have required
a hundred tongues, at least, to have answered all the
questions that were put to me, and to have acknowledged the congratulations I was overwhelmed with.
I never saw joy so general or, apparently, so heart-
felt.   That which I witnessed along the road when
I stopped on my journey, not only on your side of
the water but also on this, alone equalled it.   I have
since heard the account of the victory read, and
have seen tears flow, as it was repeated with much
emotion, " Aber Nelson gestorben ist."   Such is the
effect of the victory, and the heroism of the victor, on
all classes of people.

For myself, I have every reason to be gratified with my trip, and am considered a most lucky fellow in having been the bearer of two of the most important pieces of intelligence that Europe has been saluted with for many a year. But this would be as nothing to me without my brother's approbation; and I am well pleased to assure you that he is satisfied with the expedition with which I performed my journey to England, the course I pursued there, and my activity in resuming my journey, notwithstanding that its first object was done away with by Lord Harrowby's mission. Though to me of far less importance, you will perhaps like to know that they gave me in London 260*l.*, and the vessel gratis that brought me back.

Lord Harrowby arrived only three days before me, having made the longest journey between this and London ever known. He has taken all the important business out of my brother's hands.

24*th.*—The Russians are helping us to make up for the deficiencies of the Austrians. They have destroyed a corps of ten thousand French.

We have heard that when the Emperor Alexander left Dresden he took the road towards Prague; but before he had travelled a German mile, he received accounts of a French force of six thousand men being at Pilsen, whose object was to interrupt the communication between Prague and Vienna. Under these circumstances His Imperial Majesty thought it prudent to change his route, and took, therefore, the road to Bautzen, on his way to Breslau and Olmütz; where he and the Emperor of Germany and his Court now are.

A messenger brought last night the account of Sir R. Strahan's victory, and the capture of four French line-of-battle ships. From the spirit that now prevails amongst the public of Berlin, the general rejoicing at this fresh success over the French is unusually great.

My brother is somewhat depressed; and indeed his situation is as irksome as it well can be, and must continue so as long as Lord Harrowby remains. His lordship appears to be a confirmed, and peevish invalid.

Diaries—Nov. 24th.—I learn that the principal terms Count Haugwitz is charged to offer for the conclusion of peace—the non-acceptance of which is to form a *casus belli*—are,

1st. That Mantua should be ceded to Austria, and that the Mincio should form her Italian frontier.

2nd. That Genoa, Parma, and Placentia, shall be given as an indemnity to the King of Sardinia.

3rd. That Switzerland and Holland should no longer be occupied by French troops ; and that they should be at liberty to adopt the form of government best suited to them, as well as to erect fortifications for the security of their frontiers.

The Prussians, on the other hand, aware of the value of their co-operation at this critical moment, have driven a hard bargain on their own account, and stipulate for certain territorial acquisitions and a subsidy from Great Britain of 12*l.* 10*s.* per head for a hundred and eighty thousand men of their own army, and forty thousand Hessian and Saxon auxiliaries.

Many persons are speculating on the kind of reception Count Haugwitz will meet with, though it is not very difficult to foresee; and it is doubtful whether he will be allowed to continue his negotiation during the four weeks, at the end of which this country engages itself to begin the war. It is not expected that Bonaparte would remain inactive during that time, but it is still hoped that the combined army will be able to maintain their ground. General Kutusow, and Prince Pangrazin, who commands his vanguard, have written in good spirits notwithstanding the defeat of the Austrians and their constant expectation of having to encounter superior numbers. The latter wrote to Prince Czartoriski—in the style I am told of his military preceptor Suwarow—"We hear the Austrian army is defeated. *We* shall be victorious. *We* shall beat the French, because it is the will of God and our sovereign."

The Russian negotiator had no more hostile opponent to encounter at the conference than General Köchritz, who incessantly represented to the king the calamities attendant on a war with France. Unfortunately, this officer, himself utterly ignorant of business, and the echo of an obscure person devoted to the French interest, continues to have great influence on the opinions of the king.

The stipulations of the Treaty of Potzdam met

with the highest approval at Vienna; and the
Emperor of Germany has, on the occasion, conferred
on his minister, Count Metternich, the Grand Cross
of the Order of St. Stephen. The Russian minister,
M. Alopeus, has also received from the Emperor of
Russia the diamond star of St. Alexander.

In consequence of Bonaparte's overtures to General
Mack for peace, the Emperor of Germany wrote a
second time to Bonaparte, and sent General Count
Giulay—one of the Generals made prisoner at Ulm—
with his letter to the French head-quarters, proposing an armistice for three or four weeks, to allow
time for consulting the Emperor of Russia. This
step is highly approved of here, though it is supposed
that Bonaparte will not consent to an armistice, but
that he will push on to a general and decisive engagement, before the Russians have time to rally their
forces. General Kutusow, however, crossed the
Danube at Krems, and the first and second columns
of General Buxhövden's army arrived on the 11th in
the neighbourhood of Brunn. No further accounts
are received, and the delay causes general anxiety ;
for about the same time General Marfelt retreated
with his troops into Styria. It is thought he
may be able to co-operate with the Archduke
Charles.

Much dissatisfaction is expressed at the wavering
conduct of the Elector of Hesse. He has replaced
on the peace establishment a corps that was ready
for service ; and the officers appointed to concert
measures with him, complain that no satisfactory

result can be come to with him, though the emperor promised him both subsidy and territorial indemnity.

The reverses of the Austrians are said to have by no means damped their resolution to continue the war ; they had determined, even if Vienna fell into the enemy's hands, not to conclude a precipitate peace with him ; while, here, with the intention of making Bonaparte pause in his victorious career, the army of Prince Höhenlohe has been ordered to take up its station in the principality of Anspach ; that of Westphalia to advance as far as Frankfort-on-the-Maine, and the combined Russian and Swedish troops to attack Holland conjointly with the British force— which it was expected would be sent over for that purpose—their rear and flank to be guarded from any operations of the French by the army under the Duke of Brunswick.

To conciliate the Elector of Hesse, and to encourage him in his attachment to the good cause, the unfettered command of the Westphalian army is given to him, and much disapprobation expressed at some indiscretions of General Blücher.

Owing to a long continued prevalence of northerly winds, the King of Sweden was for some time without information of what was passing here. He therefore sent his aide-de-camp, General Löwenhjelm, with a letter, requesting to know what was the intention of the King of Prussia in occupying Hanover, and also announcing his own early arrival with an army for the purpose of taking possession of the electorate, and restoring it to the King of England.

Supposing the King of Prussia to have the same object in view, he proposed to him a pact for the operation of the two armies, similar to that which had been agreed upon. As the inquiries of His Swedish Majesty, though not offensive in themselves, were put in a very categorical style, and as no notice whatever was taken of the differences already existing between him and the King of Prussia, this letter indisposed His Majesty still more against the King of Sweden, and would have produced a very bad effect in the present state of affairs, when it is much desired to bring about a reconciliation, but for the intervention of the Emperor of Russia.

This Court requires that the King of Sweden should send a person of high rank, with a letter expressive of His Majesty's regret at the estrangement that has occurred, when the King of Prussia, on his part, will be ready to re-establish his usual relations with the Court of Stockholm. But no means yet adopted have induced the King of Sweden to alter his measures, or to soften the unfriendly tone of his communications to this Court. The messengers who were sent to him returned with orders to his aide-de-camp, Count Löwenhjelm, to leave Berlin immediately, and join him at Stralsund, which he did. This state of things is much regretted, and it is feared that the unyielding conduct of the King of Sweden may give rise to further differences that may even be prejudicial to the general success of the allies. The Emperor Alexander, on leaving Berlin, desired General

Tolstoi to go to the king, and to use his utmost
endeavours to prevail on him to make some advances
towards a reconciliation. And there is no doubt,
notwithstanding the fresh obstacles in the way of it,
that the King of Prussia will consent to it on reasonable terms, and such as may not in any degree
be felt by the King of Sweden to be personally
humiliating.

The French have sent reinforcements to Holland,
both from the army of Boulogne, and from Mayence,
and have made preparations at Greve and at
Nymegen, as though they were expecting an attack
on those places.

It seems that General Barbou, the commandant at
Hanover, wished to take with him to Hameln a
member of the executive council and a member of
the States, but that it was refused by the Prussians.
He has now collected there a quantity of Hanoverian
artillery, and has made every preparation for a
defence by destroying the houses, and cutting down
the trees and hedges round the town, a service he
compelled the inhabitants of Hameln themselves to
perform for him. He endeavoured also to lay the
country under water, and has done considerable
damage, and caused much injury and loss to a
number of persons without effecting his purpose, for
which the water does not rise high enough.

The Duke of Brunswick was to send troops to
surround Hameln, and prevent the Hanoverian
artillery from being carried away. That part of the
Hanoverian army that remained in the country was

to be brought together, and arms, which have been concealed in sufficient quantity during the French occupation, distributed to them. M. de Hardenberg, the brother of the baron, has been instrumental in effecting many arrangements that will save the country from further suffering, and accelerate the re-establishment of the electoral government.

25th.—Beym and Lombard have succeeded in persuading the king to recall Count Haugwitz to a share in the direction of foreign affairs. They were dissatisfied with Baron Hardenberg's independent manner of undertaking the business of his depart-ment, and they know, from experience, that they can fully rely on Count Haugwitz to allow them a more direct interference in it.

27th.—There is an increased degree of activity in the military preparations of this Government. The departure of the garrison of Potzdam, and the re-mainder of that of Berlin, is ordered for the 30th.

The staff of Field-Marshal Möllendorff is com-pleted. My sister-in-law's brother—who had left the service, but has again donned his uniform—is appointed aide-de-camp and brigade-major to the old Field-Marshal, who, at the age of eighty-three, is as young and active as any of his suite, and talks of nothing so much—and I dare say he is sincere—as of his wish to die the death of Nelson. He and the King of Prussia will set out for the army, it is supposed, in the course of the ensuing week. The route they will take depends on the intelligence, hourly expected, of a battle between the Russian and French armies near Olmütz. A general engagement was expected to take place on the 22nd.

The hostile armies were not more than three or four German miles from each other. The Prussians are to take up a position about a league to the west of Olmütz, where—as circumstances may render it expedient—they will either await the onset of the French, or attack them.

The Emperor Alexander meant to put himself at the head of his army, which would amount to upwards of seventy thousand men, including eighteen thousand Austrians, under Prince John of Lichtenstein.

Dec. 2nd.—Lord Harrowby is really an object of pity to everybody who sees him ; and surprise has been freely expressed that a man so thoroughly *hors de combat* should have been selected by our Government at a critical moment like this for its special negotiator. For my part, I most pity my brother, though he has, he says, made up his mind to what he could not prevent, and is disposed to judge cautiously of the conduct of a man whose infirmities are so great. He has had three fits since he came, and has suffered agonies almost the whole time ; often, as he himself told Francis, he is insensible for hours together. He is naturally of an irritable temperament, which, added to his bodily suffering, renders it both unpleasant and painful to transact business with him, during those short intervals in which he is at all capable of attending to it.

6th.—Unfavourable, though uncertain, reports are afloat respecting the fate of the allied armies. It is circulated in the city this evening that the Russians are defeated, and Alexander killed—the excitement is indescribable.

7th.—The bad news is partly confirmed. A battle was fought on Monday last, the 2nd inst., at Austerlitz, between the Russians and the French.

8th to 11th.—The Russians successfully repulsed the advanced guard of the French, but were, later in the day, completely defeated in their centre by Bernadotte's corps. It is still hoped that their right and left wings may be able to re-establish matters a little. Both emperors were in the thick of the battle, and both exposed themselves much to the enemy's fire—Alexander recklessly so. The troops followed the example of their sovereigns, and fought desperately. The nature of the ground taken up by the allies seems to have favoured their operations, and victory at one moment inclined to their side. The Russian cavalry had penetrated the French squares, and a horrible slaughter ensued. It was expected that the Russian Guard would decide the fate of the day. But again the superior generalship of Bonaparte and his marshals turned impending defeat into victory. At least, this is the cause assigned here for the disastrous result of the battle. Both sides are said to have fought with astonishing intrepidity, man to man. The Grand Duke Constantine seems to be almost the only man of his regiment that escaped. The Emperors Alexander

and Francis witnessed the final defeat of the Russian
Guard from some rising ground near the spot
where the last struggle took place. Artillery and
baggage fell into the enemy's hands. The loss on
both sides was immense; but though the returns of
the Russians are not yet received, we know that
great as was the slaughter, the number of killed and
wounded falls far short of that reported by the
French—which is, " half the Russian army, and the
rest entirely routed; of whom the greater part
threw away their arms." Equally absurd is the
statement that their own loss did not exceed nine
hundred, with about one thousand wounded; for the
fact is, that a victory like that of Austerlitz would
bear very few repetitions. Two such would go well
nigh, it is said, to ruin the French, and one defeat
would be absolute destruction. It may, perhaps, be
reserved for the Prussians to make them experience
that alternative.

The garrison of Berlin marched out in good
spirits on the 7th.

13th.—Something has passed at the head-quarters
of the hostile armies which looks like a tendency
towards peace. We have not yet received any
particulars, but we know that an armistice is concluded between the Austrians and the French.

14th.—Bonaparte's proclamation, addressed to his
victorious troops, is in the usual bombastic style.
" You have taught them," he says, " that it is more
easy to defy and to threaten than to conquer us."
Nous verrons.

Mr. F. Jackson to Mrs. Jackson.

Berlin, December 15th.

MY DEAR MOTHER,

I never remember the communication with
England so frequent and rapid as of late. Your
letter of the 5th reached me on the 12th, and found
me in much better mood than when I wrote last. I
mean, as to momentary feelings: for I shall never
forget the injustice that has been done me. I begin
to be annoyed for the progress of affairs, which
cannot be altogether what it ought to be. Lord
Harrowby is, doubtless, a man of ability; but he is
a stranger to the sort of business he has undertaken.
Everything is new, and embarrasses him, and a great
deal of time is lost. He has been for two days
unable to attend to anything, having had in that
time four or five fits. I remain quite quiet, listen
to what is said to me, and only give an opinion when
it is asked. My wish and study is only not to make
an enemy of a man who has it in his power to
do me great injury. I was as desirous on his
arrival to make him my friend; but that I see is impossible. I had determined to subdue all personal
feelings, and to assist him in working for the public
good, and I thought he would wish nothing better.
But whether it be owing to personal jealousy of
me, whether it be constitutional irritability, and an
unwillingness to confide in anybody, certain it is
that I can no more succeed with him than I should
in persuading a Russian pope to cut off his beard.

I must, therefore, wait patiently till I am restored
to my functions by his departure. I wish, with all
my heart, that I may find matters as easy of execution as when they were taken out of my hands. I
am very glad to write to you upon this subject,
because it relieves my mind and prevents me from
mentioning it to anybody else, which I should be
afterwards sorry to have done.

17*th.*—Your letter of the 9th, which came in
this morning, contains one piece of news which occasions me great anxiety. I mean with reference to
Mr. Pitt. He is ordered, I suppose, to take the Bath
waters. But I should fear something serious if he
is looking so ill as you say, and shakes so much
that he can scarce carry the glass to his mouth. I
trust most sincerely that they may prove healing
waters to him, for the nation can ill afford to spare
him.

Your prophecy is not altogether verified; for it
has not found me rejoicing, though in some measure
consoling myself for many things that have passed,
with the idea that I have not on my shoulders
the responsibility of the moment. It is right that
they who would rob me of the roses should feel the
scratchings of the thorns.

The state of affairs is just now such as might
reasonably be supposed to affect a stronger frame
than Lord Harrowby's. All may yet end well, but
this interval of suspense is distressing, and has a
most distressing effect upon his lordship. In addition
to his fits, he now has spasms every day that affect

his whole body.   He wishes very heartily that he had
not left London, and that he were well and safely
arrived there again.   And so I believe does his
whole party ; for they have a very dull time of it.
Indeed, the winter promises, upon the whole, not to
be a very lively one.   There are few people of our
society here, and of those few, several will go with
the king, when he takes the command of the army.

22*nd*—Bonaparte seems to be in a fair way to
become the uncontrolled master of the Continent.
Perhaps he may bend the bow until it breaks, which,
indeed, seems to be our best chance for the future.

Lord Harrington has arrived here.   He was
destined for an *extraordinary* embassy to Vienna,
but, under present circumstances, it seems likely that
he will not proceed further.   I suppose it was meant
only as a compliment to send a nobleman and man
of military rank.   It can hardly have been a question
of his doing any business.   Added to other incapa-
cities, a fit of the gout is come upon him, which completely ties his lordship by the leg.

F. J. J.

Letters—December 30*th.*—We are having a revival
of balls and fêtes, which, while war was impending,
had gone out of fashion.   They are even now considered by many persons rather *hors de saison.*
The Grand Duke Constantine has been here for the
last ten days, with his suite, and as he is as fond of
dancing as the queen herself, several balls have been
given by the Court, and many other gaieties are

preparing. *We,* however, do not profit much by it;
for the Court, not choosing to see M. Laforêt or any
of his party, has hit upon the expedient of excluding
the *corps diplomatique in toto.* For my part, I do
not quarrel with this arrangement; but many of the
young men, and especially those of the Russian
mission, which has seven *attachés,* think it very
hard, and wish politics, war, and Bonaparte at the
deuce, for preventing them from leading a dance.

The account you have heard of the adieus of Alexander and Frederick is true, so far as to their having
taken place in the vault. But whether any vows
were sworn over the tomb of the late king, I know
not; I never heard anything of the sort mentioned
here, and I imagine the English papers invented
it. The emperor is returned to St. Petersburg, and
I hope it will soon appear that, *il n'a reculé que pour
mieux sauter.* Much as my journey gratified me, I
cannot help regretting having missed seeing him.
The impression he made on the people is extraordinary, and they become quite enthusiastic as they
tell of what he said and did. It is certain, that had
the King of Prussia himself been in the battle of the
2nd, more anxiety could not have been evinced for
his fate than was shown for that of the Emperor
Alexander, until the particulars of the events of that
memorable, but unhappy, day reached this place.
They have struck a medallion of him to comme-
morate his visit. The likeness is said to be good; if
so, he has a fine face.

Bonaparte told Prince Dolgoruski, whom the

emperor sent to the French outposts upon his desiring to speak with him, that if Alexander wished it he might annex Moldavia and the Ukraine to his dominions, and that he not only would not oppose this measure, but would use his ·influence to render it palatable to other powers. The prince replied that his imperial master desired to enter into no such arrangements; that he sought no acquisition of territory. He was there to succour his ally, the Emperor of Germany, and had no other wish than to see Europe restored to happiness and independence. With this declaration the interview closed— Bonaparte ceremoniously desiring the prince to convey his best respects to the Emperor Alexander, and to lay him at His Imperial Majesty's feet. Since then, he has sported the magnanimous towards Russia, and has sent back Prince Repnin and some other Russian prisoners of distinction, with the observation that he would not deprive the Emperor of Russia of the services of such brave and distinguished officers.

The physicians have earnestly advised Lord Harrowby to return to England, and to withdraw entirely from business. He is getting worse, and his state of health is alarming. Last night he had a burning fever, and they were going to blister him; but this morning the fever has subsided a little, and it is determined that he shall set out on his way home as soon as he can bear the journey. With all the symptoms he has about him, poor man, he must probably soon undertake a much longer journey.·

He is much concerned at the story of his being waylaid on his road to Berlin having reached the English papers; because, he said, it would alarm his friends. I did not suppose it would cause you any anxiety on my account; knowing, as you do, how untrustworthy such "foreign news" always is. It may surprise you to hear that the reported assassination of Alexander had no foundation *whatever*, and that the "attempt on Lord Harrowby" was a very idle story, originating in the fears of a party of timid travellers. Lord Harrowby and his suite passed on their road two men, whom some of them thought very ill-looking fellows. At the next place they stopped at, they were told that two spies had just been taken up not far up from that spot, and sent to the Russian head-quarters, where they were to be immediately exalted in a manner of which the usurper who employed them was far more worthy, and that one of them was *said to be* the man who last year stopped the messenger Wagstaffe, near Lauenburg. Of course, the travellers came at once to the conclusion that these spies could be no other than the ill-looking fellows who had looked at them, and who were only prevented, they were convinced, from stopping them by the sight of the goodly array of blunderbusses and pistols with which they were armed.

Berlin is, just now, a sort of English diplomatic nest. We have Lord G. L. Gower on his way from Olmütz to St. Petersburg. Lord Harrington undecided about continuing his journey to Vienna, and Mr. Pierrepont from Stockholm. These, with our cabinet minister, and their respective appurtenances, number twenty-three persons. Besides, within the last few days, we have had an unusual influx of English travellers. Among them is Lord Kinnaird, whose father and mother both died in the space of a week, while I was in England. You will have often read this young man's speeches in the Commons. He is a very clever fellow, but a violent oppositionist. He is by no means consoled for the privation which his elevation subjects him to, by the immense fortune he has come into. Not being one of the sixteen Scotch Lords, he has no place in the upper house, and is incapacitated for a seat in the lower one. I agree with him in thinking it a hardship for an able and active-minded man.

Two officers, with beards that would astonish you, and who escaped from Verdun, after marvellous adventures that you one day may read of, amuse and astonish us with the stories they tell of their captivity, and of the almost incredible gains of the commandant and other officers by the sums they extort for "relaxations of duty." By some means, they obtained a supply of money, and agreed to pay the commandant fifty louis each for a *parole* of a day, with the privilege of reporting themselves but once, instead of twice, during the twelve hours it lasted. Twice they returned punctually. But with the third hundred louis, they considered they had paid the French general handsomely for his complaisance, and that evening both his prisoners were, of course, reported *non est inventus*.

I send you one of the Alexander medals; and
another, which is considered to be not without a
certain degree of merit, and has been lately struck
in Berlin, in commemoration of the battle of
Trafalgar and the glorious death of Lord Nelson.

31*st*.—One of the first uses made by Bonaparte of
his victory at Austerlitz is to create two kings.
The Elector of Bavaria, while out shooting one day,
received from a messenger, sent by Bonaparte, a
letter directed to " Sa Majesté le Roi de Bavière et
de Suabe, notre très chèr frère, ami, et allié." The
secret of this is, that the elector is about to give his
daughter in marriage to Beauharnois—viceroy of
Italy and Madame B's son. A princess of Würtemberg was to have shared the bed and the honours of
this hopeful youth, but we hear that she had spirit
enough to refuse him; in consequence of which her
father, the elector, who was to have been made king
first, has lost that honour, and may, perhaps, lose
some portion of the share destined for him of the
plunder of the Holy Roman Empire, about to be
distributed. Their new Majesties will be enthroned
to-morrow, and the mighty modern king-maker, de-
lighting most to honour His Majesty of Bavaria, is
expected at Munich to-day.

I am compelled to descend from this lofty theme to
a very humble one. My brother desires me, in concluding this epistle, to step, as it were, from a throne
to a beer barrel. He will be glad if you will thank
Mr. Barclay for his kind remembrance of him, and,
if he is still at Bath, will tell him, with his best

respects, that the specimen barrel he has been so good as to send him, of this year's brewing, is super-excellent.

1806.

Letters—Jan. 3rd.—Peace was signed at Presburg, on the 27th ult., between Austria and France, and upon such humiliating conditions as to resemble much more a capitulation than a treaty of peace.

4th.—The Emperor Francis has signed away all the Tyrol, the Venetian States, the Vorarlberg, and the whole of his possessions in Swabia, together with the quarter of the Inn, as far as Lintz, within a few miles of his capital. He has also acknowledged a right in his *brother emperor* to meddle, henceforth, *ad libitum*, in the interior government of what remains to him of his empire, and has received the haughty mandate of this arbitrary usurper as to what the form of that government shall be, and who the ministers to compose it.

5th.—The cowardice or ignorance — both are ascribed to them—of some of the officers who were engaged in the fatal battle of Austerlitz has proved, indeed, a heavy misfortune for Austria and her emperor; for it is now known that, at the least, much might have been done to retrieve first dis-asters if, instead of giving way to the infatuation of terror, inspired by the mere fact of the presence of Bonaparte in the field, a proper spirit had prevailed in some of those who commanded, and due exertion had been used to rally and reanimate the troops. " Better, a thousand times better," was said by more than one that came in the suite of the Prince who left the horrors of the battle-field to caper in the ball-rooms of Berlin, " that the Emperor of Germany should have perished under the ashes of Vienna, in an ineffectual struggle for the independence of his country, than that he should have subscribed to the disgraceful terms of peace proposed by his conqueror, and have allowed his name to go down to posterity connected with an act of such pusillanimity and base-ness as the signing of the Treaty of Presburg.

Yet Bonaparte was scarcely satisfied with these sacrifices, and for a long time insisted on the absolute cession of Istria and Dalmatia, with the islands dependent on it.   And it was only after a conference of more than two hours with the Archduke Charles, in which the latter declared that sooner than consent to this he would renew the war, that he thought better of it, and graciously moderated his pretensions in that respect.

When people come to know the real state of things, and are told—and it is an undoubted fact—that the whole time this negotiation, if indeed it deserves that name, was going on, the Archduke had, within thirty English miles of Vienna, an army of ninety thousand men, in the finest order and best of spirits, they will hardly believe such a result to have been possible.

6*th*.—The Bavarian coronation, it is reported, will take place to-morrow, and in a few days after the new king will give his daughter—an amiable girl, and one of the prettiest of the young German prin-

cesses—to the mighty emperor's adopted son and
heir expectant, Beauharnois. We hear that the
Princess of Würtemburg is now demanded in marriage for brother Jerome.

After the coronation and marriage at Munich,
Bonaparte is to return immediately to Paris. The
coalition has served him as a pretext for not putting
his three years' threat into execution against our
island; we shall see if he will pluck up spirit enough
again to menace us, for as to really attempting anything I believe he is far too wise for that.

It is a pity that Sir Sydney Smith should have
followed so much the gasconading system, for it
appears that all the fuss he made with his experi-
ments, &c., has ended only in smoke.

7th.—The "Morning Chronicle," and the whole
list of railing oppositionists, in their wisdom, ascribe
these continental mishaps to the policy of Mr. Pitt.
The opposers of the Administration cannot give a
stronger proof of the shifts they are reduced to.

8th.—Lord Harrowby is gone—thank God! it is
a great relief to everybody who had any business to
transact with him. I had heard in London of the
fretfulness of his temper, and although I have not,
generally, had to feel the effects of it, yet it has been
sufficiently trying to witness its effect upon others
during the last two months. As far as my brother
is concerned, his lordship's ·conduct cannot be re-
conciled to any idea of gentlemanlike feeling towards
one who was not, after all, directly under his superintendence. Francis has had, as he says, a very

difficult card to play, owing to those same dispositions having become so evident to this Government that they became heartily tired of treating with his lordship, and hinted several times that they desired to re-enter into communication with *him*.   But so far was he from yielding to those hints the least in the world, that he did not once go to the Prussian minister's house when Lord Harrowby was not there, and also declined entering into any conversation on matters of business, even with those of his colleagues with whom he has been always in the most confidential habits of intercourse.   But, as I said, he is gone, and it is well that he is, for all who were with him would soon have been as much out of their wits as Lord Harrowby, at times, is himself.   Mr. Hammond, who behaved very well through it, was near going out of his ; and it was, indeed, a severe trial of any man's temper and patience, even after all possible allowance was made for a truly miserable state of health.

We are sorry to see that you still persist, on your side of the water, in deceiving yourselves as to the issue of the battle of the 2nd of December.   The "Moniteur," and other French papers, contain many a hoax on your incredulity.

Diaries—Jan. 11th.—It is publicly reported, and credited, that Austria has undertaken to propose to the British Government terms of pacification on the part of France.   We learn also, from the same quarter, that Austria has consented to leave Istria and Venetian Dalmatia at the disposal of Bonaparte.

Nothing has publicly transpired respecting the negotiation between Prussia and France, but Count Haugwitz is to set off to-morrow to join Bonaparte at Munich ; should he have left that city he is to follow him to Paris or wherever else he may be. It was thought probable that he would return to France by way of Italy. The Count is accompanied, as before, by M. Lombard senior.

14*th*.—The Duke of Brunswick will shortly go to St. Petersburg on an extraordinary mission.

15*th*.—General Count Schulenberg is appointed to command, under the Duke of Brunswick, the Prussian troops destined to occupy the Electorate of Hanover, and waits only for the conclusion of the arrangements on that subject between Prussia and France to set out for his head-quarters—which it is supposed will be in the city of Hanover. The force under his orders will amount to about thirty thousand men. He is preparing a large military as well as civil establishment, and from this circumstance and some authentic information on the subject, we are inclined to think that he is to be charged with the superintendence of the different departments of the electorate, if not with the exclusive administration of it.

18*th*.—I much fear that the loss of his hereditary dominions in Germany will be added to the afflictions, mental and domestic, that embitter the latter days of our poor old king. Nothing, I am convinced, but a speedy peace will prevent this.

24*th*.—The preparatory measures for occupying

the electorate are going on apace, as well as those
for replacing the greater part of the Prussian army
on the peace establishment. In the meanwhile
Baron Hardenberg is invisible to the whole of the
corps diplomatique, except M. Laforêt, who, however,
declines to hold any intercourse with him; Bonaparte allowing his minister to transact business only
with Count Haugwitz, and, since his departure, with
Count Schulenberg. When the latter leaves Berlin
for his new command, we shall see whether sufficient
submission will have been made to reinstate Baron
Hardenberg in the conqueror's good graces. At all
events, we are supposed now to be free from war's
alarms, if not tired of them, but are very anxious to
know what will be said and thought in England of
these strange occurrences.

The garrison of Berlin is expected to return in
about ten days, to the great delight of all the young
women and many of the old ones.

25th. —As a means of engaging Bonaparte to
withdraw his troops from Hameln, and to renounce
his intention of reconquering the electorate, Prussia
undertakes to ensure the retreat of all troops but her
own. It is doubtful whether Bonaparte will agree
to this, or, if he does, whether he will not attach to
his acquiescence some dishonourable conditions to
which this country could not consent. However,
Prussia founds upon it her hope of being able to
disarm; the delay of which causes her a daily expenditure of one hundred thousand dollars.

In a political journal published here under Prussian

censorship, it was stated a few days ago that, in the
impending arrangements, Hanover would be divided
between the King of Prussia, and the Duke of
Brunswick, who would be created Elector of Westphalia. It was added that, at all events, that part of
the electorate between the Elbe and the Weser would
become Prussian territory. It is a new and extraordinary thing for this Government to allow a statement of its views to reach the public through the
medium of a newspaper. The circumstance is also
the more noteworthy, because the statement is in
harmony with the general expectation respecting the
ultimate disposal of Hanover.

26th.—The conduct of Count Haugwitz, when
commissioned to announce to Bonaparte the engagements which the King of Prussia had entered into
at Potzdam with the two imperial Courts, has given
great offence to Austria, he having proceeded no
further in the negotiation with which he was charged
than the production of his full powers. It appears
that he constantly evaded, under various pretexts,
making known the stipulations of the Treaty to the
Austrian minister, Count Stadion, and even refused
to confer on the subject with him.

It was the general opinion, at the time, that a
more unfortunate choice could not have been made
than that of Count Haugwitz as negotiator. Yet it
would be necessary to know, before giving full
credence to the allegation against him, *the date* of
what passed between him and the Austrian minister.
For it is certain that, at a very early period of his

stay at Vienna, he communicated the intelligence
that Austria was negotiating for a separate peace;
which assertion was so far confirmed by the events
that followed the battle of Austerlitz, that many
persons have held that he would stand justified
before them for avoiding to commit his country in a
cause already, so far, abandoned by the party principally interested in it.

At all events, the reports from Vienna are not
likely to produce any effect here. Baron Hardenberg
may express indignation, and the reports may be
laid before the king, but Count Haugwitz will find
more than one zealous advocate to plead in his
favour.

27*th*.—It is now publicly known that the discussion with France is brought to an amicable conclusion,
and it is given out that the conditions are more
favourable for this country than could have been
expected.

It is understood that Hameln and the rest of the
electorate is to be given up to Prussia for immediate
occupation. The permanent disposal of the country
to be adjourned to the time of a general peace.

28*th*.—The Russian armies in Hanover and Silesia
have begun their march to St. Petersburg.

Very pressing requests have been made for the
immediate departure of the British troops, as it is
inferred, from several circumstances that have taken
place, that Lord Cathcart intends to maintain his
position near Bremen against the occupation of a
Prussian army. He is said to be throwing up

intrenchments, and to have given an intimation to
the senate at Bremen to send away the French
consul from that town.

Fifty thousand Prussians remain on the war
establishment.

29th.—It having been notified that the continuance
of the negotiation at this Court should be entrusted
to *Lord Harrington*, much surprise was expressed at
it, and Prince Dolgoruski has especially requested to
know what is the object of his lordship's mission.

30th.—The Bavarian minister has received and
presented his new credentials. More hesitation is
felt in acknowledging the Elector of Würtemberg's
new title, owing to the engagement this court lies
under, in common with that of Copenhagen and
Hanover, to support the constitution of the states of
Würtemberg as they existed before the late innovations. But this country is now placed too much
under the control of French counsels to admit of an
independent line of conduct being followed in any
transaction.

Feb. *2nd.*—The French minister has received a
present from the king of a very valuable diamond
snuff-box, upon the occasion of the amicable settlement of the late differences between this country and
France.

3rd.—Notwithstanding this, much uneasiness is
felt here on account of the French troops having
taken up a position on the Maine and the Lahn. It
begins also to be doubted whether General Barbou
will deliver up the fortress of Hameln. The

Prussian troops, meanwhile, continue their return to their usual quarters, with the exception of the regiments of the garrisons of Berlin and Potzdam, which, yesterday, were ordered to remain on the war establishment.

4th.—The sale of their best horses and the dismissal of the furlough men, which should have taken place next week, is postponed, and thus twenty thousand men are added to the immediately disposable force of the Prussian army.

As soon as this new arrangement became known in Berlin, the public—who are very far from being satisfied with the actual state of things—were eager to learn what fresh act of hostility had given occasion for the change of orders. It is thus explained. Count Schulenberg, on arriving at Hildesheim, sent to General Tolstoi to urge the departure of the Russian troops, and was told in answer, that they could not begin their march for want of money. To remove this difficulty, the Prussian general offered to advance the sum required. The reply has not yet been received ; but no further delay on the part of General Tolstoi is expected, as the entry of the Prussians is postponed only from the 13th to the 17th. On the other hand, the French are extremely impatient for the departure of the Russians, and General Augereau has advanced towards the frontier of Hesse. He declares that he has orders not to halt until the Russians have left, and that if they are not speedily replaced by the Prussians, he shall himself undertake to reconquer the electorate.

It was yesterday publicly asserted by M. Laforêt that Bonaparte, before leaving Vienna, received proposals from that Court for a marriage between a princess of Austria and Eugène Beauharnois!

5th.—We were not a little affected by the intelligence brought here yesterday evening, by express, of the death of Mr. Pitt. The melancholy event has caused a general expression of sorrow in this city.

We have, indeed, sustained a heavy loss. God grant it may not be an irreparable one. Few, I believe, even amongst his opponents, but feel the greatness of the loss to the country, and those who were the most violent amongst his adversaries must, ere long, acknowledge it without hesitation. My brother's remark was, that " he never ceased to be great but when he yielded his own opinions to those men not so well qualified to judge as himself." For myself—to whom he was remarkably kind, and showed many civilities—having seen him so recently, and in such good spirits from the favourable turn events had then taken, the news of his death comes upon me with a heavier shock; for I placed little stress on the gossip of the Pump-room respecting his health, that came to us in our Bath letters. I am, however, inclined to say, with Tacitus, when he consoled himself for the premature death of Agricola with the reflection that he had not lived to see the republic overthrown by Domitian—for which I would substitute the overthrow of the entire Continent by Bonaparte—" he was no less happy in his illustrious life than in his opportune death."

Our common enemy, no doubt, regards this sad event as the removal of a barrier to his insatiable ambition; but, though deprived of the talents of a Pitt, and the intrepidity of a Nelson, by unanimity and exertion we may yet bring him down from his pinnacle, lustrous as "*his star*" may now seem to him to be.

From Mrs. Jackson.

Bath, February 16th, 1806.

MY DEAR GEORGE,

I well knew what your sensations would be on hearing of our national loss, and my thoughts constantly revert to Francis and you when I hear the subject canvassed, and all the consequences anticipated from it. The political world is in extraordinary confusion. All Mr. Pitt's friends are rejected. *Our* friend, Mr. Rolleston, has refused to be under-secretary of state, in which he is wise; for no one *here* thinks that Mr. Fox will be in long, so that he would literally be giving up a substance for a shadow. But R. has got his son, not yet seventeen, appointed private secretary to Mr. Fox. Lord Grenville wants a good thing for his brother, T. G.—some persons think he intends him to be speaker; but *I* don't think that in Tom's line. All the foreign ministers, they say, are to be recalled; Mr. Elliot and your brother, the only exceptions to the general sweep. I trust it may be so; for though no doubt it will be delightful to me to see you both again, that delight must be in a degree damped by the idea of Francis being removed in such a way, and at such a time.

I never remember such a clearance, even the nearest relations, Lord Chatham, and Mr. Singleton, Lord Cornwallis's son-in-law. No one thinks it can last long. There will be a new parliament; and though Fox has got the majority in the Cabinet, it is the general opinion that the Grenvilles will turn them out soon.

I did not see Mr. Pitt this winter. There was always a crowd assembled to look at him, at which he was vastly hurt. Lord Bridport told me that he had not seen him for a week when he heard that he was going away; and that he then wrote to Captain Stanhope, requesting to know if he could see him. He was admitted, and was, he says, shocked at the change, which was far beyond what he could have believed would take place in so short a time. Pitt's death, he says, was the death of a martyr; that he died for his country as much as though a ball had shot him down.

I began to be tired of hearing so much of Lord Nelson, though he was a great admiral. We have not the same complaint to make now; Mr. Pitt died and was buried without a hundredth part of the sensation the other excited. All I hear of him now is, that the last book Mr. Pitt read *here* was a novel, which interested him so much that he could not lay it down till he had finished it; so everybody is reading "The Novice of St. Dominic," and it is so much in request that I who, like the rest, am

curious to read it, cannot yet get it, though be-
spoken for me at more than one place.

Erskine, they say, is known not to be fit for a
chancellor, and is put in only that they may make
him a peer and give him a good pension. His grief
was so great at the loss of his wife—who died very
suddenly from an overdose of laudanum, or some
other narcotic—that the Bishop of London sat up
with him a whole night, but refused to consecrate his
garden, where he wished to bury her. You will not
wonder, after that, to hear he is soon to be married
to his mistress—a blacksmith's daughter.

I suppose Sir John Warren's news has reached
you. We had accounts, *viâ* Falmouth, as early as
the 5th, that he had met the enemy, and was seen
drawn up in battle array. We always get the first
news from that quarter; as we knew before you of
Trafalgar—the account being brought in by the
mails covered with laurels and ribands — to your
great annoyance, you remember, when you thought to
send me the first account piping hot from London, in
your dripping wet "extra Gazette." So much for
public news. I know you don't much regard Bath
news; but if my budget has amused you, dear
George, it has answered the purpose of

Your affectionate mother,

C. J.

Diaries—Feb. 26*th.*—My brother has just received
a despatch from Mr. Fox, in answer to one from
Berlin of the 10th. I never remember so quick an

exchange. It must have blown a hurricane both ways. We now know the final arrangements of the new Cabinet, but are a little impatient to hear how far the change is likely to affect us here.

The newspapers persist in turning out all the foreign ministers; but we ought to suppose, on seeing the composition of the new ministry, that party feelings would have little or no influence now. And it is to be hoped that the system will not prevail of regarding the diplomatic profession merely as one from which a provision can be made for political adherents; especially now that so strong an union of men and talents cannot stand in need of reinforcement by such expedients. Lord G. L. Gower had already intended to return home; and Sir A. Paget, since they have published his despatches, must retire.

27th.—Baron Hardenberg, who has been staying at his country house, returned a few days since to Berlin. On that occasion the officers of the garrison —who had marched in the preceding day from their cantonments in Upper Saxony—took the opportunity to give his Excellency a public testimony of their respect and attachment by assembling in front of his house, with the bands of their respective regiments playing the favourite military and national airs.

This homage, paid by a distinguished corps of the Prussian army to the high principle and public spirit that actuated the minister in the late crisis, was particularly gratifying to him, and, report says, was highly approved of by the king. There is, however, no doubt that the garrison of Berlin was on this occasion a faithful interpreter of the sentiments of the whole army.

Count Haugwitz has, on the contrary, drawn upon himself the severe and openly expressed censure of the public generally. For it is thought that the embarrassing position in which the country is now placed is owing chiefly to his counsels and conduct, while the popular feeling of resentment towards him is still further increased by the present proceedings and progress of the French in Franconia, under the circle of the Upper Rhine.

They are bringing together there a very considerable force, and levying heavy contributions—of which the town of Frankfort has hitherto paid the largest share. Assessments are also made on the Landgrave of Darmstadt, the Princes of Nassau, Weilburg and Usingen, as well as some other small states in that neighbourhood.

Instead of giving orders for the evacuation of Germany, Bonaparte has actually sent for fresh troops from France, and they are now on their march to cross the Rhine. No explanation is given of these proceedings, and the only construction that can be put upon them is certainly not favourable for the realization of the king's anxious wish to secure the tranquillity of Germany. But, notwithstanding the dissatisfaction expressed by all classes, it is pretty certain that whatever the plans of Bonaparte may be, this Government will oppose little or no resistance to them.

General Bennigsen, the commander-in-chief of the
Russian army in Silesia, came here a few days since
to have an interview with the king, at the request
of the latter. His troops had begun their march
homewards in the preceding week, as had also those
under the command of General Tolstoi.

The result of Count Haugwitz's mission is not made
known, but great agitation prevails in this city
respecting it, owing to the unexpected arrival of
M. de Lucchesini from Paris, on the 24th, after a
rapid journey of seven days and a half.

28th.—There is, however, no doubt that Bonaparte, whose head-quarters are now at Witzlow, has
determined not to withdraw his troops until he has
reduced the north of Germany to the same state of
subjection as the south. His immediate object seems
to be to cut off Great Britain from all intercourse
with the Continent, and to follow up his favourite
plan of transferring the electoral dominions to some
other sovereign. He insists that Prussia shall
disarm entirely, and that she shall close the ports
of the North Sea against British commerce. For
these acts of complaisance he is willing to reward
her with both Hanover and Hamburg; Lubeck he
destines for Denmark, in case she will venture to
forbid the passage of the Sound to the British flag.
The army assembling on the Lahn and Upper Rhine
is intended to intimidate Prussia and Denmark into
compliance with Bonaparte's demands, and it is the
opinion of many well-informed persons in Berlin
that Prussia, at least, as she rejects the idea of

resistance by force of arms, has no alternative but submission.

As to Denmark, Count Bernstorff, who has just left Berlin after a second private mission from his Court, said, in my hearing, that "those who knew anything of the character of the prince royal would feel persuaded that he would prefer rather to fall under the ruins of Copenhagen than suffer any infringement of the independence of his country." Whether this asseveration be worth more than the often repeated declaration of the King of Prussia, that "he would never assume the sovereignty of Hanover unless he obtained the King of England's consent," remains to be seen. Sanguine hopes have, however, been entertained of procuring that consent through the intervention of the Emperor of Russia ; and it is now pretty generally known, and, indeed, in confidence it has been acknowledged, that that is the principal object of the Duke of Brunswick's mission.

March 1*st.*—Bonaparte being now free from the fear of encountering an impediment on the side of Austria, seems to consider the present moment well calculated for the pursuance of his schemes in this quarter, as well as a favourable one for the chastisement of the king for the part he took, however unwillingly, in the transactions of November and December—at least, if we may judge from the nature of the new demands on Prussia, which have just come to our knowledge. He requires the immediate cession of Anspach, or, if that be too unpalatable to the king, that his troops should at once occupy Hanover, in order that it may be placed under the government of a member of his family; most probably General Murat.

It is also his will that Count Schulenberg should be recalled, and placed at the head of the foreign department of this country, to the entire exclusion of Baron Hardenberg, and that the king should renounce his connection with Russia, and enter into an alliance with France.

A messenger has, in fact, been sent to Hanover, to recall Count Schulenberg to Berlin. A circumstance which, if viewed as an immediate compliance with one of Bonaparte's demands, is a bad omen of the determination that may be looked for on the other two. His recall was regarded as a preparatory step to some resistance to be opposed to the advance of the French. For Count Schulenberg having the rank of lieutenant-general of cavalry must, while he remains with the army, of necessity, retain the command of it. But he has never seen service since he left the army, as a lieutenant, in early life, when the late king, as a particular mark of his regard and favour, gave him the titular rank of lieutenant-general. As he retained a predilection for military life, and it was not expected that the occupation of Hanover would lead to any active service, the command of the troops, as well as the civil administration of the country, was conferred on him as an additional mark of favour from his present sovereign. But as matters now wear a different aspect, and the advice of General Schulenberg is said to be necessary in the council about to be held, it was thought that the opportunity had been taken of appointing General Rüchel to replace him in his command. The anti-Gallican sentiments of that officer are well known, and he has been throughout the winter one of the warmest advocates for a war with France.

Allowing for exaggerations, the French troops now in Germany north of the Danube, including the auxiliaries of Bavaria and Würtemberg, probably do not number less than a hundred thousand men. And this force is so disposed between the Lahn and the Danube as to surround the principality of Anspach, to menace the Electorate of Hesse, to cut off the Westphalian provinces of this country from the main body of the Prussian troops, and to keep up the command of the resources which are now drawn from the countries on the Maine.

The Elector of Hesse, his treasure, and his army would be at the mercy of the enemy at the very first breaking out of hostilities; and there is but little doubt that the part played by the Elector of Bavaria, at an early period of the war with Austria, would be repeated in the case of Hesse.

We know that the elector is now treated with exceeding coldness by Bonaparte, and that he, as well as Talleyrand, refuses to hold any communication with M. de Möltzberg, the Hessian minister at Paris.

Before it was understood that the conclusion of an alliance with France was one of Bonaparte's injunc-

tions to this Court, it was said by the French party,
without any attempt at concealment, that Prussia
must choose between the alliance and hostility of
France and Russia; for that things were come to a
point that admitted of no other alternative.

2nd.—The king is about to establish a militia to
replace in garrison and other duties the 3rd battalion
of the regiments of the line, which, to the amount of
about fifty thousand men, will thus be added to the
effective force of the army.   The militia will only be
called out, and receive pay and clothing, in time of
war.   It will consist of all persons subject to the
military conscription who, on account of their size,
cannot be received in the line; and of all foreign
recruits who have passed the age at which they are
admitted into the regular service.

The regiment of dragoons lately under the
nominal command of the Margrave of Anspach, and
of which General Kalkrcuth is colonel, is henceforth,
by the king's command, to be called the Queen's regiment of Dragoons.   This is a distinction conferred
in this country for the first time.

3rd.—The hopes of those to whom the honour of
their country is dear are, unfortunately, not to be
realized.   Count Schulenberg returns to Hanover, and
General Rüchel to his governorship of Königsberg,
for the king cannot resolve on a war with France.
He must, therefore, comply with the conqueror's
demands, and is thus placed in the dilemma of either
giving up Anspach without an equivalent, or of
forfeiting the pledge that was given to the Emperor

of Russia that Hanover should not be alienated without His Britannic Majesty's consent.

No orders have been given for stopping the return of the troops to their usual garrisons, nor has it in any way been intimated to General Bennigsen, who, three days ago, took his final leave of the king, that there was any wish that the Russian army should halt.

The General had his family in Berlin, and they have been treated during their stay with especial marks of distinction by their Prussian Majesties. On taking leave of the king, the General was invested with the Order of the Black Eagle.

I heard it confidently asserted this morning that, as an expedient for paying off the arrears due to the French army from the Austrian hereditary dominions, it was stipulated in a secret article of the Treaty of Presburg, that the French should be privileged to levy contributions in Frankfort, Nürnberg, and other towns.

The king and his council have decided that absolute possession shall be taken of the Electorate of Hanover, and that the cession of Anspach, stipulated in the Convention of the 15th of December, shall be made without delay.

Orders have been sent to Wesel; and several civil officers employed in the department of the Franconian provinces, set out yesterday to superintend the delivery of the Margraviate to the French.

The council that discussed these measures, in the presence of the king, consisted of Baron Hardenberg, the Marquis de Lucchesini, Field-Marshal Möllendorff,

General Rüchel, General Köchritz, MM. Lombard, and Beym.

Baron Hardenberg and General Rüchel, alone, opposed them, and the former refused to counter-sign the king's order for the execution of the measures. It will, therefore, appear with His Majesty's signature only. The baron has again expressed his wish to retire from office. He is distressed in the greatest degree at what has occurred, and the utmost dejection prevails amongst those few persons connected with this Government who have any sort of feeling for the honour and dignity of their country and their king.

Letters—March 3rd.—You have become quite violent in your politics, my dear M., since you went into opposition. Your letters, just received, are absolutely scurrilous. Francis desires me to remind you that letters are sometimes opened before they reach our hands, especially in the present state of things, and entrusted, as yours were, to the ordinary post. What is said in the innocence of Bath gossip might be thought very objectionable here, and be revenged on the receivers. This looks a little like turn-ing the tables upon you for the lecture you wrote me when in Paris four years ago ; and I confess I would rather my brother had himself given you a hint to be more guarded in repeating the opinions expressed in Bath of the King and Queen of Prussia. He is, however, too fully occupied with business to write a line to-day, and the letter especially complained of was also addressed to me. I own to you that, I don't think your people are very far wrong in saying the

King of Prussia is no better than Bonaparte. For a vigorous resistance to his encroachments would certainly have prevented much mischief that would seem now to be irreparable. As to the story of the lace gowns, &c., it has been abominably misrepresented, and the consequences drawn from it are altogether erroneous. Madame Bonaparte's decorations have never been worn by the queen, or Bonaparte's Eagle by the king.

All I have to say on the subject of your politics is, that you know my brother is not a party man. Though a great admirer of Mr. Pitt, it does not prevent him from doing justice to Mr. Fox, and believing that he has the good of the country sincerely at heart.

Everybody's attention is so much taken up with the events of the moment that we have little or nothing going on in the way of amusement, and there are very few English, for the threatening aspect of affairs has made them anxious to get home. We have one amusing specimen of our countrymen in a Rev. Mr. Cox, an old Westminster, and whose son was a frequenter of Dean's Yard at the same time as myself. He has been travelling with a Russian, Prince Bariatinski, who has lived much in England, and is now on his way thither to marry a daughter of Lord Sherborne. Mr. Cox is famous for shooting with a long bow, and for wholesale dealing in superlatives. For all that, perhaps because of that, he is most diverting, and is besides a most good-natured, generous fellow; but he has never been able,

clever as he is, to master the French language,
though he has spent a great part of his life on the
Continent, which, as he has a great deal to say, and
is by no means backward in his wish to say it, is
unfortunate. He was introduced at our house; a few
evenings ago, to the Countess Voss, a fine stiff old
lady of the old school, in its fullest sense—being one
of the highest bred, and of the most ancient family
of her set—when, meaning to be very *amiable and
polite*, Mr. Cox stammered out, " Que, comme lui
était le petit cochon du Prince Bariatinski, qui le
suivit partout, elle, grande-maîtresse, était *le petit
cochon de la reine*," a style of address that greatly
astonished the dignified old lady.

Mr. Cox, I hear, is the author of several tours,
more amusing than veracious.

The countess had had an interview with a mad-
man on the preceding day—a gentleman of the
name of Koas, who had arrived in Berlin from the
country, and put up at one of the principal inns.
The people of the house noticed the agitation of his
manners, and his constant repetition of " Oh, I have
missed my purpose—but, another time, another time
I shall succeed," &c. On examining his room, a
pair of loaded pistols was found on his table, and
soon after it was known that he had been to the
palace, and mistaking, probably, the queen's apartment for the king's, had demanded admittance, but
had been turned away by a servant who, fortunately,
was in the antechamber.

It is the custom here for the officers, coming to

report themselves, or having other military business, to go into the king's room without being announced, and had this man done so the consequences, most likely, would have been fatal. However, not gaining admittance to the queen's rooms he went to those of the *grande-maîtresse*, the Countess Voss, to whom he made a long, incoherent communication, and put many startling questions, then rushed away, and returned to his inn. Shortly after he was arrested by the police. He unhesitatingly declared to them that his purpose was to take the king's life, which several sovereigns of Europe, and particularly the King of Sweden, had commissioned him to do. That he should then marry the queen, and that his intention was to govern the country upon a very different system from that in favour with the present king.

It has been ascertained that this unfortunate person was formerly in the Danish service, but has, of late, lived on his estate in Mecklenburg. He is connected with the first families of the Duchy, and is to be sent to his friends, with the intimation, that should he again appear within the Prussian territory he will be confined for life.

Adieu, my dear M.—We place no reliance on the report that Lord *and Lady* Holland are likely to supersede my brother at Berlin.

Diaries—March 6th.—Scarcely had the humiliating intelligence become known, that Anspach was to be delivered up in compliance with the demands of Bonaparte, than a fresh pang was added to it by the

arrival of a Prussian officer with the information
that the French, without waiting for the decision of
the King of Prussia upon the points submitted to
him for consideration and acceptance, had taken
possession of Anspach, with a corps of fifteen thousand
men, on the 24th ult., the very day on which M. de
Lucchesini reached Berlin from Paris. The number
of troops has since been increased to near forty
thousand. The French have taken possession of all
the public offices, besides a considerable sum of money
found in them.

8th.—The king and queen are gone to Stettin,
but are expected back shortly. His Majesty has
sent the Black Eagle to General Tolstoi, and the
Red Eagle to several other Russian officers. The
object of this journey is to see the Russian army
pass through Stettin on its homeward march.

9th.—The insignia of the Order of St. Andrew,
very richly set in diamonds, have just been received
from the Emperor of Russia, by Baron Hardenberg ;
and M. de Lucchesini, who leaves for Paris to-day,
with his letters of credence to the King of Italy,
carries with him valuable presents from the king for
different members of the French Government.

11th.—As every other part of Count Haugwitz's
convention is being carried into execution, it is not
unlikely that the report is correct of the stipulated
offensive and defensive alliance being also agreed to.
This is, however, denied. Perhaps, because modified
by the omission of the words offensive and defensive,
the alliance still subsisting. What Bonaparte may

ultimately decide upon respecting Hanover, no one,
at present, ventures to conjecture.

12th.—The inhabitants of Anspach, not aware
that they were to fall, almost without notice of their
fate, into the hands of the enemy, forwarded a
petition to the king, which arrived at the same time
as the news that the French, anticipating the king's
determination, had already entered and taken possession.   They implored that their country might
not be alienated from the Prussian dominions, and
offered to forego every exemption from personal
service in order to support His Majesty in a war for
their defence; proposing also to raise money and
men for that purpose to the utmost extent the country
would possibly admit of, and concluding with the
strongest expressions of attachment, and a declaration of their sentiments of loyalty towards their
sovereign.

The king is said to have been much affected by
this earnest prayer of his faithful subjects; and could
he then have resolved on daring to do, that which he
would, there is no doubt, have been glad to do,
the inhabitants of Anspach might have received an
answer more worthy, alike of him, and of them.   The
king, in reply to their petition, said, " The proof
they had given of their fidelity and attachment
to their sovereign would never be forgotten by
him."

The large force placed in Anspach is intended as
a check upon Austria, of whose future intentions
Bonaparte is said to be suspicious.   The army on the

frontier of Hesse will operate in the same way upon Prussia.

15th.—The British minister at Hesse, passing through Berlin on his way to England, has been prevented, by order of the king, at the command of the French Government, from making the few days' stay he had proposed doing in this capital. Passports were furnished for continuing his journey immediately on his arrival, and the Prussian minister was exceedingly anxious until assured that Mr. Taylor was off again post haste. The Government feared the possibility of his arrest, and the consequences that must have resulted from it. Yet it is a known and recognized fact, that Bonaparte could not substantiate any charge whatever against Mr. Taylor. And that his intercepted letters and despatches, which were published in the " Moniteur," could not, by even the most perverse construction, be twisted into a justification of the incessant persecution he was for a considerable time subjected to by the myrmidons of Bonaparte, while resident at the Court to which he was accredited.

The King of Prussia cannot surely bow more lowly and more humbly before the mighty conqueror, if he is still to be regarded as a king.

The Landgrave of Darmstadt, who remained firm in his allegiance to the emperor and the empire, and resisted every temptation to join the French army, has been abandoned to Bonaparte's resentment; a deaf ear has been turned to the supplications of the king's faithful subjects in Anspach, and the Govern-

ment has felt, and confessed, that the capital of the
kingdom is no safe asylum, even for a few hours, to a
subject and representative of a friendly power, should
he be an object of Bonaparte's displeasure. No wonder
that it should have been said in bitterness of feeling
by one strongly attached to his sovereign and his
country, " Who, but must now despair of rousing
our king to a sense of his duty; to himself as a
man, to his people as their ruler !"

17*th.*—The accounts just received from Paris state
that ratifications have been exchanged between
M. de Haugwitz and Talleyrand, of a treaty agreeing
in all respects with the Convention of Dec. 15th,
with the one exception of the alliance being defensive, but not offensive.

19*th.*—In consequence of the great dissatisfaction
openly expressed, at the lamentable proceedings of
this Government, as well by the military as by the
general public, an order has been issued to the
officers of the garrison of Berlin to abstain, under
severe penalties, from speaking of the state of public
affairs; and it has been in contemplation to publish
an edict, prohibiting the public at large from discussing questions of state policy. This measure is,
however, deferred, under the hope that the course
adopted to silence the garrison may produce, generally, the desired effect. As yet it has failed to
do so; and the satire, the sarcasm, and the *jeux
d'esprit* directed against the chief members of the
government were never so bitter and so frequent as
now, and never were sentiments more opposed to

each other than are those of the nation and those
of its rulers.

20th.—Part of the army of Frankfort, under
General Augereau, has marched to take possession
of the duchy of Berg.   The other part is on its way
to occupy Cleves, on the right bank of the Rhine.
These troops were to be replaced by fresh detachments, that would remain in Frankfort until the
contribution of four million florins should be fully
paid to the French Government.

22nd.—The fortresses of Hameln and Wesel were
to be evacuated on the 18th; but when a detachment of Prussian troops marched from their cantonments to take possession of the fortresses, General
Barbou refused to deliver over that of Hameln until,
as originally arranged, the French troops had received their pay, up to the 1st of April.   General
Schulenberg, finding that payment was absolutely
insisted upon, required it to be made by the States.
They represented their total inability to raise the
necessary sum, and, finally, the General was obliged
to take upon himself to make good the deficiency.
Upon these terms *one gate* of the fortress was given
up to the Prussians.

24th.—Since that, General Rapp has brought
orders from Paris for the evacuation ·of Hameln ;
and Schulenberg having collected upwards of two
hundred thousand dollars from the public chests of
Magdeburg and Hildesheim, and satisfied the demands of General Barbou, that officer took his
departure.   This act of complaisance on the part of

Count Schulenberg would, however, have failed to move the French from Hameln, as General Barbon himself made known, had he not received the orders brought by General Rapp. The King of Prussia has ordered the artillery of the fortress of Wesel to be given up to the French, and has consented to take, in exchange for it, the iron guns that remained at Hameln after the Hanoverian artillery was carried away last autumn.

It is now generally understood that the *transactions* between this country and France are *closed for the present.* The only immediate anxiety felt is to know what steps these transactions will lead to on the part of England and Russia.

25th.—The Duke of Brunswick is returned from St. Petersburg. He travelled so rapidly that he was but eleven days on his journey. The emperor has not expressed, it appears, so much dissatisfaction on the subject of Hanover as was expected; and from all we learn, it is not likely that Russia will interfere very warmly on the occasion.

The duke and his suite were received and treated by the emperor and his Court with every possible mark of personal favour and distinction.

26th.—It has transpired that his serene highness was charged to make proposals for a marriage between Prince Henry of Prussia and the Grand Duchess Catherine. And, in order to render the proposals more acceptable to the Court of St. Petersburg, to offer to form an establishment for the prince at Hanover—for the support of which the revenues

of the electorate should be assigned. The duke
brought with him the insignia, superbly enriched
with diamonds and other valuable gems, of the Order
of St. Catherine; conferred by the emperor on the
duchess. They have been sent on to her to
Brunswick, the duke intending to remain here some
days.

27*th*.—The King of Prussia's proclamation for the
final assumption of the sovereignty of Hanover will
very shortly appear. It has been sent to Paris for
approval; Bonaparte having been much dissatisfied
with that of the 27th of January. Lubeck and the
ports of the German Sea are to be closed to the
British flag. For this the king takes much credit to
himself, and considers that he has earned the gratitude of the continental powers by thus thoroughly
carrying out his *système pacifique* and securing, at
all sacrifices, the tranquillity of Northern Germany.
There are, however, many who take a very different view of the matter; who think the honour of
the Prussian name sullied by the course the king
has pursued, and deplore the fate of their country,
subjugated as she is, with every means of resistance
in her hands, to the tyranny and mad ambition of
the Corsican adventurer.

The resignation of M. de Hardenberg has not
been accepted, but he has received unlimited leave of
absence; which would seem to be a means adopted
by the King of Prussia to conceal from himself his
having yielded to Bonaparte's injunction to dismiss
his minister. M. de Haugwitz will resume the

entire direction of foreign affairs, and the whole conduct of the business of government will be under the exclusive influence of French authority.

Amongst those persons who are not wholly devoted to the French interest, and who, from the nature of their avocations, are more particularly acquainted with, and therefore the more desirous to avert the consequences that may ensue from the measures now decided upon, the utmost uneasiness exists respecting the decision of the British Government in this crisis of affairs. They do not scruple to acknowledge that the very greatest distress must arise from the suspension of the commerce of the above-named ports, and the effect it will produce on the Prussian revenue—of which a fourth part is derived from the excise duties.

The public, also, have not failed to observe that the injury put upon Great Britain is not only gratuitous, and unprovoked, but that the form and manner of it are of a character in many respects altogether irreconcilable with any principle of good faith or fair dealing ; especially when the terms are considered on which the retreat of His Majesty's troops from the Continent was obtained. Hopes, however, are cherished that war may yet be prevented. They are founded on the belief that the commercial interests of Great Britain will not allow of her taking the closure of the ports of the North Sea as a provocation to hostilities, and that she will be disposed to content herself with the advantage of having the ports in the Baltic still open to her.

The personal friendship existing between the Emperor of Russia and the King of Prussia will induce the former, it is thought, to use his endeavours to prevent the commencement of hostilities, or, at all events, to refrain from taking part in them himself; while the interests both of England and Russia will render them, it is considered, unwilling to consolidate the union between France and Prussia by any attack on the latter power.

General Murat arrived yesterday se'nnight at Düsseldorf, with a numerous suite. That town is to be made the seat of government of the duchies of Berg and Cleves. Murat will be constituted sovereign, with a vote at the Diet of Ratisbon, and with the rank, it is said, of elector. Louis Bonaparte is to take possession of Holland; but whether he will assume the title of king, or one more analogous to that of stadtholder, is not yet made known.

A battalion of hussars is under orders to march towards the frontiers of Mecklenburg; and seventeen thousand men, under General Count Kalkreuth, and Lietenant-General Schmettau, are to take up a position on the borders of Pomerania and Perleberg, as a demonstration against Swedish Pomerania, and to compel the King of Sweden entirely to evacuate Lauenburg, where he has left a detachment of about five hundred cavalry. It was known that he had determined not to withdraw them, and some violent measures, it is feared, will be resorted to, to compel him to retreat.

A Russian force lately appeared off Cattaro, and

took that, and the other forts commanding the bays called *les bouches de Cattaro.* The Austrian officer had refused to admit the Russians, alleging that his orders directed him to deliver the forts to the French. An attack ensued, which was followed by a capitulation. The French arrived the day after it was signed.

General Blücher has sent his son to Berlin with information of the French having taken possession of the abbeys of Essen and Werder, bordering on Cleves. On the arrival of the troops, General Blücher immediately sent four battalions of infantry and a strong detachment of cavalry into the same quarters that the French had occupied, and prohibited the inhabitants from supplying the latter with provisions or other necessaries.

In the same way, the French have since possessed themselves of several Prussian fiefs—amongst them the county of Gimborn, held, under the crown, by Field-Marshal Walmoden. All these encroachments are made under pretence of engagements, expressed or implied, in the recent treaties between Prussia and France.

Count Haugwitz is daily expected from Paris, and it is supposed that he will bring an account of further cessions made by him on behalf of this country. Meanwhile, his signature has been put to the proclamation for the taking possession of Hanover.

I am off to England to-night.

Cuxhaven, March 31st, 1806.

Letters.—Everything has favoured and facilitated my journey thus far. I reached Hamburg yesterday morning, and found Mr. Thornton not altogether unprepared for the news I brought. It was determined that I should get down to this place by water, without loss of time ; and at daylight I arrived here with a letter to the commanding officer of His Majesty's ships and vessels at the mouth of the Elbe.

This letter, without letting him into all the circumstances of the case, contained an intimation that it was necessary to stop the entrance into the Elbe of two convoys of great value, daily expected from Leith and Hull, until further notice from Mr. Thornton, as well as British merchant ships in general that might be entering the Elbe or Weser, and to keep them in these roads under the protection of his guns.

The second object was, if possible, to detain the Prussian courier, who, by-the-bye, only arrived yesterday morning; but unfortunately he is gone. However, the packet he sailed in is one of the slowest, and I may therefore, not improbably, pass him. As yet there are no Prussian troops here. They are to begin marching in to-morrow, at the rate of one hundred and fifty each day until the whole have entered. The governor is gone to meet them. The inhabitants here have already scent of what is going forward, and are, accordingly, in a great fright. Prussian commissaries arrived here a few days ago,

but the townspeople say they would much rather
have the French than the Prussians.

At Hamburg, the state of things is but too generally known. Rapp gave the alarm, and Bourrienne
talks openly of it at the card table. There are about
fifteen British merchant vessels at Hamburg ; six or
seven are already laden, and they, at all events, will
soon have sailed.

The packet is getting under way. Wind fair,
but blowing hard, so that I have a good chance of a
quick passage.

G. J.

Reilly's Hotel, April 5th—Midnight.—How surprised you will be, my dear mother, to receive a
letter from London, and that not to tell you I have
arrived, but that I am off, after forty-eight hours'
stay. I have not had a moment unoccupied. I
have been twice with Mr. Fox—very gratifying
interviews, both as regards Francis and myself.

Half an hour ago, I thought I might venture to
turn in for the night, and to-morrow I purposed
to write you a long letter. But a messenger arrived
with despatches just as I got into my room, and it
is notified to me that, a determination being
come to relative to my business, I must set off
immediately on my return. The horses are ordered,
and in an hour hence I shall be on my road to
Harwich. As I send this in the form of a parcel,
I may tell you, that the contents of this night's
" Gazette " have been followed up by the order I take

for my brother to return to England with all possible
expedition, and without taking leave. I mention this,
because I know how anxious you would be; but, for
heaven's sake, don't let it be known, or even hinted
to any living soul. I don't know what the consequences might be *to me* if you were even to have the
appearance of expecting Francis.

Adieu, dearest mother. I regret that I must leave
England without seeing you; but you will agree
with me that, even for that pleasure, I could not
abandon the post of duty.

G. J.

Berlin, 18*th April.*—I arrived only this morning,
my dear mother. The winds and the waves proved
as unfavourable for my return as they were prosperous in wafting me over. It was my fate to cross in
one of the worst of the packets, and to be one of
the twenty-five people in a cabin with only twenty
berths. But the delightful scenes of that ten days'
voyage are now forgotten; for I am again snug in
port, and I hasten to give you that news to dispel
the anxious fears which I know you have felt on my
account. My brother will probably be detained here,
by certain arrangements, nearly three weeks longer.
Bartle Frere will be off in two or three days, and
with the departure of the next messenger, our official
correspondence will be closed.

My friend, Otto Löwenstern, alarmed at the warlike
appearance of affairs, began to fear that by further
delay he should render his long-projected journey to

England, less easy, if not impracticable : he therefore hastened his departure, and I had the mortification of learning, at the first stage out of Hamburg,
that he had passed in the contrary direction only an
hour before.   In fact, as far as I am personally concerned, my last trip—setting aside the importance
of the business on which I was despatched—was
attended with as little pleasure as could possibly be,
and from the time I left Berlin until I returned, I
literally had my clothes off but three times.   If you
see Otto before my return, receive him, my dear
mother, as your son, as such I have been received,
and affectionately welcomed, by his family for the
last three years.   G. J.

Diaries— *April* 20*th.* — My brother, in consequence of orders I brought from England to that
effect, yesterday requested the Prussian minister,
Count Haugwitz, to forward his passports immediately, as he was directed to quit Berlin without
delay.   The greatest consternation is excited by this
prompt decision of the British Government.

Baron Hardenberg announced, on the 15th, his
retirement from office on unlimited leave of absence.
He carries with him the respect and esteem of all
classes of persons in this country, as well as the
goodwill and regard of his sovereign.   He has
thought it advisable to reply, in the " Berlin Gazette,"
to a violent attack upon him in the " Moniteur " of
the 21st of March.*

* See Appendix, No. 9.

21*st*.—Count Haugwitz has been received with
the strongest public marks of general disapprobation, no less so by his friends than by those
openly opposed to him; for the interests of the
former are materially compromised by the lamentable
state of things he has been mainly instrumental in
bringing about, and in many instances, these selfish
considerations, rather than any worthier motives,
have led them to abandon him. The queen, and the
persons who compose her Court, have been most
pointedly reserved and cold in their manner towards
him, and some members of the government have
even declined to transact business with him.

23*rd*.—The Count has represented to my brother
that the present state of Prussian affairs is not
thought here, any more than in England, to be
one that can possibly be tolerated for any length of
time. He therefore urges him to put off his departure, and to employ whatever means may be in his
power to prevent an open rupture between the two
countries.

25*th*.—On Thursday night, during Count Haugwitz's absence from home, the windows of his house
were completely demolished by some persons unknown, and who have hitherto contrived to escape
detection. It is, however, strongly suspected that
the mischief has been done by some of the military of
this garrison, as carabine bullets were chiefly used
for the purpose. The same destructive smashing
occurred some nights before, on two successive occasions. The damage was repaired, and the Count

intended to take no notice of what had happened. But since the last attack, a party of police patrols the street in which he resides.

26th.—General Kalkreuth's regiments are to hold themselves in readiness to march at the shortest notice. The garrison of Berlin has been placed under his orders. The furlough men of the different regiments are recalled, and everything wears the appearance of some approaching military operations. The cause assigned for these measures is, the expectation that the King of Sweden will oppose the attempt to take possession of Lauenberg by the Prussian troops already despatched thither for that purpose, and that, if compelled to yield to a superior force, he will make an attack on some other part of the Prussian frontier. But they may be merely intended to intimidate His Swedish Majesty, who has made a public declaration of his intention to continue to protect the Electorate of Hanover at all risks.

27th.—The detachment of troops under Colonel Beeren, employed for the occupation of Lauenburg, entered that province on the 23rd, near Ratzeburg, where the Swedish cavalry was drawn up in a body. An officer, with a trumpeter, was sent to summon their commander, Count Löwenhjelm, to withdraw. He refused, and ordered his men to fire on the Prussians. The fire was returned, and resulted in the retreat of the Swedes. They afterwards entered the duchy of Magdeburg, near Gadebusch. A lieutenant and a private of Beeren's regiment were wounded ; the Swedes had one hussar killed, and

several wounded.   This Government intends to take
no notice of the affair, but it is doubted whether the
King of Sweden will be equally quiet.   General
Kalkreuth has orders to be prepared to resent any
further operations which His Swedish Majesty may
think fit to undertake.

May 4*th.*—The recent history of this Court may,
I think, be comprised in a few words :—

After the Emperor of Russia and his young
ministry abandoned the field of battle in Moravia,
with as much haste as they had gone to it, they
naturally lost a great part of their influence here.
They abandoned, at the same time, all the advantages which Bonaparte's rashness and Alexander's
meritorious efforts had obtained for us in this quarter,
and they made no struggle to retain or to recover
any part of them.   The consequence has been that
the French party resumed the upper hand, and has
now, more than ever, possession of His Prussian
Majesty's councils.   M. de Haugwitz has been the
principal instrument and actor employed by the
cabinet secretaries, and has ended by replacing himself
at the head of the foreign department.   He now
desires to call to his assistance, Count Keller, as a
sort of a make-weight, of which, indeed, he stands in
much need ; being himself so light as almost to kick
the beam, and, in fact, he hardly dare show himself
in public.

With regard to *our* immediate grounds of complaint, the spirited manner in which Great Britain
has resented the injustice and insolence of those

Gallic-Prussian measures, has both surprised and disconcerted the authors of them. It was not thought that we should take the thing so much amiss, or, if we did, that we could do so much mischief as is now apprehended. They are, therefore, endeavouring to cajole us by the promise of modifications, and connivance at the continuance of our continental commerce ; a promise which, even were it satisfactory, they, with the best dispositions, could keep no longer than it would take a courier to go from Berlin to Paris, and back again.

5th.—There has been a sort of coquetry between our Government and Bonaparte, but it does not appear likely to lead to anything more than an exchange of prisoners.

7th.—My brother left Berlin yesterday morning. I went with him as far as Bötsow, and returned in the evening. Until his furniture and effects are disposed of, I remain here, to look about me, and to accompany my sister-in-law, now recovering from an illness, to England.

The Court came from Potzdam yesterday, for the play that was given for the benefit of Schiller's widow. Their Majesties gave fifty louis, and the Duchess of Courland a subscription of thirty. They remain in Berlin for the special reviews of to-day and to-morrow.

8th.—M. de Bronikowski, one of the king's aides-de-camp, set out yesterday for the King of Sweden's head-quarters, with instructions to say that if His Swedish Majesty will remain quiet, and will take off the embargo on Prussian vessels, this Court will be satisfied. But that if he persists in his hostility a Prussian army will march, without delay, to the attack of Pomerania. Everybody seems to think that Bronikowski will not even be received, but will be served as Löwenhjelm was last year at this Court.

General Kalkreuth has been taken very ill at Pasewalk. M. de Massenbach is gone to take a share of his duties. The king sent off an express for Huffland, and he has set out for Pasewalk to attend the General.

9th.—Last night a mob again assembled round Count Haugwitz's house, and were about to repeat their acts of violence when a party of police came up; but the delinquents made so precipitate a retreat that none of them were taken.

10th.—Count Baudissin has just told me, he has received *official* advice from the Danish consul at Memel, that orders had been given to allow of the free ingress and egress of all British vessels at that port; and I have learnt that a similar permission has been, or is to be, given in regard to Lubeck and Embden. I must send off this news to Francis, though I believe that this sort of modification with which Prussia hopes to pacify our Government will produce no effect whatever, and that a straightforward course will be kept till all the measures we so justly complain of are redressed.

11th.—Count Keller has not accepted the post that was offered him, or rather, he has attached so many conditions to his acceptance of it, that it is thought it will not be pressed further upon him. He was very unwilling to be associated with M. de Haugwitz in the direction of public affairs; and, as a *sine quâ non* of his taking office, he required, in order to exempt him from a certain kind of suspicion that might attach to his doing so, that the king should add to his official instructions a positive order that no present of any kind, should be received by him from any foreign power, upon any occasion, or on any pretext whatever.

Mr. F. J. Jackson to G. Jackson.   On board the " Ariadne."

May 10*th.*—I embarked yesterday at eleven o'clock at Hamburg, in a small vessel Lord Falkland had sent for me, and came on board this frigate at nine last evening. His lordship is a fine handsome Scotchman, of whom I had before heard that he piqued himself on being at once a first-rate seaman, and a man *comme il faut*, qualities not often united; but I am bound to say that he has received me with the frankness of a sailor, and the courtesy of a gentleman.

Albemarle Street, May 13*th.*—I arrived to-day at one o'clock, and can say little more than that I have had a fine passage. I find all the world entirely taken up with Lord Melville's trial, so that I have seen no one but Mr. Fox, and him, only for a few minutes. I have an appointment with him for to-

morrow. I must remind you of my parting injunction at Bötsow. For you cannot be too careful,
while you look about you with your eyes well open,
not to let it be known, in any manner, that you
now take any interest or concern in public affairs.
In a word, all you have to do is to take care
that, while nothing escapes your notice, no notice
whatever is taken of you by the Government of the
country.

16*th*.—I have time only to tell you that the result
of a great confusion and clashing of ideas, and of perplexing pros and cons of a long discussion, is, that
it was yesterday decided that war should be formally
declared against Prussia. It is *possible* that Baron
Jacobi has given his Court information of this by a
messenger he despatched last night. But you may
remain perfectly quiet, and quietly settle all I left
unsettled in Berlin.

I was at the king's levée on Wednesday. There
were not more than twenty persons there, for only
official people now attend them. Afterwards I had a
private audience, of upwards of half-an-hour, in the
course of which many pleasant things were said to
me, and many *pleasant* questions asked. Yesterday
I kissed the queen's hand—she gave me a very
gracious reception.

17*th*.—I manage to steer clear of balls and routs,
for I am a good deal fagged with the business of the
moment. I dine to-day with the Duke of York,
which inconveniences me greatly, as it forces me to
give up a dinner party which Cavendish had made

on purpose for me, at his father's, and to which several persons were invited to meet me. Tell Count Göertz that I am induced to recommend, as the result of my inquiries, that the ships laden with corn, on account of the elector, should run for Lubeck as soon, and as fast, as they can ; the truth is, that Lubeck, notwithstanding our declaration, is not yet blockaded. As for the vessels under Prussian colours, it is difficult to give any advice, because, independent of the blockade, they will be seized by our cruisers wherever they are met with.

F. J. J.

Diaries, May 15th.—M. de Bronikowski returned yesterday from his mission to the King of Sweden. His Majesty received, and treated him very courteously, and he has brought his reply to the King of Prussia's letter. After an interview with Count Haugwitz, he went on to Potzdam, and in the course of the day was followed by the count. The substance of the King of Sweden's reply, a copy of which I have seen, is, that His Prussian Majesty could not have more at heart than himself the maintenance of peace and good understanding between the two countries. That, as a proof of it, he was willing to put a stop to those measures he had found it necessary to adopt, as soon as Prussia should consent to recall her troops from Lauenburg, to restore the country to the King of England, and that no port of the Baltic was closed to the British flag. An intimation was added that, in case these conditions were not complied with,

a squadron, already fitted out for the purpose, would
proceed to blockade those ports.

17th.—The effect produced by this answer may be
easily imagined. Orders have been sent to this
garrison for a corps of infantry, and a detachment of
artillery, to be held in readiness to march at a
moment's warning, and everything has assumed a
warlike appearance. Prince Louis, whose undisguised
reprobation of the recent measures of this Court
excites some uneasiness, is appointed to the chief
command of the expedition. That there is forth-
with to be war with Sweden is now in everybody's
mouth. Further orders are received, for the troops
to begin their march on the 20th.

19th.—To-day the above orders are countermanded,
for the present. This is owing to the arrival, on
Saturday, of a Major de Chapmann—son of the famous
admiral of that name in the last reign—with a second
letter to the king, modifying the demands of the
first. The major went on immediately to Charlottenburg. He was invited to the Sunday morning
parade, and afterwards to dine with the king. He
was placed at the marshal's table, and was treated
with the same marks of distinction as M. de Bronikowski received from the King of Sweden at
Stralsund. After dinner, the King of Prussia's
answer was delivered to him, with which he took his
departure the same evening. It corresponds with
the tenor of a conversation Count Haugwitz had
with M. Lützow on the subject. The king renews
the assurances of his pacific dispositions, and his

desire that the differences between the two countries should be amicably settled ; a desire of which, he says, he gives the most unequivocal proof in his readiness to overlook, and to consider as *non avenu*, as well what passed in Lauenburg, as the embargo, and the seizure of the Prussian vessels. But he rejects, in the most positive terms, all idea of combining the interests of His Swedish Majesty with those of his ally. This resolution he is determined to adhere to, both on the ground of his not recognizing the right of the King of Sweden to interfere in the affairs of England, as .that such an intervention, so far from facilitating, could only tend to protract, and render more intricate the negotiations with that country.

The last step taken by the King of Sweden appears to have given much satisfaction to all those who have no immediate interest in misrepresenting or denying it. He no longer persists in his demands respecting Lauenburg; but he requires peremptorily, and definitely, the re-opening of the Elbe. He has thus, as it were, turned the tables on the King of Prussia; for in proportion as the King of Sweden's former proposal was regarded as unconciliatory and inadmissible, his present one is allowed to be marked by moderation, and to require only what honour and justice would seem to dictate.

20th.—Thus matters stand at present. The general opinion is that neither party will give way, and that the King of Sweden, having gone to the utmost extent of concession, will found his right to interpose, on the appeal of His Britannic Majesty in his manifesto as Elector, and will resolutely persist in this last condition. Whether, in this case, this Court will immediately proceed to extremities appears very doubtful. It will certainly make every *demonstration* of an intention to commence hostilities. But so much forbearance has hitherto been shown on that head, and so great a disposition evinced to *ménager* the King of Sweden, that M. d'Alopeus tells me he trusts no decisive measures will be taken, until the return of a messenger who was sent to St. Petersburg with the letter brought by M. de Bronikowski from Stralsund.

It has been reported here that Louis Bonaparte has refused the crown of Holland; that Murat is the person now fixed on in his stead, and that the duchy of Cleves and Berg will be given to the hereditary Prince of Bavaria. It has always been said that Bonaparte intended the duchy for a German prince.

21st.—One of the syndics of Hamburg is come to Berlin for the purpose of soliciting some relaxation of the embargo, for the towns of Ritzebuttel and Cuxhaven, and a free passage for small flat-bottomed boats on the Jade. Count Haugwitz says that his request will be granted.

22nd.—Baron Binder has told me that he received orders a few days ago, from Count Stadion, to apply to this Court for passports for Sir A. Paget and suite to pass through the Prussian territory. They were instantly granted, and forwarded to Count Zorley at

Dresden ; Haugwitz, at the same time, observing to
Baron Binder that the demand was altogether an unnecessary one, as it was not, and never had been,
intended to ,put obstacles in the way of any English
travelling in this country.

23*rd.*—The military preparations are still going
on, but with abated vigour. The gendarmes have
always one foot in the stirrup, but the word of
command, to mount, is not yet given.

24*th.*—Intelligence reached us last night that the
King of Sweden had actually put into execution the
threat held out in his first letter, and that the ports
of Dantzig, Memel, and Pillau were blockaded in the
most vigorous manner by a Swedish squadron.

Count Keller has again been offered a place in the
cabinet. He has declined it, and has stated unre-
servedly to the king that his reasons for doing so
are, that the terms on which M. de Haugwitz proposed he should hold office tended to render him a mere
cipher in the government and incapable of being in
any way useful to his country.

The king, meanwhile, continues to keep up a
regular but private correspondence with Baron Hardenberg, frequently despatching couriers to Cassel,
where the baron is now staying. He had intended to
withdraw altogether from public affairs, but he is so
much occupied by the king's correspondence, that he
is frequently engaged the greater part of the night
in writing.

25*th.*—A *Feld-jager*, despatched by General Kalkreuth, brought yesterday a letter for the king, which

had been sent to the Prussian outposts by the King
of Sweden, after the return of Major de Chapmann.
As far as I can learn, its contents are a mere recapitulation of his former letters, and a positive refusal
to recede from his last demand. It appears to have
produced nothing decisive here. The garrison has
certainly received the *marche route*, but, hitherto, no
final orders to make use of it.

28*th*.—Count Kalkreuth, the General's nephew,
has arrived from the Prussian head-quarters, to
report the appearance of Swedish gunboats at the
mouth of the Pene.

29*th*.—He returned to Pasewalk in the evening.
A Prussian courier from St. Petersburg, who came
in this morning, may have brought accounts that
will lead to more decisive measures against the King
of Sweden ; that is to say, in the way of demonstration, for though this garrison expects to march, it
does not expect to fight the Swedes. At all events,
no answer whatever will be given to the letter sent
by the king to the Prussian outposts, and which, it
appears, was penned by His Majesty himself. For
M. Brinckman wrote to Count Lützow, who has
been good enough to read his letter to me, that he
was for two hours with the king, dissuading him
from sending it, after it was written, but without
avail. It was M. Brinckman who induced the king to
modify his first demands, and to despatch Major de
Chapmann to Berlin after the departure of M. de
Bronikowski ; but His Majesty has declared that he
will not be prevailed upon to retract any further.

There is a story in circulation in society here, the truth of which M. de Bray, the Bavarian minister, says he is inclined to doubt, but which was certainly reported to this Government as a fact, that the Princess of Bavaria, *vice-reine d'Italie*, has returned unexpectedly to her father, in consequence of Beauharnois having ended some marital dispute by striking the princess *très rudement*, as the account has it. This treatment from her *roi et maître*, though it might be a *mode de Paris*, she was not prepared to receive or tolerate, therefore, *faisait ses paquets au plus vite*, and decamped. The king, her father, was surprised at her visit, and was, naturally, much grieved on learning the cause of it; but he has endeavoured to induce his daughter to return to her noble husband, and, with the assistance of Bonaparte's paternal authority, the quarrel, it is supposed, will be made up and another motive be assigned for her journey.

30th.—Advices just received state that, the King of Sweden has extended the blockade of the Baltic ports to all flags, without exception. This last step was taken by the king without either consulting or informing his advisers. But there is, it appears, much jealousy, as well as uneasiness, amongst those who take part in the councils of His Imperial Majesty. M. Brinckman sent off an express to M. Lützow, begging him, for God's sake, not to interfere any further with this Government on the king's behalf, but to let things take their course.

The courier from St. Petersburg brings a letter,

expressive only of the emperor's regret that the differences between Prussia and Sweden cannot be amicably terminated.

About the same time a messenger from Count Goltz, the Prussian minister at that Court, reached Berlin, and his report of the friendly dispositions of the Emperor towards the King of Sweden will probably deter the King of Prussia from proceeding to extremities against him. The former has been urged by His Imperial Majesty to desist from his hostile measures, or at least to suspend them.

This Government received an *estafette* from Baron Jacobi this morning, which prepared me for the news brought a few hours later by the mail of the 16th. But news to the 19th, *viâ* Holland, has since arrived, which not only contradicts a preceding report— that letters of marque were issued on the 15th—but mentions that the Declaration, &c., had not appeared in the Saturday's " Gazette," and that, in consequence, all hopes of an accommodation were not entirely given up. The non-arrival of the messenger seems to accredit this intelligence.

Mr. F. J. Jackson to G. Jackson.

York Hotel, Albemarle Street,
June 5th, 1806.

DEAR GEORGE,

I have your sister's letter of the 24th ult., but of what *you* are doing in Berlin I know nothing since the 19th and 20th. Parts of those and of letters of preceding dates have been seen, *à qui de droit*, and have obtained for you the commendation your vigilance merits.

I adhere to my original plan of meeting you at Hamburg, for although Elizabeth says of you " Je n'ai qu' à me louer de son amitié, et de ses attentions soutenues," I think she will be better satisfied that I should cross the water with her. I purpose leaving this on the 10th, and, with a tolerably fair wind, may expect to be at Hamburg about the 15th.

As soon as you receive this, you must, yourself, deliver the enclosed letter to Count Haugwitz. The necessary papers with which he will furnish you for the entrance of the packet I beg you to forward by *estafette* to Mr. Thornton at Hamburg.

This town was in a blaze last night. I, of course, paid my respects on the occasion to the king. He seems to me somewhat improved in general health, but his sight is decidedly impaired. The day before I dined with Burghersh's father. Lady Westmoreland is one of *les élégantes* of the day. It was a curious dinner; the company, chiefly Russians—as much out of their element in English society as I feel myself to be, after the sociability, ease, and elegance of that of foreign Courts, to which I have so long been accustomed.

I am satisfied with your report of the sale, even with the probability of the "state coach" being brought back to England. But as Countess Metternich has so set her heart on having it, I am willing to take the fifteen hundred dollars, as proposed. Yet I fancy that when the matter is laid before the count on his return, he will be compelled to answer her, " Though ready to gratify you, how am I to raise the needful for payment ?"

I look forward with pleasure to the prospect of getting out of this dusty town after being cooped up in Albemarle Street.

The " Winter in London," which you ask for, to read on your voyage, I can tell you, from having run through it myself—as I found it a subject of fashionable, though as I think unprofitable, discussion—is a wretched performance.

This novel of the day is a work miserably put together to serve a most miserable aim.

I will say nothing of politics until we meet. There is, indeed, little to be written from hence, in point of fact, though, in the way of reflection on that little, a great deal might be said, but that would be too long to enter upon now. If Prince Hatzfelt or Alvensleben should broach the subject you may tell them, as from yourself, that none of the suggested modifications can have the smallest effect here.

F. J. J.

Diaries—June 15th.—An *estafette* from Mr. Thornton brought us last night a letter from my brother, enclosing one for Count Haugwitz. I lost no time this morning in waiting upon his Excellency, but did not see him until my second call, about ten o'clock, when, apologizing to him for so early an intrusion, I delivered my brother's letter. He said he was ever happy to receive anything that came

from him; and having read it, he told me that, so
far from any apology being necessary, he felt himself,
on the contrary, obliged for the opportunity my
brother afforded him of showing with what pleasure
he seized the occasion of being useful to him, and of
proving the sincerity of these sentiments of regard
and good-will which he trusted were mutual.

He expressed his sorrow that the journey my sister
was about to undertake should be necessary, but as it
had unfortunately become so, no endeavours, on his
part, should be spared to render it as little incon-
venient to her as possible. The king, he said,
participated in that feeling, and, for himself, to the
regret with which he saw my brother's departure in
a public point of view, he must add that which he
experienced from his loss in his private capacity.
" This," he went on to say, " is not the language of
mere commonplace civility, but proceeds from the
real esteem I feel for your brother, from the long
and close connection, both public and private, I have
had the satisfaction of holding with him."

He then told me, that he knew too well His
Prussian Majesty's sentiments to make it necessary
that he should take his orders on the subject of the
letter. He would not, therefore, defer the answer.

I mentioned that the packet my brother was to
come in would be under Pavillon Parlémentaire.
He answered, " Mais Pavillon Anglais suffit."

In a word, nothing could be more obliging than
the manner in which he received my brother's
request.

To give full effect to it, and to prevent the possibility of any delay or misunderstanding, Count Haugwitz immediately despatched an *estafette* to Count Schulenberg with the necessary orders, and has, besides, already sent the maritime passport, which I have forwarded to Hamburg, and to-morrow we leave Berlin.

In the course of our conversation, Count Haugwitz more than once referred to the change which the packets had made from Cuxhaven to Husum. He assured me that this Government had never intended to prevent their coming, as formerly, to Cuxhaven, and he begged that I would represent this to my brother. As I was leaving he repeated this request, and I promised to report what he had told me. I then bade him adieu, with many acknowledgments for his kind expressions of good will towards myself, and for the obliging readiness he had shown to comply with my brother's wishes.

London, Aug. 1*st.*—Contrary winds detained us a fortnight at Hamburg. We reached London on the 24th ult.· I return to it from Bath to-day, to set off again by to-night's mail to join my friend Otto Löwenstern at York, thence to make a tour together in Scotland.

As to my future prospects, I am totally in the dark; and, perhaps, at this early period I am hardly justified in my impatience on the subject. Whether Mr. Fox will only resign his office in Downing Street, or his office upon earth, seems to be a question. He is to be tapped, they say, to-morrow, which looks as if he could not last long. Lord Lauderdale, I hear, will negotiate the peace.

They are already speculating at the office as to who will be Mr. Fox's successor. Some say, Lord Spencer is a very likely man, and a very proper one, too. The *regulars*, they say, would have a very tolerable chance with him against the many *irregulars*, whom it seemed F.'s system to employ in the foreign line. I hope it may so turn out, but for my own part I had grounded some expectations not only on Mr. Fox's manner of receiving me when I came over in March, but on some words he let fall when I saw him the second time. However, I am off to bonnie Scotland, and *après?—après nous verrons.*

APPENDIX.

No. 1.

LE Senatus Consulte détermine pour l'avenir la dénomination, les formes et la transmission du pouvoir souverain en France ; les seules choses que dans l'organisation du gouvernement de la République n'étaient pas proportionnées à la grandeur et au besoin de l'état.

Dans cette circonstance le premier soin de Son Excellence le Ministre des Relations Extérieures de Sa Majesté Impériale, a été de charger le soussigné de notifier au Ministre de Sa Majesté le Roi de Prusse, que Sa Majesté Impériale Napoléon, Empereur des Français, est investé par les lois de l'état de la dignité impériale, et que ce titre et cette dignité seront transmis à ses descendans en ligne directe et masculine, ou, à défaut de cette ligne, à la descendance directe et masculine de leurs Altesses Impériales les Princes Joseph et Louis Bonaparte, frères de l'empereur.

En exécutant les ordres qu'il a reçus, le soussigné a l'honneur de faire observer, au Ministere d'Etat que les communications officielles doivent cesser jusqu'à ce que les dénominations anciennes soient remplacées par celles du Protocole Impériale, tant dans les lettres de créance des ministres accrédités en France que dans celles des ministres de Sa Majesté Impériale accrédités dans les cours étrangères.

Le soussigné n'a pas besoin de déclarer que la grande loi qui vient d'accomplir l'organisation de l'état d'une manière conforme à la dignité du peuple Français, n'apporte aucun changement dans les rapports politiques, seulement en les plaçant sous la sauvegarde d'un gouvernement investé de plus d'éclat et revêtu d'une dignité plus analogue à la nature des choses. La France assure plus de force et de consistance à la réciprocité d'avantages que les nations amies peuvent attendre d'elle, et en même tems elle attache plus d'importance aux égards que tous les gouvernemens recévront du sien, et qu'à leur tour ils doivent lui rendre.

Le soussigné saisit, etc., etc.,

Signé   LAFORÊT.

À *Berlin, le* 7 *Prairial, An.* 12.

27 *Mai,* 1804.

No. 2.

Le soussigné, Ministre d'Etat et du Cabinet, a porté sans délai à la connoissance du roi l'office que M. de Laforêt lui a fait l'honneur de lui remettre au sujet du Senatus Consulte, qui vient déterminer pour l'avenir la dénomination, les formes, et la transmission du pouvoir souverain en France.

Le roi partage la satisfaction que cet éclatant témoignage de reconnoissance et de dévouement de la nation Française aura causé à Sa Majesté l'Empereur. Elle s'empresse de l'en féliciter, et de lui exprimer ses vœux pourque ce glorieux événement, en assurant le bonheur de la nation par l'établissement d'une base permanente et stable de son gouvernement pour l'avenir, serve encore à fixer, et à rehausser, par le retour prochain d'une heureuse paix, cette prospérité nationale qui est le grand but des soins de ce monarque, et qui fera la gloire de son regne.

Sa Majesté Impériale voudra bien compter de la part du
roi sur une persévérance inébranlable dans les sentimens
dont il a plus d'une fois eu l'avantage de pouvoir lui donner
des preuves convaincantes, et Sa Majesté en faisant observer
dans ses relations avec l'empire Français les formes qui vien-
nent d'y être établies, se tient assurée à son tour que, par
une juste réciprocité de sentimens, l'empereur loin de permettre que ces rélations d'amitié et d'heureuse intelligence
éprouvent quelque altération, sera disposé à en écarter de
son côté tout ce qui pourroit contribuer à les relâcher le
moins du monde.

Le roi, en réconnaissant que les communications officielles
des ministres respectifs ne pourront qu' éprouver une interruption momentanée jusqu'à l'arrivée des lettres de créance
dans la nouvelle forme, est prêt à abréger cette interruption
autant qu'il dépend de lui, et vient en conséquence de pour-
voir dès à présent son ministre à Paris de celle dont il a
besoin, dans l'attente certaine qu'à son arrivée celle de
M. de Laforêt lui aura également déjà été transmise.   En
attendant, le soussigné sera empressé de cultiver avec ce
ministre les communications confidentielles que les affaires
pourroient exiger, et profite avec un très grand plaisir de
cette occasion, etc., etc.

                                Signé   HARDENBERG.
Berlin, le 6 Juin, 1804.

- - - - - - -

No. 3.

Bulletin du 24 Juin, 1804.

La Cour de Cassation vient de confirmer l'arrêt rendu par
la cour de justice criminelle contre les prévenus de conspiration.

Le dénouement de ce procès était devenu un problème
fort difficile à résoudre aux yeux des hommes qui savent les

dangers qu'entraine quelquefois la condamnation des grands coupables. Nous ne parlons pas ici des hommes *vomis en France par l'étranger*, que l'indignation et le mépris public avaient poursuivis avant leur arrestation.

La difficulté est principalement dans celui que sa carrière avait *jetté* aux premier rangs de la révolution. Cet individu, lié par des preuves irrésistibles avec des conjurés, déjà convaincu moralement par sa conduite au 18 Fructidor, n'avait d'excuse réele que dans sa. faiblesse, et peut-être aussi dans des vertus privées, qui n'empéchent pas quelquefois d'être bien coupable envers la patrie. Aussi ses défenseurs ont ils pris grand soin de cacher l'homme et de ne montrer que le général : ils ont atténué des circonstances graves par des faits étrangers : ils ont émû la pitié publique parceque le peuple ne réfléchit guère : il éprouve des sensations, et les sensations déterminent son jugement.

Il faut applaudir à cet esprit d'humanité redevenu le caractère national. Cela prouve quels progrès le gouvernement a faits, et quels services il a rendus à la France et à l'Europe.

La cour de justice criminelle avait voulu distinguer les personnes, les fautes, et les crimes, mais son arrêt, en satisfaisant à la justice, n'avait pas pourvû à tout. La clémence de l'empereur vient de donner la solution si importante de cette affaire.

Le Général Moreau, condamné à deux ans de réclusion, a demandé, par une lettre addressée à l'empereur, sa grace avec la liberté de passer aux Etats Unis d'Amérique. S'il doit ce conseil à ses défenseurs, c'est ce qu'ils ont fait de mieux pour son bonheur et pour sa réputation.

L'empereur, qui avait désiré de ne point le trouver coupable, s'est laissé aller à l'intérêt que pouvait lui inspirer un homme qui dans d'autres tems avait rendu des services : et des services militaires sont d'une grande valeur auprès d'un héros : aussi l'empereur a tout accordé.

De quelque manière qu'on envisage ce dénouement du procés, tous les intérêts s'y trouvent conciliés—Moreau faible, égaré, humilié, est dèsormais séparé du nouvel ordre de choses.

Il fut un moment où il devoit franchement s'unir au chef de l'état, et sans doute alors son influence sur les destinées de la République eut pû être distinguée. Mais des passions étrangères l'ont arrêté. Aujourd'hui, Moreau, jouissant de sa fortune et de sa réputation militaire en Amerique, ne verra point dépendre son sort des crises de l'état, ou des intrigues de l'étranger, ou de celles de l'intérieur, auxquelles son nom pourrait servir de prétexte ou de ralliement.

Il est noble à l'empereur de chercher l'extinction des fautes plutôt que la punition des coupables. La faiblesse du caractère de Moreau l'auroit nécessairement compromis : à la première intrigue son nom eut été prononcè ; il se fut encore trouvé par consentement ou par quelque connivence le véritable chef, ou le point de ralliement des conspirateurs. Alors le chef de l'état, ne pouvant plus consulter que les intérêts de la nation, qui l'a chargé de ses destinées, aurait été forcé par devoir de tarir la source éternelle de l'inquiétude publique, et d'étouffer enfin la dernière étincelle d'un feu qui, sans pouvoir faire de mal bien réel, pouvoit cépendant inquiéter et compromêttre des hommes faibles et non malintentionnés.

Moreau était dangereusement placé pour l'état et pour lui-même. Il était hors de la nation, organisée comme elle est aujourd'hui. Il n'était plus que dans la dissolution des choses, ou dans un reste de factions. Ce n'était plus qu'un phare pour éclairer les intrigans de la nuit. Son éloignement, devenu nécessaire pour lui-même, plait au public, autant qu'il avoit été désiré par ses amis. C'est a lui de faire oublier par sa conduite, comme il l'a promis dans sa lettre, les torts qu'il a pû avoir, et les intrigues auxquelles il a pris part.

Turin, le 2 Floreal, An. 13.

Comme il est souvent arrivé qu'on s'attachait à donner aux opérations de Sa Majesté Impériale de fausses interprétations, j'ai cru devoir vous présenter, Monsieur, sous leur véritable jour les événemens qui ont porté Sa Majesté d'accepter la couronne d'Italie. Il n'est pas à présumer que vous ayez à répondre aux inductions que pourroit en tirer la malveillance. Cependant j'ai rassemblé ici quelques une des suppositions qu'on peut lui prêter afin de vous mettre à portée de les répousser, si, contre toute attente, l'occasion s'en présentoit.

Le royaume d'Italie remplace la République Italienne; ces deux désignations se correspondent, la première ne peut indiquer aucune prétention nouvelle; elle n'a rien de plus alarmant pour les autres puissances, et, celles-ci ayant déjà réconnu la République Italienne, on ne conçoit pas comment le titre de Roi d'Italie pourroit leur inspirer quelque ombrage.

La France, l'Espagne, le Portugal, tous les états qui environnent la Méditerranée, ont-ils cru leur indépendance menacée par l'Empereur d'Autriche parcequ'au lieu de se borner au titre d'Empereur d'Allemagne, il prend celui de chef du Saint Empire Romain, qui avait autrefois compris tout le monde connu? Le Pape se croît-il moins souverain de Rome parcequ'un fils de l'Empereur d'Allemagne prend le titre du roi des Romains?

La circonscription d'un état, ses relations avec les autres puissances, le rang qu'il occupe au milieu d'elles, voilà les seuls objets qui puissent les intéresser. Rien n'est changé dans les limites, dans les rapports politiques, ni même dans la désignation du royaume d'Italie; ils sont les mêmes que ceux de la République que ce royaume a remplacée.

Si l'innovation d'un titre avoit pu servir de prétexte aux interprétations c'était contre celui de République Italienne qu'elles avoient depuis trois ans, à se diriger. La conservation de ce titre, reconnu aujourd'hui dans toute l'Europe, ne laisse aucune prise à la malveillance.

La dénomination actuelle se trouve même plus particulièrement consacrée dans l'histoire du pays et dans l'opinion publique; et, si l'on peut comparer entr'eux deux événemens dont les circonstances sont analogues, et qui appartiennent aux deux plus grandes époques de notre monarchie, le même territoire avec des limites à peu près semblables, composa autrefois le royaume d'Italie.

Le pays auquel on a rendu son ancienne désignation était gouverné en république lorsque son indépendance a été reconnu par le traité de Luneville. Mais le même traité a réservé aux habitans la faculté d'adopter telle forme de gouvernement qu'ils jugeroient convenable. Cette clause, et leur indépendance permettoit de répasser au système monarchique, qui sous des formes différentes, les avoit long-tems gouvernés.

La France était république lorsque le traité de Luneville fut conclu. Cette circonstance et l'établissement d'une république en Italie devait inspirer à l'Autriche plus d'inquiétude ; aujourd'hui les mêmes motifs d'éloignement n'existent plus. La France a répris son ancienne forme de gouvernement. D'autres états ont imité sa sagesse. La République Italienne est rendu à la monarchie et toutes les puissances ont une garantie de plus contre le système des innovations.

Si l'on demandait l'indépendance actuelle du royaume d'Italie, vous auriez, Monsieur, à faire remarquer que ce royaume se trouve dans la même situation que la République Italienne. On n'avait pas regardé comme contraire à l'esprit des traités que le premier consul en fut déclaré président ; il ne leur est pas plus contraire que l'Empereur de France soit nommé Roi d'Italie. Le titre seul est changé : les rélations des deux états sont les mêmes : les motifs de securité, qui faisoient sentir à la République Italienne le besoin d'un protecteur, subsistent encore ; ce pays ne peut acquérir, qu'à l'abri d'une autre puissance, les moyens de se soutenir un jour comme royaume indépendant.

Sa Majesté Impériale a marqué le terme où il renoncerait à la couronne du royaume d'Italie. Ce terme étoit indéfini lorsque l'Empereur étoit président de la République Italienne, et dès lors les autres puissances auroient pu s'en alarmer d'avantage : aujourd'hui Sa Majesté ne demande, pour transférer la couronne d'Italie, que l'éxécution des traités qui ont assuré l'indépendance des Sept Isles *et celle de Malte.* Elle ne veut que pouvoir compter sur le repos et la sureté du midi de l'Europe, pour que ce royaume puisse jouir sans danger de son indépendance.

Ce sont les vœux de ses habitans qui ont changé la forme de ce gouvernement et qui ont déferé la couronne à Sa Majesté Impériale. La constitution Italienne leur reservé le droit de faire, au bout de trois années, des changemens dans leur institutions. Ce terme arrivé ils ont senti le besoin de les modifier.

J'ai eu l'honneur de vous transmettre le procès verbal de cet événement. Vous y aurez remarqué dans les discours de M. de Melri, dans les vœux qu'à exprimés la députation Italienne, dans les arrêtés qui en ont été la suite, les motifs qui ont porté Sa Majesté l'Empereur à accepter la couronne d'Italie, et les vues de modération qui l'ont animé, même en cédant aux vues des habitans.

Vous jugerez, par ces observations, et par les faits qui y ont donné lieu, de l'opinion qu'on doit naturellement se former d'un événement dont le principal objet est de consolider le repos et la sûreté de cette partie de l'Europe qui, par la nouveauté de son organisation, et par la direction qu'ont prise quelques événemens militaires, seroit la plus

exposé à de nouvelles vicissitudes, si elle n'avoit pris de sages
mesures par s'en garantir.

Agreez, Monsieur, etc.,

Signé   CH. M. TALLEYRÀND.

No. 5.

*Explication Verbale de M. de Laforêt d'après les
Dépêches de Milan.*

Si la Russie, ou toute autre puissance du continent, voulait
intervenir dans les affaires du moment et *péser également*.
sur la France et l'Angleterre, l'Empereur Napoléon ne le
trouvera pas mauvais et fera avec plaisir des sacrifices équi-
valens à ceux que l'Angleterre feroit de son côté. Mais
si au contraire on n'exigeoit des sacrifices que de la France
seule, alors, quelle que fut l'union que l'Angleterre eut
trouvé moyen de former par l'intermédiaire de la Russie,
l'Empereur Napoléon se serviroit dans toute son étendue,
de son bon droit, de ses armées, de son génie.

L'Empereur Alexandre serait tout-à-fait trompé, s'il
s'était laissé persuader que l'évacuation de Malte fut un
sacrifice suffisant de la part de l'Angleterre. L'affaire
de Malte est d'un intérêt très secondaire, et, si après le
message du Roi d'Angleterre la France s'est refusée a trans-
iger sur ce point ainsi qu'il le vouloit, ce n'est point à cause
de la valeur réele de cette isle ; mais parcequ'en consentant
à la laisser dans les mains de l'Angleterre, la France eut
reconnu ce droit étrange de demander *des garanties;* c'est
à cause du message calomnieux et insultant du Roi d'Angleterre ; c'est encore par la raison qu'en négociant dans cette
circonstance pour maintenir la paix, la France auroit reconnu à l'Angleterre le droit de la calomnier et de l'insulter
publiquement, toutes les fois qu'un pareil calcul pourroit

entrer dans les vues des factions du ministère et contribuer
au succès de quelques mesures d'administration intérieure.
Enfin, lors des négociations d'Amiens la valeur intrinsique
de Malte a été apprécié. Son évacuation n'est qu'une conséquence du traité, et la France, qui la réclame comme son
droit, ne pourrait jamais la considerer comme l'objet d'une
compensation. Si l'on exige qu'il y ait dans le traité entre
la France et l'Angleterre une clause défavorable à la France
qui ne se trouve pas la traité d'Amiens, il faudroit qu'on
insérât dans le même traité une clause équivalente au dés-
avantage de l'Angleterre et qui seroit de compensation aux
sacrifices que la France aurait à faire.

Tels sont les sentimens de l'Empereur Napoléon sur la
traité à intervenir entre la France et l'Angleterre, et ses
dispositions sont de même nature relativement à la Russie.

Il consentira à évacuer Naples, lorsque la Russie de son
côté évacuera les Isles Ionniennes. Ces deux conditions sont
équivalentes. Mais si la Russie voulait faire insérer dans
la traité quelques dispositions défavorables à la France, il
faudrait qu'elle s'attendit de son côté à l'insertion de quelques
clauses à sa charge.

N'est il pas extraordinaire en effet que Petersbourg devenu
l'écho des déclamations astucieuses de Londres, prêche
partout contre la prétendue ambition de la France, lorsque
la Russie, non contente de l'immense étendue de son territoire et des réunions qu'elle n'a cessé d'y faire, veut forcer
la Porte Ottomane à renouveller le traité de 1798, et qu'elle
opprime deux des plus beaux et des plus puissantes empires
du monde—la Turquie et la Perse—de manière à ne leur
laisser aucune indépendance. Si l'on demanda des explications à la France, il faut que la Russie en donne elle-même
sur ce traité de 1798—si funeste à la Porte.

Il faut qu'elle fasse connoître ses limites avec la Perse,
qu'elle déclare si la Géorgie doit faire partie de l'empire
de Russie, ou en demeurer séparée.

Il est de la plus exacte vérité que l'Empereur Napoléon ne désire rien tant que la rétablissement de la paix, mais il la veut *égale et honorable.* Il consent à faire les *sacrifices qui seront nécessaires pour parvenir à ce but,* mais dans le cas seulement où l'Angleterre et la Russie feroient de leur côté des *sacrifices ou des concessions équivalentes.*

Comme c'est déjà un grand pas de fait vers le succès d'une négociation lorsque les deux parties sont informées respectivement des bases sur lesquelles chacune est disposée à traiter, et dont on ne veut pas s'écarter, il n'y aura aucun inconvénient à ce que les idées renfermées dans cette *conversation* parviennent à la connoissance du Gouvernement Anglais.

No. 6.

Lorsque Sa Majesté Impériale de toutes les Russies consentit à la demande de Sa Majesté Britannique d'envoyer le soussigné auprès de Bonaparte pour répondre à une démonstration pacifique que celui-ci venoit de faire à la cour de Londres, elle fut guidée par deux motifs également puissans, également uniformes à ses principes et à ses sentimens connus, l'un de seconder un souverain prêt à faire des efforts et des sacrifices pour le repos général, et l'autre de tirer avantage pour tous les états de l'Europe d'un désir de paix qu'on auroit dû croire bien sincère à la solemnité avec laquelle on l'avait annoncée.

Les rapports existans entre la Russie et la France eussent pû supposer des obstacles insurmontables à une négociation de paix par l'organe d'un ministre Russe. Mais Sa Majesté Impériale ne balança point à passer sur tous les sujets qu'elle avoit de mécontentement personnel, sur toutes les formalités usitées. Elle profita de l'intervention de Sa Majesté Prussienne en faisant demander des passeports pour son plénipotentiaire, elle se borna à déclarer qu'elle ne les accepterait, que sous la double condition bien précise, que son plénipotentiaire traiteroit immédiatement avec le chef du Gouvernement François sans reconnoître le nouveau titre, qu'il s'étoit donné, et que Bonaparte assuserait positivement qu'il était encore animé du même désir de paix générale qu'il avoit parû vouloir manifester dans sa lettre à Sa Majesté Britannique.

Cette assurance préalable devenoit d'autant plus importante, que Bonaparte immédiatement après la réponse donné par Sa Majesté Britannique à sa lettre du 1re Janvier, s'etait revêtu du titre de Roi d'Italie, titre, qui pouvoit mettre par lui seul des nouvelles entraves à la pacification désirée.

Sa Majesté Prussienne ayant transmis la réponse formelle du cabinet des Tuileries, qu'il persistoit dans l'intention d'y prêter les mains sincèrement, Sa Majesté Impériale accepta les passeports avec d'autant plus d'empressement que le Gouvernement François avoit affecté d'en mettre à les envoyer.

Une nouvelle infraction aux traités les plus solemnels vient d'opérer la réunion de la République Ligurienne à la France. Cet événement en lui même, les circonstances qui l'ont accompagné, les formes qu'on à employés pour en précipiter l'éxécution, le moment même, qu'on a choisi pour l'accomplir, ont formé malheureusement un ensemble, qui devoit marquer les dernières bornes aux sacrifices que Sa Majesté Impériale venoit de faire aux instances de la Grande Bretagne et à l'espoir de ramener par la voie des negociations la tranquillité nécessaire en Europe.

Sa Majesté Impériale n'eut sans doute pas arrêté dans ces bornes sa complaisance et ses sacrifices, si le Gouvernement François avoit permis d'espérer, qu'il respecteroit les premiers liens qui unissent la société et qui soutiennent la confiance des engagemens parmi les peuples civilisés. Mais assurément il seroit impossible de croire que Bonaparte en

expédiant les passeports accompagnés des protestations des
plus pacifiques, songeat sérieusement à les suivre, puisque
dans l'intervalle, qui devoit s'écouler entre l'expédition des
mêmes passeports et l'arrivée du soussigné à Paris, il hâtoit
des mésures, qui bien loin d'apporter des facilités au rétablissement de la paix, sont de nature à en détruire
jusqu'aux élémens.

Le soussigné en rappellant à son excellence le Baron
Hardenberg des faits bien particulièrement connûs du
cabinet Prussien, doit lui faire part qu'il vient de recévoir
de Sa Majesté Impériale l'ordre exprès du $\frac{9}{21}$ Juin dernier
de remettre sans délai les passeports ci-joints et de prier son
excellence de vouloir bien les renvoyer au Gouvernement
François, en lui annonçant que dans l'état actuel des choses
ils ne sauroient être d'aucun usage.

Le soussigné saisit cette occasion, etc., etc.,

Signé   NOVOSSILTZOW.

Berlin, $\dfrac{28\ Juin}{10\ Juillet}$, 1805.

No. 7.

Le soussigné Ministre d'Etat et de Cabinet se voit obligé
à son plus grande regrét de faire part à M. de Laforêt,
Ministre Plénipotentiaire de Sa Majesté l'Empereur des
François, de l'office que M. de Novossiltzow vient de lui
addresser, pour lui rendre le passeport François ci-joint en
original et lui annoncer l'ordre que Sa Majesté l'Empereur
de toutes les Russies lui à fait passer à la suite des derniers
changemens en Italie, et nommément de la réunion de la
République Ligurienne à l'empire François, de ne pas pour-
suivre son voyage en France.

Le Roi n'a pû que ressentir une peine infinie, en voyant
ainsi se confirmer les inquiétudes, que dès la nouvelle de cet

événemont inattendu on n'avait pû s'empêcher de concevoir
sur l'effet qui pourroit en resulter relativement à la négociation salutaire qu'il s'agissoit d'ouvrir. Le vif désir du
rétablissement de la paix générale, dont Sa Majesté n'a cessé
d'être animé, et qu'elle a si souvent manifesté, est un sûr
garant des sentimens douloureux, qu'elle éprouve dans cette
occasion.

Le soussigné a l'honneur, etc., etc.,

Signé   HARDENBERG.

Berlin, le 11 *Juillet,* 1805.

APPENDIX.—No. 8.

Dans ce moment où l'Empereur de toutes les Russies,
mon auguste maître, et Sa Majesté le Roi de Prusse vont
s'expliquer et s'entendre sur les plus grands intérêts qui
jamais ayent occupé les souverains, il m'a paru d'une urgente
nécessité de rétablir par des explications franches des faits
singulièrement altérés qui jettent un faux jour sur les principes, les sentimens, et les vues de Sa Majesté Impériale.

Bonaparte, au moment où il avoit manifesté l'intention
la plus prononcée d'entamer une négociation qui devoit préparer les voies au rétablissement de la paix entre l'Angleterre et la France, se porte à de nouvelles usurpations. Non
seulement que par cet acte de la plus révoltante déloyauté
il détruit jusqu'à l'ombre d'une naissante mais timide confiance, il fixe encore l'opinion que l'Empereur devoit prendre
des égards qu'il est intentionné de marquer à Sa Majesté
Impériale dans le cours de la négociation prête à s'ouvrir.

Dès ce moment, le seul parti à choisir étoit celui de ne
point s'exposer à un traitement contre lequel se révolterent
l'honneur, la dignité et même l'intérêt de tous les états
indépendans. Aussi l'Empereur ne balança pas un seul
instant. La cause de tous les souverains, de toutes les

nations étant devenue même personellement la sienne, pouvoit-il—dévoit-il—se permettre le plus léger doute sur l'empressement avec lequel on se joindroit à lui ? Ce n'étoit plus le cas de perdre, par des négociations, le tems devenu singulièrement précieux.

L'Empereur ayant mis ses armées en mouvement, elles s'approchent des frontières de l'Autriche et de la Prusse dans la persuasion qu'on les accueillera partout avec cet empressement qu'inspire un intérêt commun. On ne demande que le passage, lors même que dans ces états on jugeroit à propos de ne pas se joindre à elles : payemens en argent comptant ; indemnisations de tout genre sont offertes. De plus grands avantages réels vont devenir la partage de ceux qu'une accession active associe à la glorieuse entreprise de réprimer une ambition également folle qu'elle est vaniteuse, révoltante et qualifiée à inquiéter jusqu'au dernier individu sur son avenir.

L'Autriche, sans contredit éminément intéressé à la généreuse entreprise de Sa Majesté Impériale, ouvre ses barrières. Les armées Russes sont accueillies avec amitié et joie.

Les ouvertures que j'ai eu l'honneur de faire au ministre de Sa Majesté le Roi de Prusse, que n'ont elles pas éprouvés la même faveur ?

Il n'y en a pas eu une seule où avant toute chose l'intérêt de la monarchie Prussienne n'ait été consulté. Je ne parle pas seulement de celui de l'Europe, dont la Prusse ne sauroit jamais se détacher. Jamais un mot n'est sorti de ma bouche qui ait dénoté de loin l'intention de ma cour d'avoir recours à des mésures violentes. Mais ce qui détruit jusqu'à l'ombre d'un tel dessin prêté à la Russie, et auquel des contes absurdes ont donné une vogue que la malveillance et la crédulité ont pris à tâche de répandre par tout le pays, c'est la position que maintiennent deux grandes armées Russes sur la frontière de la Prusse. Je demande à tout homme impartial dans la monarchie Prussienne, se seroit-on laissé arrêter pendant plusieurs sémaines sur le même point, si l'intention avoit été de forcer le passage ? Auroit-on attendu que le roi eut rendu mobile toute son armée ? Mais on pouvoit entrer sans éprouver de la résistance ; on désarmoit 20,000 à 30,000 hommes avant que la résistance pouvoit même être organisée.

Voilà ce qu'eut fait Bonaparte dans une situation semblable. Le grand cœur d'Alexandre, lors même que la politique, l'intérêt des nations opprimées des peuples foulés aux pieds, et la voix étouffée de victimes innombrables sacrifiées à la soif de la domination, de l'or, et de la folle ambition d'un homme obscur l'eussent exigé impérieusement. Le grand cœur d'Alexandre réjette une telle mesure. Cet auguste souverain s'attende de l'amitié, de l'intimité, de l'union cimentée à Memel et de tous les sentimens qui en derivent, que son royal ami, sentant et appréciant l'importance de la conjoncture actuelle, loin de traverser ses généreux desseins les seconder efficacement. Ce sera là le résultât de l'entrevue dont l'Europe, l'univers, l'humanité attendent leur salut. La Prusse lui devra sa tranquillité et un avenir dont le bonheur et la félicité seront garantis par la consolidation d'une alliance que Frederic II. regardoit pendant la longue durée de son regne prospère comme le boulevard de sa monarchie.

Signé   ALOPEUS. ·

No. 9.

From the Berlin "Gazette" of April 10th, 1806.

Le "Moniteur" du 21 Mars, en imprimant une lettre adressée par moi, le 22 Decembre, 1805, à Lord Harrowby, me somme de dire si elle est véritable ou supposée, et l'accompagne de plusieurs remarques.

Ce qui rend les devoirs et la situation d'un homme d'état

particulièrement pénible, c'est l'obligation où il se trouve le plus souvent, de se renfermer dans le silence, lors même qu'il est méconnu ou calomnié.

Cependant, je dois au roi et à moi-même de déclarer, que la lettre en question, quoiqu'altérée dans plusieurs expressions essentielles, est officielle et écrite par ordre de Sa Majesté. Je le dois au roi, parcequ'à la cour de Berlin, quelqu'y soit le protocole cité par le "Moniteur," les ministres n'osent se permettre des démarches de cette nature à l'insçu du souverain ; à moi-même parceque je ne puis voir avec indifférence qu'on me croye capable de manquer à mes devoirs et de m'exposer à être désavoué après avoir agi en son nom.

Le 22 Decembre le roi et tout le monde ignorait à Berlin qu'un traité avoit été signé le 15 à Vienne par M. le Comte de Haugwitz ; celui-ci ayant réservé toute information sur ce sujet à son rapport oral, et n'étant arrivée à Berlin que le 25 Decembre. On se trouvait, comme il est exprimé dans ma lettre à Lord Harrowby, dans une incertitude totale sur les intentions de Sa Majesté l'Empereur des François. De part et d'autre les armées étoient en campagne et sur le pied de guerre. Le Général-Major de Pfuhl fût envoyé au quartier-général François et à M. de Haugwitz, pour s'expliquer sur l'arrangement intermédiaire qui fait le sujet de la lettre à Lord Harrowby, et qui avoit été proposé par M. de Haugwitz. M. de Pfuhl rencontra ce ministre en chemin, retournant à Berlin avec un traité définitif, et naturellement l'arrangement intermédiaire dût tomber. Voilà le fait avec le plus exacte vérité. Un jugement impartial saura apprécier les remarques du "Moniteur."

Je m'honore de l'estime et de la confiance de mon souverain et de la nation Prussienne ; je m'honore des sentimens des étrangers estimables avec lesquels j'ai été en relation, et c'est avec satisfaction que je compte aussi des François parmi eux. Je ne suis pas né en Prusse, mais je ne le cède en patriotisme à aucun indigène, et j'en ai obtenu les droits tant par mes services, qu'en y transférant mon patrimoine et eu y devenant propriétaire.

Si je ne suis pas soldat, je sens que je n'aurois pas été indigne de l'être, si le sort m'avoit destiné à défendre les armes à la main mon souverain et ses droits, et la dignité, la sureté, et l'honneur de l'état. Ceci en réponse aux remarques du "Moniteur." Au reste, ce ne sont ni les bulletins des gazettes, ni les remarques de leurs rédacteurs, qui pourront jamais me déshonorer.

Voici le véritable texte de ma lettre du 22 Decembre à Lord Harrowby. En le comparant à celui inséré dans le "Moniteur," on observera entre autres, qu'il n'y est pas question ; *ni de confédérations à former qui puisse s'adapter aux événemens*, mais du défaut d'un concert adapté aux circonstances ; *ni de gagner du tems pour prendre des mesures plus décisives*, mais de l'avantage qui résulteroit de l'arrangement intermédiaire, de voir plus clair ; ni *d'un plan* que j'aurois soumis à Lord Harrowby, mais de l'arrangement intermédiaire qui lui fût présenté pour empêcher que rien ne troublât les négociations dont on se promettois le maintien de la paix entre la Prusse et la France et peut-être l'acheminement à la paix générale.

Signé   HARDENBERG.

À Berlin, le 8 Avril, 1806.

Lettre du Baron de Hardenberg à Lord Harrowby.

MY LORD,—A la suite de la réponse préalable que j'ai eû l'honneur d'addresser à votre excellence sur la question qu'elle m'avoit fait rélativement à la sûreté des troupes de Sa Majesté Britannique dans le nord de l'Allemagne, je m'empresse de lui transmettre sur cet sujet les assurances positives dont j'ai la satisfaction de pouvoir m'acquitter.

Votre excellence connoit la position actuelle des affaires. Elle sera la première à sentir qu'au point où les choses en sont venúes après la malheureuse bataille d'Austerlitz entre l'Autriche et la France, qu'après la rétraite de la grande armée Russe, et dans l'incertitude totale où nous nous trouvons sur les intentions de Napoléon à l'égard de la Prusse, la plus grande circonspection dévient indispensable. L'armée la plus valeureuse ne peut pas toujours compter sur les chances de la fortune, et il est sans doute non seulement de l'intérêt de la Prusse, mais de l'intérêt le plus général de prevenir qu'elle ne soit pas attaquée dans ce moment où tout le poids de la guerre tomberait sur elle et pendant qu'aucun concert adapté aux circonstances n'a été formé, car dans le cas de malheur de ses armées le dernier rayon d'espoir de pouvoir maintenir encore la sûreté et l'indépendance des états du continent de l'Europe seroit évanoui.

Le roi toujours animé du même vœu de rétablir la tranquillité générale sur un pied stable et autant que possible satisfaisant pour tous, n'a pu que désirer vivement, de voir sa médiation stipulée par la Convention signé le 3 Novembre à Potzdam, acceptée par la France.

Dans un entretien que M. de Haugwitz eût le 28 Novembre avec Napoléon, ce souverain se montra disposé à l'admettre sous la double condition: 1. Que durant la négociation aucunes troupes de Sa Majesté Britannique, Russes, ou Suédoises ne dépasseroient les frontières de la Hollande pour y porter la guerre en partant du nord de l'Allemagne; 2. Qu'on assurerait à la forteresse de Hameln, un rayon un peu plus étendu, afin d'obvier à l'embarras des ses subsistances.

Le roi ne pouvait accepter ces conditions dans les circonstances du moment où elles furent faites, mais celles-ci ont entièrement changé, et dans les conjonctures présentes, cette double demande a paru non seulement admissible à Sa Majesté, sous la condition que l'Empereur de son côté s'engage à ne faire entrer aucun corps de troupes dans le nord de l'Allemagne pendant la durée de la négociation, et à ne rien entreprendre durant cet intervalle contre le Hanovre, mais même favorable parcequ'elle laisse le tems de voir plus clair, et de se préparer à tout événement, soit que la guerre eût lieu, soit que cet état de choses intermédiaire pût conduire à une négociation définitive. Pour ne point perdre de tems, Sa Majesté vient d'envoyer le Général M. de Pfuhl au quartier-général François afin de terminer cet arrangement. En même tems M. de Haugwitz a reçu les instructions nécessaires, en date du 19 de ce mois, et le roi fait connoître à la France qu'il regarderait la réoccupation du pays d'Hanovre par les troupes Françoises comme une mesure hostile contre lui.

D'après ce que je viens d'exposer, le roi m'autorise à vous déclarer, milord, à la suite des assurances précédément données, pour le cas où les troupes de Sa Majesté Britannique et Russes eussent essuyés des malheurs, qu'il se charge de la sûreté des troupes de Sa Majesté Britannique qui sont dans le pays d'Hanovre et leur donne pleine faculté de se replier au besoin, sur l'armée Prussienne et sur les états du roi, avec les modifications suivantes que les circonstances rendent nécessaires.

1. Quelles prennent des positions en arrière des troupes Prussiennes et s'abstiennent pour le moment pendant la durée de la négociation intermédiaire de tout mouvement et de toute démarche qui serait provocatoire contre la Hollande.

2. Que si une attaque des troupes Prussiennes de la part des François avoit lieu, Sa Majesté puisse compter avec une entière certitude sur le soutien et la coöpération des troupes de Sa Majesté Britannique pendant qu'elles resteront dans le nord de l'Allemagne. Sa Majesté fait avancer un corps respectable en Westphalie et prendra en outre les mésures de sûreté et de défense nécessaires. Les troupes Russes, sous les ordres de Général Tolstoi, se trouve déjà actuellement à la disposition entière du Roi, l'Empereur Alexandre s'en étant remis à lui d'en disposer à son gré, aussi

bien que de celles qui sont en Silésie sous les Général Bennigsen.

Je prie votre excellence de vouloir bien écrire le plutôt possible, en conséquence, à Lord Cathcart commandant les troupes de Sa Majesté Britannique et de l'engager à prendre sans délai les mesures nécessaires à ces divers égards, et en particulier à se rendre à l'invitation qui, d'après les ordres du roi, lui sera adressée par le Général de Kalkreuth pour s'aboucher personellement à un endroit convenu, avec lui et le Général Tolstoi, rélativement aux positions que les troupes de Sa Majesté Britannique, Russes et Prussiennes, auront à prendre en consequence de l'arrangement exposé au dessus.

Les troupes Suédoises se trouvant sur la même ligne avec les troupes Anglaises et Russes, il est fort à désirer qu'on puisse engager Sa Majesté Suédoise à se conformer à ces arrangemens. J'espère que vous voudrez bien vous employer à cet effet, milord, de concert avec le Prince Dolgoruski, chargé par l'Empereur de toutes les Russies de ce que régarde la destination de l'armée Russie. Au cas que Sa Majesté Suédoise fasse suivre à ses troupes la direction que leur donnera M. Tolstoi, le roi est prêt à leur donner la même garantie qu'il offre aux troupes de Sa Majesté Britannique, pendant leur séjour dans le nord de l'Allemagne.

3. Quand à l'approvisionnement de la forteresse de Hameln, on a jugé que l'attribution d'un rayon où la garnison pourvoiroit elle-même à ses subsistances, seroit sujette à de très grands inconvéniens tant à l'égard des sujets de Sa Majesté Britannique que des collisions qui en résulteroient entre les troupes. Il a donc paru préférable de fournir le nécessaire à cette garnison du pays d'Hanovre, au moyen d'une personne intermédiaire à laquelle le Général Barbou indiqueroit les besoins pour sa consommation journalière et sur les réquisitions de laquelle le ministre Hanovrien auroit soin de faire livrer ces objets aux endroits dont on conviendroit.

Le Général Barbou de son côté devra s'engager à se tenir tranquille dans la ville de Hameln. D'après ces idées le roi envoye à Hanovre le Colonel Kreusemark, aide-de-camp de F.M. Möllendorff. Je le charge d'une lettre de ma part pour le ministere de Sa Majesté Britannique, et d'une autre pour le Général Barbou, afin que les arrangemens nécessaires pour fournir de cette manière momentanément à l'entretien de la garnison de Hameln, puissent être réglés et mis en exécution sans délai.

Il ne me reste qu'à me référer à tout ce que j'ai eû l'honneur de vous dire de bouche, milord, et à vous prier de vouloir bien vous porter en général à toutes les démarches que vous croirez propre à l'exécution de tout l'arrangement que j'ai eû l'honneur de vous présenter. Je vous prie de vouloir bien expliquer à Lord Cathcart que ce n'est qu'autant qu'il jugera convenable d'acceder à cet arrangement, et de prendre les mesures que dependéront de lui pour en assurer l'exécution que Sa Majesté Prussienne pourra suivre l'engagement positif de garantir la sûreté des troupes. Il est cependant nécessaire pour le cas d'une attaque de la part des François, que la direction parte d'un seul point, et il paroit naturel que le général le plus ancien en grade se charge alors du commandement. Le Général Comte de Kalkreuth y seroit appelé par conséquent, tant par cette raison que parceque se trouvant le plus près de l'ennemi il seroit le mieux en état de juger des mesures à prendre.

Je réitère avec empressement l'assurance, etc., etc.,

Signé   .HARDENBERG.

Berlin, le 22 Decembre, 1805.

END OF VOL. I.

LONDON :
PRINTED BY W. CLOWES AND SONS, STAMFORD STREET
AND CHARING CROSS.

www.ingramcontent.com/pod-product-compliance
Lightning Source LLC
Chambersburg PA
CBHW052331110726
47901CB00005B/1203